Student Collection
Seven Day Loan

Return date

D0297710

THE HARMONISATION OF EUROPEAN CONTRACT LAW: IMPLICATIONS FOR EUROPEAN PRIVATE LAWS, BUSINESS AND LEGAL PRACTICE

After an extended period in which the European Community has merely nibbled at the edges of national contract laws, the bite of a 'European contract law' has lately become more pronounced. Many areas of law, from competition and consumer law to gender equality law, are now the subject of determined efforts at harmonisation, though they are perhaps often seen as peripheral to mainstream commercial contract law. Despite continuing doubts about the constitutional competence of the Commission to embark on further harmonisation in this area, European contract law is now taking shape, with the Commission prompting a debate about what it might attempt.

A central aspect of this book is the report of a remarkable survey carried out by the Oxford Institute of European and Comparative Law in collaboration with Clifford Chance, which sought the views of European businesses about the advantages and disadvantages of further harmonisation. The final report of this survey brings much needed empirical data to a debate that has thus far lacked clear evidence of this sort. The survey is embedded in a range of original and up-to-date essays by leading European contract scholars reviewing recent developments, questioning progress so far and suggesting areas where further analysis and research will be required.

Volume 1 in the Series: Studies of the Oxford Institute of European and Comparative Law

Studies of the Oxford Institute of European and Comparative Law

Editor

Professor Stefan Vogenauer

Board of Advisory Editors

Professor Mark Freedland, FBA
Professor Stephen Weatherill
Professor Derrick Wyatt, QC

Volume 1: The Harmonisation of European Contract Law: Implications for European Private Laws, Business and Legal Practice
Edited by Stefan Vogenauer and Stephen Weatherill

Volume 2: The Public Law/Private Law Divide
Edited by Mark Freedland and Jean-Bernard Auby

Volume 3: Constitutionalism and the Role of Parliaments
Edited by Katja Ziegler, Denis Baranger and A W Bradley

The Harmonisation of European Contract Law

Implications for European Private Laws, Business and Legal Practice

Edited by

STEFAN VOGENAUER
and
STEPHEN WEATHERILL

·HART·
PUBLISHING

OXFORD AND PORTLAND, OREGON
2006

Published in North America (US and Canada) by

Hart Publishing
c/o International Specialized Book Services
920 NE 58th Avenue, Suite 300
Portland, OR 97213-3786
USA
Tel: +1 503 287 3093 or toll-free: (1) 800 944 6190
Fax: +1 503 280 8832
Email: orders@isbs.com
Website: www.isbs.com

Hart Publishing, Salter's Boatyard, Folly Bridge, Abingdon Rd, Oxford, OX1 4LB
Telephone: +44 (0)1865 245533 Fax: +44 (0)1865 794882
Email: mail@hartpub.co.uk
Website: http//:www.hartpub.co.uk

British Library Cataloguing in Publication Data
Data Available

ISBN-13: 978-1-84113-591-5 (hardback)
ISBN-10: 1-84113-591-7 (hardback)

Typeset by Forewords, Oxford
Printed and bound in Great Britain by
TJ International, Padstow, Cornwall

Contents

Contributors

Guido Alpa is Professor of Law at the University of Roma La Sapienza and President of the Italian Bar Council.

Baroness Ashton of Upholland is Parliamentary Under Secretary of State at the Department for Constitutional Affairs.

Hugh Beale is Professor of Law at the University of Warwick and a Law Commissioner for England and Wales (Commercial and Common Law).

Ulf Bernitz is Professor of European Law at Stockholm University and Director of the Oxford/Stockholm Wallenberg Venture in European Law.

Aurelia Ciacchi is a Fellow of the Centre of European Policy and Law (ZERP) and a Lecturer in Comparative Law at the Hanse Law School, Bremen.

Sir David Edward is Emeritus Salvesen Professor of European Institutions at the University of Edinburgh and a former Judge at the European Court of First Instance and at the European Court of Justice.

Martijn W Hesselink is Professor of European Private Law at the Universiteit van Amsterdam.

Ewan McKendrick is Professor of English Law at the University of Oxford and a Fellow of Lady Margaret Hall.

Dirk Staudenmayer is Head of Unit at the European Commission, Health and Consumer Protection Directorate General. He is Honorary Professor at the University of Münster.

Sir John Vickers is Drummond Professor of Political Economy at the University of Oxford and a Fellow of All Souls College. He was Director General/Chairman of the Office of Fair Trading from 2000 to 2005.

Stefan Vogenauer is Professor of Comparative Law at the University of Oxford and a Fellow of Brasenose College. He is Director of the Oxford Institute of European and Comparative Law.

Stephen Weatherill is Jacques Delors Professor of European Community Law at the University of Oxford and a Fellow of Somerville College. He is a Deputy Director of the Oxford Institute of European and Comparative Law.

Daniela Weber-Rey is Partner at Clifford Chance LLP in Frankfurt and Head of the German Financial Institutions Group. She is a Member of the Advisory Group on Corporate Governance and Company Law at the EU Commission.

Reinhard Zimmermann is Director of the Max Planck Institute for Foreign Private Law and Private International Law in Hamburg and Professor of Private Law, Roman Law and Comparative Legal History at the University of Regensburg.

Series Editor's Foreword

This book is the first volume of the 'Studies of the Oxford Institute of European and Comparative Law', a new series that is meant to provide a forum for publications arising from the research pursued at the Institute. The Institute is one of the Research Centres of the Law Faculty of the University of Oxford. It was established in 1995 and inaugurated 10 years ago, on 17 January 1996, originally as the 'Centre for the Advanced Study of European and Comparative Law'. The function—I hesitate to say the 'mission'—of the Institute is to facilitate and promote the Faculty's work in the areas of European and comparative law. In doing so, it can build on the Faculty's traditional strength in both fields and add a further dimension in focusing on the intersection of the two disciplines, which have become increasingly intertwined in recent years. The Institute aims to achieve this by contributing in various ways to the research and teaching of the Faculty in European and comparative law, and by supplying a supporting structure of specialised staff and relevant activities. As far as research is concerned, the Institute's activities mainly consist in organising conferences, symposia and workshops, which are frequently held jointly with one of our partner institutions, both within Oxford and abroad, and both within academia and beyond. The 'Studies of the Oxford Institute of European and Comparative Law' will serve as a focal point for making the results of these events accessible to a wider audience, thereby replacing previous mechanisms of dissemination through publications produced by various publishers and bodies, both in print and electronically.

It is hoped that the present volume provides a good example of the kind of research pursued at the Institute and of future publications to be expected in this series. European contract law is, like so many issues of European and comparative law these days, a topic which is very much on the agenda of both disciplines. On the one hand, it has become impossible to conduct a meaningful comparison of the domestic contract laws in Europe without taking into account the existing body of EC contract law. On the other hand, this body is still emerging, and it does so on the basis of thorough comparison of the rules and principles of the Member States' contract laws. It makes sense, therefore, to tackle the subject of European contract law with comparatists and experts in European law joining forces.

The close link between the two disciplines and the rich diversity of the work undertaken within the Institute should also become apparent in the following two volumes in this series. Volume 2, edited by Mark Freedland and Jean-Bernard Auby, will compare the divide between public law and private law in England and in France, and will show, inter alia, how the influence of European law has helped to overcome the strong divergence that used to prevail on this issue between the two jurisdictions. Volume 3 will be edited by Katja Ziegler, Denis Baranger and Anthony Bradley. It will look at constitutionalism and the role of Parliament in France, Germany, the United Kingdom and the European Union.

The present volume is also characteristic of the Institute's work in that the contributions contained in it are based on papers given at a conference which brought together academics and practising lawyers from all over Europe (on which more at the end of the first chapter). The conference had the same title as this book: 'The Harmonisation of European Contract Law: Implications for European Private Laws, Business and Legal Practice'. It was hosted by the Institute in conjunction with its major benefactor, global law firm Clifford Chance. Clifford Chance has been supporting the Institute's activities from its very first days, and it is more than appropriate to acknowledge their crucial support here. Neither the conference nor the ensuing publication would have been possible without their help for which we are more than grateful.

Some further words of thanks are due. Professors Mark Freedland, Stephen Weatherill and Derrick Wyatt, all of whom are institutionally linked with the Institute in one way or another, kindly agreed to serve on the Board of Advisory Editors for this series so that an appropriate balance between European and comparative law would be struck. Richard Hart was most supportive and showed enormous patience in the process of establishing the new series, particularly in the run up to this first volume. Finally, Vanessa Mak, Graduate Teaching Assistant at Oriel College, Oxford, did a sterling job in preparing the papers for publication.

Stefan Vogenauer
Director of the Institute
Oxford
January 2006

Table of Cases

Decisions of the European Court of Justice

Decisions of the English and Scottish courts

Decisions of the US Supreme Court

Decisions of the European Court of Human Rights

Table of Domestic Legislation

Italy

The Netherlands

Scandinavia

UK

Table of EC Legislation

Regulations

Directives

Table of International Legislation and Principles

1

The Spectre of a European Contract Law

STEFAN VOGENAUER

'A spectre is haunting Europe'—'un spectre hante l'Europe'—'ein Gespenst geht um in Europa'.[1] It is not the spectre of communism, as it was in the days of Marx and Engels some 150 years ago. It is the spectre of a European contract law. European contract law has all the characteristics of a true ghost. People are almost certain that it had a real and glorious life in the past, in the almost mythical era of the *ius commune*. Back then, from the twelfth to the late eighteenth century, there was a basic unity of the general law of contract, taught and practised all over Europe. It slowly vanished with the arrival of the great codes on the continent and has not been resurrected since.

Like every supernatural appearance, European contract law is somewhat elusive and for the most part not really tangible. We realise this as soon as we try to grasp it, as soon as we ask hard legal questions, such as 'Does this agreement constitute a valid contract under European contract law?' or 'Which remedies does European contract law provide for this situation?' The answer will invariably be a counter-question: 'Which European contract law?' Only occasionally, where relevant EC law applies, might we be able to score a hit. In all the other cases we are not sure whether a 'European contract law' really exists, whether it is in force and whether it can be applied.

However, there is undeniably a strong impression that there is something out there. There are people who claim to have seen the European law of contract. The author of the leading textbook, for instance, concedes that 'there are as yet no actual rules of European law apart from European legislation. But', he continues, 'all that is needed to constitute European private law is to recognise it.'[2] So people are constantly on the lookout, waiting for apparitions.

As is usually the case with supernatural phenomena, this has generated an

---

[1] Cf the opening sentence of K Marx and F Engels, *Manifesto of the Communist Party* (1848).
[2] H Kötz, *European Contract Law* (Oxford University Press, 1997) v.

industry of its own. There is a major textbook on 'European Contract Law' from which I have just quoted. A casebook has been co-edited by one of the contributors to the present volume, Hugh Beale,[3] and it will see a second edition soon. A journal, the *European Review of Contract Law*, was launched in 2005. In the preceding year, the Oxford Law Faculty had introduced a new graduate course entitled 'European Private Law: Contract'. It was heavily oversubscribed. Finally, the title of this volume assumes that there is such a thing as European contract law.

Spectres generate different responses. Some observers are terrified, others are fascinated. There are many, both in academia and in the professions, who wish to lay the ghost to rest once and forever. They have various legitimate reasons for this. Others would like to resurrect it, giving it substance and providing for more than a shadowy outline. These also include academics and, to a lesser extent, practitioners. And, more importantly, the European Commission has committed itself to this course of action. Again, there are different reasons, and they are considerable.

Most arguments that are advanced in the current debate concern the feasibility and the methodology of further harmonisation in the area of contract law: in view of the diverging national contract laws, is it actually possible to create a common European contract law? And what is the way to achieve this end: a restatement, the search for a 'common core', an EC regulation, a non-binding 'optional instrument', or the production of further scholarly literature? The one question that should logically precede all this is often somewhat neglected: is the creation of a European contract law necessary or at least desirable? After all, uniformity or harmonisation as such is not an end in itself. There must be compelling reasons of a moral, political or economic nature if we are to abandon the status quo.

This volume is an attempt to give at least a limited answer to this question. The starting point is, somewhat unsurprisingly, the status quo. Ewan McKendrick gives an overview of the degree of harmonisation already achieved in the area of contract law and of the various arguments for and against going ahead. One of the major reasons advanced for change is the tension currently arising between the domestic contract laws and the emerging contract law of the EC. Different legal systems in Europe have adopted different strategies to cope with the problem. Three of them are looked at in this volume. The strategy chosen in England is investigated by Hugh Beale, Martijn Hesselink looks at that for the Netherlands, and Reinhard Zimmermann considers Germany.

The latter two countries were chosen in particular as they might hold in store some additional lessons for a further harmonisation of European contract law. Both Germany and the Netherlands underwent large-scale

---

[3] H Beale, A Hartkamp, H Kötz and D Tallon, *Casebooks on the Common Law of Europe: Contract* (Oxford, Hart Publishing, 2002).

revisions of their contract laws relatively recently. Obviously, these reforms cannot be compared with a similar—and even more daunting—enterprise on a supra-national scale. However, they might give us some indication as to the transition costs, ie the expenses incurred in switching from one contractual regime to another, which might be expected at a European level. Supposing, for a minute, that the introduction of a new contract law has a number of beneficial effects: will they ever outweigh the expenses generated by the introduction and implementation of the new regime, such as the preparation and drafting of new provisions, the necessity to amend the contracts generally used by businessmen and the legal training needed to prepare lawyers for their new challenge?

Framing the question in this way does not even take account of the potential cultural and political 'losses' and 'gains' that are to be expected by the introduction of a European contract law and that continue to dominate the current debate as to the necessity and desirability of taking such a step. These are highly important policy questions which merit further discussion. However, adopting a strictly legal viewpoint for the moment, the most pressing issue on the agenda is a clarification of the constitutional competence of the EC to enact a more comprehensive contract law of any sort. This is dealt with by two contributions in this book. First, Steve Weatherill outlines the constitutional framework and argues that there are good reasons for the Commission's reluctance to tackle the constitutionality question head-on. Then Stefan Vogenauer and Steve Weatherill present the results of a major survey amongst European businesses engaging in cross-border transactions. Its purpose was to establish whether the diverging contract laws in Europe really form a barrier for international trade and impede on the proper functioning of the European economy. Only if this question can be answered in the positive are the requirements of Article 95 EC, the most promising candidate to provide a legal base for further harmonisation, met.

More general issues about the codification of a European contract law are highlighted in Guido Alpa's contribution. Then the focus changes to some of the areas of contract law which are of particular interest in the context of the current debate: consumer contracts, standard terms, suretyships and insurance contracts. John Vickers, Ulf Bernitz, Aurelia Ciacchi and Daniela Weber-Rey deal with these in turn, and it becomes apparent that there is no single answer to the question of whether further harmonisation is necessary or desirable.

The book concludes with observations by policymakers. Dirk Staudenmayer of the European Commission gives a view from Brussels. Baroness Ashton of Upholland presents the United Kingdom Department of Constitutional Affairs' perspective, which was not only crucial during the second half of the year 2005, when the United Kingdom held the Presidency of the European Union, but remains of huge importance in the political process lying ahead.

The contributions to this book are revised and updated versions of papers given at a conference that was held in Oxford on 18 and 19 March 2005. Both the speakers and the almost 120 conference delegates represented a variety of European legal systems and made for a rare mix of academics, students, practitioners, judges and policymakers: we welcomed barristers from London, solicitors based in various places from Budapest to Yorkshire, and a representative of the Council of the Bars and Law Societies of Europe. We hosted judges from the Italian Supreme Court and the Royal Courts of Justice. We encountered members of the European Consumers' Association, the Federal Association of the German Industry, the Spanish College of Land and Mercantile Registers, and the interest group representing the retail, wholesale and international trade sectors in Europe. We met a Member of the European Parliament, as well as representatives of the Department of Constitutional Affairs, the Law Commission of England and Wales, and the Office of Fair Trading. And academics and students came from such diverse places as Paris, Northumbria and Lower Bavaria. Small wonder that there were vigorous and highly informed discussions about all sorts of issues relating to European contract law.

The conference was chaired by Professor Sir David Edward, formerly Judge of the European Court of Justice. Sir Jonathan Mance, then a Lord Justice of Appeal, was in the chair at one of the sessions. We are grateful to them both. The conference was jointly organised by the Oxford Institute of European and Comparative Law and Clifford Chance, the London-based global law firm. The constant and generous support lent to the Institute by Clifford Chance has already been mentioned in the Foreword to this volume. With respect to this conference and the ensuing publication, we are even more indebted to them than usual since Clifford Chance were not only instrumental in devising the questionnaire for the above-mentioned business survey, but also provided the considerable financial means to have it conducted by a professional agency. Our thanks go to their Senior Partner, Stuart Popham, and to the other Partners involved in the preparation, particularly Julia Clarke and Simon James.

It is not claimed that this volume gives a conclusive answer to the questions of whether we should imbue the spectre of a European contract law with life, whether we ought to hope for it to vanish into thin air or whether we should actively force it to withdraw. But far-reaching decisions will be made soon, and it is important that this is done on an informed basis. If this book were to assist in this process it would have achieved its aim.

2

Harmonisation of European Contract Law: The State We Are In

EWAN McKENDRICK

What state are we in? This question can be answered from different perspectives in relation to the harmonisation of European private law. The word 'state' has different meanings. It can refer to the Nation State, and in that sense can be used to identify the Nation State or jurisdiction in which we happen to be at the time at which the question is posed. Alternatively, it can refer to our 'condition' or our 'manner of existing', and in this sense is used to denote the condition in which we find ourselves. We are not concerned with the first of these meanings in this chapter, even though the future scope of the Nation State may be vitally affected by the ongoing attempts to bring about a greater degree of harmonisation of European private law. The aim of this chapter is to examine our 'state' in the latter sense and to provide an overview of the current position in relation to the harmonisation of European contract law. In this sense it is hoped that the chapter will set the scene for the discussion which follows in subsequent chapters.

The chapter is divided into three parts. The first part considers the principal steps on the road to our current position, ie how we got here. The second part considers the arguments generally advanced in favour of further harmonisation of European contract law. The third part considers some of the objections routinely put forward (at least by the English[1]) against further harmonisation or integration of European contract law.

I. HOW DID WE GET HERE?

The road towards a greater degree of harmonisation of European contract

---

[1] In this essay I do not purport to speak for Scotland, which is a separate jurisdiction from England and Wales. Some of the objections discussed in the third part of the chapter may also be voiced by Scots lawyers, but I do not purport to represent their views (whether academic lawyers or lawyers in practice).

law has been a long one. In many ways it is difficult to identify the precise starting point of the journey. Some might be tempted to go back to the medieval *lex mercatoria*. But the link between the medieval *lex mercatoria* and the modern debate on the further harmonisation of European contract law is at best tenuous. The world has changed so radically in the last few hundred years that it is impossible, in my view, to draw any meaningful comparison between the regulation of the medieval world and the regulation of the world today.

A more realistic starting point for the modern debate may be the work of the great Austrian jurist Professor Ernst Rabel. He began work on the creation of an international uniform sales law in the late 1920s and, largely at his suggestion, UNIDROIT adopted the project and commenced the task of preparing a draft international sales law. This work began in earnest in the 1930s but was suspended on the outbreak of the Second World War. Work was resumed on the project after the end of the war and ultimately bore fruit in the form of two Hague Conventions, namely the Uniform Law on the International Sale of Goods and the Uniform Law on the Formation of Contracts for the International Sale of Goods. The texts for both instruments were agreed in 1964, but neither instrument came into force until 1972, when they obtained the necessary ratifications. However, neither Convention can be termed a resounding success. Only nine States ratified them.[2] However, it would be a mistake to conclude that they were therefore devoid of practical significance. Professor Schlechtriem, one of the leading authorities on sales law, has offered the following conclusion on the Hague Conventions:

> the Hague Sales Law in the end proved to be very successful. In 1987, when my Institute [in Freiburg] published a collection of cases decided under this Uniform Sales Laws and asked all district courts and courts of appeal to send us cases decided by them in which these Uniform Sales Laws were applied, we received almost 300 decisions, although only 5% of the courts responded to our request.[3]

This conclusion is, however, rather more favourable to the Hague Conventions than the generally accepted view, which is that they failed to have the impact for which those responsible for their creation had hoped.

The primary significance of the Hague Conventions is probably to be found in the fact that they provided a significant starting point for the drafting of what was to become the Vienna Convention on Contracts for the

---

[2] United Kingdom, Belgium, West Germany, Italy, Luxembourg, Netherlands, San Marino, Israel and Gambia.

[3] P Schlechtriem 'Uniform Sales Law—The Experience with Uniform Sales Law in the Federal Republic of Germany' (1991–92) 3 *Juridisk Tidskrift* 1, 2. It would, however, appear to be the case that the Hague Conventions exerted their greatest influence in Germany, Italy and the Benelux countries.

International Sale of Goods (CISG). While it is true that the CISG did depart from the Hague Conventions at a number of points, it did so only after careful consideration of the competing issues. The CISG is now, of course, a hugely influential Convention. It has been ratified by most European States[4] and its significance has extended into the domestic law of some Nation States, notably Germany.[5] The CISG came into force on 1 January 1988 and there now exists a huge academic literature on the Convention[6] and a considerable volume of case law, much of which is relatively easily accessible courtesy of some excellent websites.[7] The extent to which the CISG has succeeded in the aim of harmonising sales law across the world is a matter of some debate.[8] There is evidence to suggest that courts and arbitrators remain prone to interpreting the Convention through the lens of domestic law.[9] Even making an allowance for a certain 'homeward bound' tendency in the interpretation of the Convention, it can nevertheless be considered a resounding success. One of its principal successes has been the development of an agreed framework for the analysis of some of the complex legal issues that can arise in the law of sales and, more generally, in the law of contract. One may disagree with some (or, perhaps, many) of the solutions prescribed in the CISG, but one cannot doubt that these solutions are now of great practical and academic significance.

The next major stage in the development of a harmonised European contract law can be said to be the work done on the Principles of European Contract Law (PECL). The PECL were prepared by scholars drawn from the Member States of the European Community under the chairmanship of Professor Ole Lando (hence the frequent description of the group working on the Principles as 'the Lando Commission').[10] The PECL were published in three phases: Part I was published in 1995, Parts I and II in

---

[4] The principal exceptions being the United Kingdom, Ireland and Portugal.

[5] On which see further R Zimmermann, 'Remedies for Non-performance: The Revised German Law of Obligations, Viewed against the Background of the Principles of European Contract Law' (2002) 6 *Edinburgh Law Review* 271 and W Lorenz, 'Reform of the German Law of Breach of Contract' (1997) 3 *Edinburgh Law Review* 317.

[6] See generally P Schlechtriem and I Schwenzer (eds), *Commentary on the UN Convention on the International Sale of Goods (CISG)* (2nd (English) edn, Oxford University Press, 2005).

[7] Such as those operated by PACE (http://www.cisg.law.pace.edu) and the University of Freiburg (http://www.cisg-online.ch).

[8] See, eg H Flechtner, 'The Several Texts of the CISG in a Decentralised System: Observations on Translations, Reservations and other Challenges to the Uniformity Principle in Article 7(1)' (1999) 17 *Journal of Law and Commerce* 187 and RA Hillman, 'Applying the United Nations Convention on Contracts for the International Sale of Goods: The Elusive Goal of Uniformity' [1995] *Cornell Review of the Convention on Contracts for the International Sale of Goods* 21.

[9] See, eg Flechtner, *ibid*.

[10] See also the preliminary draft of a European Contract Code produced by the Academy of European Private Lawyers (the Pavia Group) under the direction of Professor Giuseppe Gandolfi. The text of a preliminary draft of that code is to be found in O Radley-Gardner et al, *Fundamental Texts on European Private Law* (Oxford, Hart Publishing, 2003) 439.

2000,[11] and Part III in 2003. The work of those responsible for drafting the PECL was very much influenced by the work of those who had gone before them. Thus the significance of the CISG can be seen at numerous points in the Principles, even though the Principles frequently go beyond the solutions prescribed in the CISG[12]—and, in this way, the members of the Lando Commission made the best use of the opportunity to learn from the problems and gaps that had become apparent in the final text of the CISG. Further, the fact that the members of the Lando Commission were not aiming to produce a legally binding text gave them greater latitude in developing novel or 'best' solutions to some old and some new problems in the law of contract.[13] The work on PECL was also influenced, at least in part, by the UNIDROIT Principles of International Commercial Contracts. These were first published in 1994, and were thus available to members of the Lando Commission when they were preparing the early drafts of their text. However, the Lando Commission quickly began to catch up on the work of UNIDROIT and, indeed, Part III of PECL was produced before the second edition of the UNIDROIT Principles made its appearance in 2004. It would perhaps be fair to say that, latterly, the two Principles operated in tandem (or even in competition with one another), and that the learning experience was not necessarily a one-way process (with PECL always drawing on the experience of UNIDROIT).

As has been noted, the PECL is a very different type of instrument from the CISG in that the Principles were not drafted as, nor were they intended to be, a legally binding set of rules. Professors Lando and Beale, in their editorial introduction to *Principles of European Contract Law: Parts I and II*,[14] set out a number of purposes for which the Principles are designed. First, they state

---

[11] The production of Part II resulted in various changes being made to the version of Part I which was published in 1995 and, consequently, an amended version of Part I was also published in 2000.

[12] See, eg Art 6:111, which deals with change of circumstances. This is a much more elaborate provision than that to be found in Art 79 of the CISG.

[13] This follows from the fact that it was not necessary to secure the agreement of all members of the Commission in order to obtain approval for the text. In this way, the possibility of one member of the Commission holding the others to ransom was substantially reduced, if not eliminated. The process of reaching agreement in the CISG was much more fraught, largely as a result of the need to produce a text which Nation States would be willing to ratify. A good example of this process is provided by Art 78 of the CISG, which deals with the payment of interest. The controversy surrounding the entitlement of a party to recover interest was such that it was only possible to secure agreement in Art 78 to the principle that interest should be paid (on which see generally C Thiele, 'Interest on Damages and Rate of Interest Under Art 78 of the UN Convention on Contracts for the International Sale of Goods' (1998) 2 *Vindobonda Journal of International Commercial Law and Arbitration* 3). The Article is silent on matters such as the rate at which interest is to be paid. Article 9:508 of PECL, which deals with the payment of interest, is, by contrast, more elaborate. The fact that there was no need to achieve unanimity on the text of the Article doubtless made it easier to reach agreement on the content and the scope of Art 9:508.

[14] O Lando and H Beale (eds), *Principles of European Contract Law Parts I and II* (The Hague, Kluwer, 2000).

that the Principles may form a foundation for European legislation, including a possible first step in the work of preparing a future European Code of Contracts. Secondly, the Principles are stated to be suitable for express adoption by contracting parties, who can declare that their contract is to be governed by the PECL. However, the ability of contracting parties to incorporate the PECL into their contract in this way is limited by Article 3 of the Rome Convention on the Law Applicable to Contractual Obligations. While contracting parties are free to incorporate the Principles as a set of contract terms, they cannot incorporate them into the contract as the applicable law, at least in the context of litigation in national courts. Article 3 requires the parties to choose the law of a country as the applicable law,[15] so that any choice of the Principles can only take effect subject to the national law that is found to be applicable to the contract, applying the usual conflict of law rules. Thirdly, Lando and Beale state that the Principles are a 'modern formulation of a *lex mercatoria*' (in other words, they can be applied by arbitrators in the case where a contract is stated to be governed by 'general principles of law' or 'the *lex mercatoria*'[16]). Fourthly, they are a model for judicial and legislative development of the law of contract. Finally, they may form the basis for the harmonisation of contract law among the Member States of the European Union. Lando and Beale conclude:

> [T]he Principles have both immediate and longer-term objectives. They are available for immediate use by parties making contracts, by courts and arbitrators in deciding contract disputes and by legislators in drafting contract rules whether at the European or the national level. Their longer-term objective is to help bring about the harmonisation of general contract law within the European Union.[17]

Thus far, no mention has been made of the impact of European community law on the development of a European contract law. This omission must now be rectified. Community law has had an impact on national contract law, although it is probably fair to say that its intervention has been rather episodic or selective to date. However, its role is steadily increasing. The principal examples of the contribution of community law to the development of a harmonised contract law take the form of the various Directives which have been introduced over the last twenty years. These Directives cover subjects such as doorstep selling,[18] self-employed commercial agents,[19] package

---

[15] See A Briggs, *The Conflict of Laws* (Oxford University Press, 2002) 159.

[16] See Art 1:101(3)(a) of the PECL. It is, however, open to question whether the drafters of the Principles are able, by their own assertion, to constitute the Principles as part of the *lex mercatoria*.

[17] See above n 14, xxiv.

[18] Council Directive 85/577/EEC of 20 December 1985 to protect the consumer in respect of contracts negotiated away from business premises [1985] OJ L372/31.

[19] Council Directive 86/653/EEC of 18 December 1986 on the coordination of the laws of the Member States relating to self-employed commercial agents [1986] OJ L382/17.

travel,[20] unfair terms in consumer contracts,[21] timeshares,[22] sale of consumer goods and associated guarantees,[23] and late payment in commercial transactions.[24]

A more expansive role for the EU has been signalled in recent years. On 13 July 2001 the European Commission issued a Communication on European Contract Law to the European Parliament and the Council. The purpose of the Communication was to broaden the debate on the creation of a European contract law by encouraging contributions from consumers, businesses, professional organisations, public administrations and institutions, the academic world and all interested parties. The Commission was concerned about possible obstacles to cross-border trade within the internal market caused by the differences between the various national contract laws in Europe and sought to ascertain the extent to which differences between national laws created difficulties for commercial parties. The Communication discussed options for the future of contract law in the EC and set out a non-exhaustive list of four options to stimulate discussion:

— *Option I: no EC action*, leaving interest groups and others to advise on cross-border trade and solve problems encountered in it;
— *Option II: promote the development of common contract law principles leading to more convergence of national laws*, encouraging the development of non-binding restatements of principles;
— *Option III: improve the quality of legislation already in place*, concentrating attention on reviewing existing Directives, modernising, extending and simplifying them so as to produce a more rational and coherent set of laws; and
— *Option IV: adopt new comprehensive legislation at EC level*. This could take the form of a Directive, a Regulation or a Recommendation, and could range from an optional set of rules to be incorporated by the parties to rules that apply unless excluded or even to a mandatory code. The level of harmonisation that would be effected would depend very much on the form and extent of the model chosen.

Following the publication of the Communication, the Commission received contributions from some 180 stakeholders, the largest number coming from

[20] Council Directive 90/314/EEC of 13 June 1990 on package travel, package holidays and package tours [1990] OJ L158/59.

[21] Council Directive 93/13/EEC of 5 April 1993 on unfair terms in consumer contracts [1993] OJ L95/29.

[22] Directive 94/47/EC of the European Parliament and of the Council of 26 October 1994 on the protection of purchasers in respect of certain aspects of contracts relating to the purchase of the right to use immovable properties on a timeshare basis [1994] OJ L280/83.

[23] Directive 99/44/EC of the European Parliament and of the Council of 25 May 1999 on certain aspects of the sale of consumer goods and associated guarantees [1999] OJ L171/12.

[24] Directive 2000/35/EC of the European Parliament and of the Council of 29 June 2000 on combating late payment in commercial transactions [2000] OJ L200/35.

the academic and business communities, with a considerable number from governments and legal practitioners. In addition, the European Council, the European Parliament and the Economic and Social Committee each produced responses to the Communication. This interest of the Community Institutions and stakeholders shows the importance of the debate launched by the Communication. Of the four options put forward, the majority of contributors rejected Option I on the grounds that it was unrealistic and inadequate, and that it failed to give sufficient protection to weaker parties. By contrast, Option II attracted more favourable comment, although a number of respondents saw this as merely a step on the way to a new legal instrument at the community level (Option IV). Option III seemed to be the most favoured solution, receiving support from governments, business, consumer organisations, legal practitioners and academic lawyers. Opinions varied on Option IV. Some respondents saw a uniform and comprehensive European civil code as the best solution to the problems identified, whereas others were strongly opposed to the creation of a civil code.

In 2003 the Commission produced a further communication in the form of an Action Plan.[25] In this document the Commission identified various areas in which problems may undermine the proper functioning of the internal market and the uniform application of community law. It noted support for Option II and that the 'overwhelming majority' of respondents supported Option III, and therefore proposed to continue a broad strategy of sector-specific legislation as well as non-regulatory measures. Steps to promote standard EU-wide cross-border contract terms were launched immediately.

However, the central plank of the Action Plan was more ambitious and consisted of a plan to produce a Common Frame of Reference (CFR). The CFR was to consist of a delineation of fundamental principles of European contract law (such as the principle of freedom of contract), definitions of legal terms (the examples given were 'contract' and 'damage') and possibly model rules. The CFR was intended for use when existing legislation was being reviewed and new legislation drawn up so as to improve consistency in community legislation; it was also hoped that the CFR would be taken into account in the drafting of national legislation and so further encourage the convergence of contract legal rules throughout Europe. Finally, it was hoped that the CFR would provide the foundation for the development of an optional instrument, should that option be pursued. Over 120 responses to the Action Plan were received and published on the website, again from a wide range of stakeholders. There was some scepticism about the efficacy and desirability of measures intended to increase the use of EU-wide standard

---

[25] Communication from the Commission to the European Parliament and the Council, 'A More Coherent European Contract Law: An Action Plan', COM(2003) 68 final, available at http://europa.eu.int/comm/consumers/cons_int/safe_shop/fair_bus_pract/cont_law/com_2003_68_en.pdf.

contract terms. With regard to the CFR, there was broad support, although perhaps some confusion as to what exactly it entailed.

On 11 October 2004 the Commission issued a further Communication on a European contract law and the revision of the *acquis*: The Way Forward.[26] In this document the Commission stated that it would 'pursue the elaboration of the CFR.' It is clear that the CFR will play a crucial role in the development of a European contract law. At present, the Commission considers that 'the CFR would be a non-binding instrument,' although it acknowledges that this is an issue on which divergent views have been expressed and which it may be necessary to re-visit. The main role of the CFR will lie, at least initially, in the improvement of the existing *acquis*. To this end, there will be a review of eight consumer Directives in order to determine whether the Directives meet the Commission's consumer protection and internal market goals.[27] But the CFR will not be confined to the present and future *acquis*: a more extensive role for the CFR is envisaged. Thus it is suggested that the CFR could: (i) be taken into account by national legislators 'when transposing EU directives in the area of contract law into national legislation'; (ii) be used in arbitration to 'find unbiased and balanced solutions to resolve conflicts arising between contractual parties'; (iii) be developed 'into a body of standard contract terms to be made available to legal practitioners'; and (iv) 'inspire the European Court of Justice when interpreting the *acquis* on contract law.' The preparation of the CFR will be undertaken, at least initially, by a group of researchers who will be expected to deliver a final report to the Commission in 2007. This research

> will aim to identify best solutions, taking into account national contract laws (both case law and established practice), the EC *acquis* and relevant international instruments, particularly the UN Convention on Contracts for the International Sale of Goods.

The proposed structure of the CFR bears a remarkable resemblance to the structure of the Principles of European Contract Law (although the Communication does not expressly acknowledge this) with the addition of chapters on sales contracts and insurance contracts. A number of workshops have been held in Brussels at which drafts prepared by the researchers have been considered by stakeholder experts.[28] Once the report prepared by the researchers has been received by the Commission, it will consider the report and subject it

---

[26] COM(2004) 651 final. The Communication has been considered by the House of Lords European Union Committee and is the subject of a report: 'European Contract Law—The Way Forward' (12th Report of Session 2004–5, HL Paper 95, 5 April 2005).

[27] The Commission is still in the 'diagnostic phase' of this work but some 'preliminary findings' are set out in the 'First Annual Progress Report on European Contract Law and the Acquis Review' COM(2005) 456 final (23 September 2005), section 3.

[28] A brief report of these workshops and the initial difficulties in running them effectively can be found in COM(2005) 456 final, above n 27, paras 2.6.2–2.6.3.

to a 'practicability test on the basis of concrete examples of the anticipated uses of the CFR,' and will consult with a wide range of interested parties. It is hoped that the adoption of the CFR will take place in 2009, when it will be published in the Official Journal of the European Union and reviewed as necessary.

The Communication of 11 October 2004 also deals with the promotion of the use of EU-wide standard terms and conditions, but there is little here that is new. The Commission stated that it would 'host a website' on which market participants could exchange information about EU-wide standard terms and conditions which they were currently using or planning to develop. However, the Commission has since changed its mind and decided that it is not appropriate to host such a website, largely because of the costs involved in setting up and maintaining such a site and its likely limited utility.[29] In particular, the Commission pointed out that standard terms and conditions tend to be drafted for a specific sector, have a limited life-span and, if they were to be held out as enforceable terms in all European jurisdictions, would have to satisfy the 'most restrictive national law' (and a standard term which was drafted in order to comply with the most restrictive national law would be of limited utility to traders who enter into transactions in Europe but not in the jurisdiction which happens to have the most restrictive national law).

Finally, the Communication of 11 October 2004 raises the more difficult issue of 'an optional instrument in European contract law.' Here the Commission states that it intends 'to continue this process in parallel with the work on developing the CFR.' But the message which emerges from this section of the document is ambiguous. On the one hand, the document states that 'it is premature to speculate about the possible outcome of this reflection,' but on the other hand it states that

> it is neither the Commission's intention to propose a 'European Civil Code' which would harmonise contract laws of Member States, nor should the reflections be seen as in any way calling into question the current approaches to promoting free circulation on the basis of flexible and efficient solutions.

Nevertheless, the linkage of the optional instrument to the progress of the CFR suggests that it would be premature to dismiss the possibility of a European civil code at some time in the medium to long term. Quite what will emerge from this process is hard to predict, but the CFR may (together with the Principles of European Contract Law) turn out to be one of the first significant steps on a road that will end with a European code of contract law.

---

[29] *Ibid*, para 4.1.

II. WHY SEEK TO CREATE A EUROPEAN CONTRACT LAW?

It is now time to turn to the second issue, namely the arguments that are commonly advanced in favour of further harmonisation of European contract law. A number of different arguments have been advanced in support of this view.

1. Increase in Cross-border Transactions

Businesses increasingly do not confine themselves or their activities within national borders. To use the jargon of the day, we now live in a global economy, and in that economy national boundaries are said to assume far less significance. The emergence of the global economy is of primary significance for businesses but it cannot be said to be confined to the world of commerce. It also has significance for consumers; not only do they travel more extensively than they once did, but widespread access to the internet has enabled potential purchasers to discover the existence of products and sellers in other jurisdictions and has enabled sellers to advertise their products on a global scale. It has been argued that, in light of this increase in cross-border transactions, the harmonisation of contract law would be beneficial, both for businesses and for consumers.[30]

2. Differences in Contract Law as a Barrier to Trade

The argument that the differences between the various national contract laws can act as a barrier to trade is a simple one; it rests on the assumption that one contracting party is less likely to be willing to enter into a transaction when that transaction is governed by the law of another state. Take, for example, the case of negotiations between a German seller and an English buyer. Neither party may be willing to conclude a contract which is governed by the law of the other party. In such a case, an impasse may be reached. An internationally accepted set of rules has the potential to break that impasse, in that it can be adopted and applied by parties from different jurisdictions. A harmonised law of contract has the appearance of neutrality that the law of a Nation State lacks. The existence of such a harmonised law would therefore reduce, if not eliminate, the battle over the law that is to govern the contract and thus remove one potential stumbling block to the formation of that

---

[30] This is not necessarily an argument in favour of the creation of a *European* law of contract. It can be argued that a global economy requires the creation of a global or an international law of contract and not an instrument which aims at regional (European) harmonisation of contract law. This point also applies to some of the other arguments which are advanced in favour of the creation of a European contract law.

contract. It is, of course, difficult, if not impossible, to ascertain the extent to which the differences between the various substantive contract laws of Nation States act as a barrier to trade. In some markets, differences between national contract laws do not appear to act as a significant barrier to trade at all. The United Kingdom provides an example in this respect.[31] Although there are substantial differences between the law of contract in Scotland and the law of contract in England, these differences do not appear to impede trade between the two countries. One must therefore be careful not to claim too much for this particular argument. Nevertheless, there would appear to be some substance to the claim that differences in national contract laws do act as a barrier to trade, if only because a lawyer in practice will in all likelihood warn her client of the legal difficulties that may follow from the conclusion of a contract which is subject to a law with which both the lawyer and the client are largely, if not wholly, unfamiliar.

3. The Growth in Standard Form Contracts and the Growing Use of Boilerplate Clauses

A boilerplate clause is a standard form clause which lawyers habitually incorporate into the contracts they draw up on behalf of their clients: examples include a choice of law clause, a jurisdiction clause, a retention of title clause, a force majeure clause, an exclusion clause and an arbitration clause. These clauses tend, however, to be neglected in the academic literature on contract law.[32] Textbooks, monographs and practitioner works (at least in England) tend to focus on the black-letter rules that make up the law of contract and pay scant consideration to the terms that are commonly to be found in modern commercial contracts. The same tendency can be seen in much of the current debate on the harmonisation of private law within Europe and beyond. When we focus on harmonisation we tend to concentrate on the black-letter rules, whether these rules are legally binding, as in most national legal systems or in instruments such as the CISG, or non-binding, as in the case of PECL or the UNIDROIT Principles of International Commercial Contracts. The debate on harmonisation has not given standard contract terms the attention that they deserve. These terms may play a very significant role in practice. Indeed, a plausible argument can be made to the effect that harmonisation is more likely to take place as a result of the increasing use of standard terms in commercial contracts than it is through the harmonisation

---

[31] Another example is the United States of America, where there are differences between the laws of the various States of the Union. The Restatements of Contract Law and the Uniform Commercial Code help to ensure a substantial degree of uniformity between the various States, but they do not require uniformity.

[32] See more generally E McKendrick, *The Creation of a European Law of Contracts—The Role of Standard Form Contracts and Principles of Interpretation* (The Hague, Kluwer, 2004).

of black-letter rules of law. Most major law firms and commercial parties have their own standard terms of business which they seek to use in the transactions which they conclude. Although there are undoubtedly differences between these standard terms, their similarities tend to be greater than their differences. These standard form clauses are as important as, if not more important than, the black-letter rules to be found in national legal systems. In this respect, we have to remember that most rules of contract law in national laws are default rules; that is to say, they apply unless they are excluded by the terms of the contract. Mandatory rules, at least in the commercial context, are relatively few. This being the case, the rules of law can be, and frequently are, displaced by the terms of the contract concluded between the parties. Thus it is the terms of the contract, rather than the rules of law, that play the principal role in the regulation of the relationship between the parties.

The claim that the standard terms to be found in modern commercial contracts are of great significance for legal practice is an important one in terms of the current debate on the harmonisation of contract law. In particular, it suggests a rather different agenda for those involved in the process of harmonisation. Rather than focus on issues of legal doctrine, such as consideration, cause and good faith, greater attention ought to be given to the rules and principles applied by the courts when interpreting contractual documents. This is so for three reasons.

First, commercial parties generally have their own standard terms and conditions of business, and the meaning of these terms is a matter of great significance to them.

Secondly, these terms are often used not only for domestic transactions (that is to say, contracts concluded between parties within the same jurisdiction) but also for international or cross-border transactions. This use of standard terms in contracts between parties from different jurisdictions makes the development of a common understanding of these terms a matter of greater importance. If standard contract terms are interpreted in different ways in different jurisdictions, or if the parties' understanding of these terms differs, then greater difficulties are likely to arise when seeking to conclude an international transaction.

Thirdly, many contractual disputes turn on the proper interpretation of the terms of the contract that has been concluded between the parties. That this is so can be illustrated by the fact that the most cited case in modern English contract law is *Investors Compensation Scheme v West Bromwich Building Society*,[33] a case in which Lord Hoffmann re-stated the principles to be applied by the courts when interpreting contractual documents. A

---

[33] [1998] 1 WLR 896. A LEXIS search conducted on 14 October 2002 revealed that the case had been cited in over 180 cases. The case continues to be cited regularly in the courts. See further E McKendrick, 'The Interpretation of Contracts: Lord Hoffmann's Re-Statement' in S Worthington (ed), *Commercial Law and Commercial Practice* (Oxford, Hart Publishing, 2003) 139.

common approach to the interpretation of contracts could play a significant role in the development of a common understanding of the meaning of standard contract terms and could also assist in the reduction of disputes (or help make such disputes as do arise easier to resolve).

4. National Laws Unsuitable for International Transactions

The argument that national rules of contract law may be unsuitable for international transactions is rather difficult to evaluate because it rests ultimately on the quality of the legal rules that are to be found in national legal systems. It is undoubtedly the case that the laws and legal systems of many Nation States in the world are not suited to the regulation of international transactions. However, this argument has limited application within Europe, where the quality of national contract laws is generally high. In any event, the remedy for this problem may be said to lie in the hands of the parties, namely not to choose the unsuitable law as the law applicable to the contract.

It has sometimes been suggested that individual rules of law within national legal systems may not be suitable for international transactions. Professor Lando[34] gives the example of a provision in the Scandinavian Sale of Goods Act which provided that the buyer who wishes to 'invoke a late delivery of the goods must give notice immediately upon delivery.'[35] He states that this rule is 'not fit for international sales'[36] and that it may act as a 'trap' for non-Scandinavian buyers who are unaware of the existence of the rule. Much better, he argues, is Article 49(2) of the CISG, which gives to the buyer a reasonable time in which to give notice to the seller. Every legal system has rules of this nature. They do little harm within the context of the national legal system because the lawyers know the rules or can be assumed to know them, but this does not necessarily hold good at the international level. For example, while English lawyers can be assumed to know that the phrase 'time is of the essence' means that a failure to comply with a time stipulation will give to the other party the right to terminate further performance of the contract, it cannot be assumed that all foreign lawyers will realise the consequences which follow from an agreement to make time of the essence. Thus it can be said that the elimination of rules which are unsuitable for international transactions or which cause an element of what may be termed 'unfair surprise' will help to promote international trade. While there is much to be said for this argument in theory, the problem in practice lies in identifying those rules of national law which are thought to be particularly unsuitable for international transactions. This is an issue which is likely to produce disagreement between lawyers in national legal systems. However, it may be

[34] O Lando, 'The Lex Mercatoria in International Commercial Arbitration' (1985) 34 *ICLQ* 747.
[35] *Ibid*, 753.

possible to recast the argument by relying more heavily on the notion of 'unfair surprise'. One problem with national rules of contract law is that lawyers working in other jurisdictions may not easily discover them. To this extent, they may create a problem which the lawyer from the 'foreign' jurisdiction could not have recognised. This same problem should not arise with international rules (or, perhaps more accurately, it should not arise to the same extent). This is particularly so in the case of instruments such as the CISG, where the text of the Convention, the case law interpreting its provisions and much academic commentary thereon is freely available via the internet. Lawyers who conclude contracts that are subject to the CISG are not well placed to take the point that they could not ascertain the consequences to their client of the application of the CISG to their contract.

5. The Growth of International Commercial Arbitration

International arbitration as a means of resolving disputes is growing. Arbitrators are less constrained than judges in national courts in terms of the materials upon which they can draw when making decisions. Unlike state courts in Europe, arbitrators can apply the PECL as the law applicable to a contract, at least where the arbitral rules so allow.[37] The use by business parties of arbitration as a means of dispute resolution may indicate that they are not necessarily committed to the resolution of their disputes in accordance with national laws. To this extent, transnational or supranational standards or principles seem to have an accepted role to play in the resolution of international commercial disputes.

6. National Laws Cannot Solve the Problems which Currently Confront Those Who Enter International Transactions

National laws cannot solve all of the problems that currently confront international commerce, particularly when we move from the realms of contract law and into the law of secured transactions. The Convention on International Interests in Mobile Equipment provides a useful illustration of this. How can developing nations acquire assets such as aeroplanes and satellites at reasonable cost? The willingness of financial institutions to advance money to developing nations in order to enable them to acquire such expensive items of equipment depends upon the ability of the financier to obtain an adequate security over the asset. Yet it can be no easy task to obtain such a security. In

---

[36] *Ibid.*
[37] The problem for national courts lies in Art 3 of the Rome Convention on the Law Applicable to Contractual Obligations, on which see further p 9 above.

this context, the difficulty is that an asset such as an aeroplane is constantly travelling from one jurisdiction to another. The financier is obviously in a vulnerable position if the debtor can defeat his security by the simple expedient of causing the aeroplane to take off from the home jurisdiction to land in another in which the creditor cannot enforce his security. This is a problem which cannot be resolved at the level of the Nation State. It requires cooperation between Nation States and the recognition of an 'international interest' which is recognised and enforced in different Nation States. This argument carries less force in the context of contract law because contractual rights are generally personal in nature and thus are enforced against an identified party rather than against an identified or identifiable asset. Contractual rights cannot be defeated with the same ease as a security interest over an asset which is constantly moving between jurisdictions. While this is so, it is important not to create an unnecessary gulf between the law of contract and the law of securities. Many security interests are the product of agreement between the parties. A harmonised contract law has the potential to provide a secure foundation upon which those who frame rules in other areas of law (such as securities) can build.

III. WHY OBJECT TO THE CREATION OF A EUROPEAN CONTRACT LAW?

The case for further harmonisation of European private law is not, however, beyond dispute. Indeed, many voices have been raised against further harmonisation and some have even argued that we have already gone too far down the road towards the creation of a harmonised European private law. Many, but by no means all, of these criticisms have emanated from England. The aim of this section is to identify the principal arguments which have been advanced by those who are hostile to the harmonisation process. This account is drawn from the objections raised by various British respondents to the European Commission.[38] It is possible to dismiss these objections on the ground that they are peculiar to the English and are not of wider significance. A widespread belief among civilian lawyers is that the English are motivated simply by a concern to preserve the common law tradition. There is undoubtedly some truth in this belief. There is indeed a concern in some quarters that the global significance of the common law will suffer if national laws of contract are to be replaced by a European contract law. However, if we examine the responses to the Commission Communications—in particular the response issued by the Bar Council to the 2001 Communication, which considers the issue in some depth—it becomes clear that this is not an emotional concern, but a fundamentally pragmatic one. As the Bar Council

---

[38] The account that follows draws heavily on work done by my research assistant, Rachel Kapila, to whom appropriate acknowledgement must be made.

emphasises, every year a large number of international commercial contracts are concluded which provide for English law as the governing law and which subject the parties' disputes to the jurisdiction of the English courts, even though they have no other obvious connection with England.[39] The reason for this is said to be that certain features of English law are seen as 'extremely attractive' to the international business community; in particular, its commitment to the principles of freedom of contract, certainty and consistency in dispute resolution. The effect of this, the Bar Council maintains, is that:

> ...English law is acting as an invisible export from the UK, and often (where businesses domiciled in non-contracting states are involved, as is frequently the case) from the European Union: creating work for the lawyers involved in the drafting of such contracts; and for lawyers assisting in the resolution of disputes arising out of such contracts.[40]

According to a report commissioned by the Lord Chancellor and published in February 2001 ('the Cap Gemini Report'),[41] by the end of the last millennium UK legal services attracted about £800 million a year in invisible earnings. If a mandatory scheme of harmonised European contract law were introduced, the Bar Council argues, considerable volumes of international legal business would be lost to the United States and other non-EU jurisdictions; further, they claim that this would do 'serious and irreparable damage to a large sector of the European economy.'

Given these financial considerations, English concerns about any possible threat to the global significance of the common law are understandable. Notwithstanding this point, however, it is submitted that the belief that the English are motivated solely, or even chiefly, by a desire to preserve the common law tradition is misconceived. There are in fact numerous reasons why English stakeholders are unenthusiastic about the development of a European contract law, all of which could be maintained by stakeholders from other Member States.

Underpinning all the English submissions (and no doubt most of the submissions emanating from other Member States) is the view that harmonisation should not be pursued 'just for the sake of it', but should be pursued only where there is a demonstrable need for such action, and after careful

---

[39] This is confirmed by the survey for the conference at which this paper was given (see the contribution of Vogenauer and Weatherill in this volume, ch 7, p 121). Participants were asked which law was the most used when conducting cross-border transactions. UK law ('for these purposes, probably synonymous with English law') was much the most used, at 26%; no other single country scored more than 11% (France). If those who said that they did not know or refused to answer are excluded, the figure for the use of UK law rises to 49%.

[40] Response to COM(2001), para 6.

[41] Cap Gemini Ernst & Young, *Commercial Court Feasibility Study*, prepared for the Lord Chancellor's Department, issued in February 2001.

consideration of the impact of the change on businesses and consumers. This was expressly stated by the UK government as follows:

The UK Government considers it axiomatic that:

— any action at EC level should be in response to a demonstrable need for action at that level to deal with a real (not just a theoretical) problem;
— there should be a reasonable likelihood of achieving agreement;
— the measures proposed should be proportionate to, and targeted on, the problem in question; and
— action should be taken only after a careful assessment of the net effect of the change on business and consumers to ensure that it was, on balance, beneficial.[42]

It is essentially a belief that these requirements are not satisfied which motivates English scepticism towards the development of a European contract law. Using the UK government's 'axioms' as a framework, the English arguments can be divided into four main categories, each of which is considered in turn.

1. Divergent Laws Do Not Act as a Barrier to Trade

Several English responses to the Commission Communications emphasise that the coexistence of different national laws of contract is not, in itself, necessarily inimical to the functioning of an effective internal market. Thus, the UK government points out that the UK itself is a long-standing example of a 'perfectly functioning single market', notwithstanding the fact that significant differences exist between the legal systems in Scotland and in England and Wales. The states of the USA can be said to furnish another example of different laws of contract operating effectively within a single market.[43]

Given that, in principle, an internal market is capable of functioning with different national laws, it has been argued that it is necessary to look for specific, 'real' problems arising from the different national laws of Member States before action at the EU level can be said to be necessary. The crux of many contributors' arguments is that no such problems can be identified; or alternatively that, while problems can be identified, they are not sufficiently serious to require the development of a European contract law. Thus, the UK government, in discussing paragraph 28 of the 2001 Communication, which considers the possibility that cross-border trade could be obstructed if

---

[42] Response to COM(2001), para 5; response to 2003 Action Plan, para 3.
[43] It is, however, important to note the role played by the Uniform Commercial Code (and, to a lesser extent, the various Restatements prepared by the American Law Institute) in bringing the laws of the various States closer together. The Uniform Commercial Code has exerted enormous influence, not only within the USA, but also in jurisdictions further afield.

different national contract laws contained contradictory mandatory rules, states that:

> No example of an existing contradiction between national mandatory rules is cited, and the UK Government is not aware of any.[44]

Similar comments are made by the Financial Services Authority (FSA) and the Consumers' Association. Other contributors, eg the Law Society and the Society of Public Teachers of Law (SPTL), accept that there are, or may be, problems in practice arising from different national laws, but argue that these problems are not insurmountable. As the Confederation of British Industry (CBI) observes, the 2001 Communication is viewed by many as being 'a solution in search of a problem'.[45]

Several arguments are put forward by contributors in support of the proposition that there is no 'real' problem, and therefore no 'demonstrable need' for action at the EU level. First, the SPTL points out that the differences between national systems of contract law should not be overstated:

> [I]n a number of areas there are already broad and extensive similarities between the laws of Member States, due in part, no doubt, to their common origins. This is often the case in those areas of law where rules are derived from the mediaeval *lex mercatoria*, such as the law of bills of exchange.[46]

The view that Member States' national laws of contract are wholly divergent and contradictory is misconceived; despite their dissimilar methods of reasoning, these national systems often produce similar results.[47]

Secondly, many contributors argue that there are other, more significant barriers to trade than the diversity of laws. The FSA cites 'language, culture and currency,' to which the SPTL adds 'logistical problems' and the 'practical difficulties of enforcing rights.' The CBI lists numerous barriers, including: fiscal differences between Member States; interpretation and enforcement of existing directives; lack of coordination between directives; lack of a consistent country of origin principle; different civil justice procedures and pre-contractual differences between Member States; and the Commission's

---

[44] Response to COM(2001), para 7.

[45] This is not to say that this perception is correct. The survey for the conference at which this paper was given (see above n 39) reveals that there is a significant perception among those surveyed that obstacles to cross-border trade do exist between EU Member States (see further ch 7, pp 125–7 below).

[46] Response to COM(2001), para 11.

[47] Some support for this proposition can be gleaned from the Trento project (the Common Core of European Private Law). Some of the studies concluded as part of this project demonstrate that the differences between the laws of the various European states can be overstated. In particular, the divide between the common law and civilian systems is not as sharp as some would have us believe. In many cases, the common law and civilian courts reach similar results, albeit by rather different routes: see, eg R Zimmermann and S Whittaker, *Good Faith in European Contract Law* (Cambridge University Press, 2000).

own decision-making procedures. Similar sentiments are expressed by the Consumers' Association and the Law Society. There are two points being made here. The first is that there are other, more significant barriers to trade than the diversity of the rules of law that make up the law of contract. As Clifford Chance emphasises, in its response to the 2003 Action Plan, contract law 'cannot be viewed in isolation'; it overlaps with many other areas of law, 'including restitution, prescription and property.' Any attempt to remove legal barriers to trade

> would necessitate not just a review of contract law, but a far wider exploration of the Member States' laws and judicial procedures.

The second point is that there are other more significant barriers to trade than the diversity of laws in general. Even if all legal barriers to trade were removed (including those outside the law of contract), the various non-legal barriers, such as language and culture, would remain.[48]

The third argument in support of the proposition that there is no 'real' problem, and therefore no 'demonstrable need' for action at the EU level, is that choice of law clauses reduce the problems caused by differences in national laws of contract. In the words of the Bar Council:

> In the United States, the different states have different systems of private contract law. This has not hindered cross-border trade within the US. The reason why the difference[s] in national contract laws are not a real impediment to inter-state trade (whether in the US or the EU) is because the parties to a cross-border transaction can currently stipulate for a choice of law clause to govern their relationship, and effect will generally be given to that choice of law clause. Within the EU this is done pursuant to Article 3(1) of the Rome Convention (enacted by all the EU Member States).[49]

This argument is not, however, conclusive because it tends to overlook the difficulties which can and do arise in terms of securing agreement on the law that is to govern the transaction. As has been noted,[50] it can be argued that the need to secure agreement on matters such as the choice of the governing law itself can act as a barrier to trade.

The final argument is that such problems as do exist are to some extent ameliorated by existing international instruments. These instruments can assume different forms. In some cases they aim simply to harmonise the rules of private international law, whereas in other cases the aim is the more

---

[48] That said, the survey for the conference at which this paper was given (see above n 39) revealed that factors such as language and culture seem to have less of an impact than matters such as tax and the cost of obtaining foreign legal advice. Thus it would appear that specifically legal matters do seem to count for more in the equation than the softer, non-legal issues.
[49] Response to COM(2001), para 16.
[50] See above p 14.

ambitious one of harmonising the underlying substantive law. In this context, the CBI emphasises the important role played by the CISG, while the SPTL focuses on the Rome Convention on the Law Applicable to Contractual Obligations and what is now the Council Regulation on Jurisdiction and the Recognition and Enforcement of Judgments in Civil and Commercial Matters (more commonly known as Brussels I).[51]

2. Such Problems as Do Exist Do not Demand the Creation of a European Contract Law

Many of the English responses to the Commission Communications stress that, even if there is a 'real' problem arising from the diversity of national laws, this does not mean that legislative action at EC level is required. Two main arguments are advanced to this effect.

In the first place, it has been argued that there is considerable scope for the market to develop solutions to potential problems. This can be done, for example, by the development of cross-border model contracts for voluntary use in particular sectors, such as the Master Agreements developed by the International Swaps Derivatives Association. Also of importance in this context are the 'boilerplate' clauses to be found in many modern commercial contracts.[52] Given that many rules of contract law are default rules, these standard clauses frequently oust the otherwise applicable rules of law and thus are of enormous significance in the practice of contracting across the world. The UK government argues thus:

> A particular advantage of the market option is that it is likely to be more flexible and responsive, particularly in the face of rapid technological developments, than a legislative solution.[53]

This sentiment is echoed by the CBI, the Consumers' Association and the Commercial Bar Association. It is also echoed by the SPTL, which offers, as a further example, letters of credit,

> where there is already a large measure of international harmonisation as a result of the widespread use of the Uniform Customs and Practice for Documentary Credits prepared by the International Chamber of Commerce.

The London Investment Banking Association (LIBA) expresses the argument as follows:

---

[51] Council Regulation 44/2001 of 22 December 2000 [2001] OJ L12/1.
[52] On which see further McKendrick, above n 32.
[53] Response to COM(2001), para 18.

The Commission should give full weight to the ability of the market mechanism to overcome problems: this applies particularly in inter-professional markets, where the level of circumspection and bargaining power of the parties to the contract is similar, and they can therefore be relied on to arrive at an appropriate resolution of any problems without outside intervention. In professional financial services markets extensive use is made of standard contract clauses which have been developed by the industry itself specifically to eliminate any problems caused by conflict of laws: it would be inappropriate for legislators to interfere with this well-functioning mechanism.[54]

The second argument advanced is that a practical and proportionate response to problems caused, essentially, by unfamiliarity with different laws is not to harmonise those laws, but to focus on improving access to information and guidance about them. As the UK government in particular argues, such efforts could readily be targeted on those sectors experiencing significant problems. The UK government goes on to suggest, in its response to the 2003 Action Plan, that psychological barriers could effectively be addressed by a 'thesaurus' which would allow economic actors to 'translate' concepts from one legal system to another. The CFR, it argues, could fill this role. In a similar vein, the CBI suggests that it might be helpful to business if the Commission could publish a comparative table setting out the main differences in contract law between different Member States:

> That way businesses could be alerted to differences before entering into contracts and it would also provide a more specific and useful basis for consultation with members as to difficulties encountered.

The Consumers' Association states simply that: 'Information and education is key.'

Regarding both arguments, the point being made in the English submissions is an important one: even if there are problems arising from the diversity of national contract laws, it does not follow that harmonisation is the solution. There are other, arguably superior, ways in which these problems can be addressed.

Viewing the submissions outlined so far together, a third, related argument comes into play. Several English contributors argue that, given the doubts as to whether there is a 'real' problem in need of a solution, and the view that even if there were such a problem legislative action would not be an appropriate response, to adopt a new instrument at EC level would be disproportionate and likely to cut across the principle of subsidiarity. This argument is adopted, in particular, by the UK government, the FSA, the LIBA, the Consumers' Association and Clifford Chance. It is also endorsed by the Bar Council, which observes that in the current political climate—following

---

[54] Response to COM(2001), 2.

the Maastricht and Amsterdam amendments to the EC Treaty—the principles of subsidiarity and proportionality have become 'entrenched'. These principles, the Bar Council argues, are 'fundamental'; they cannot simply be pushed to one side when considering the course of action which should be taken.

3. The Disadvantages of Harmonisation

A further set of arguments focuses on the practical difficulties and disadvantages of developing a European contract law. To use the language of the UK government's 'axioms',[55] the basis of these objections is first, that there is no 'reasonable likelihood of achieving agreement'; and secondly, that the net effect of the change would not necessarily be beneficial.

Virtually all the English submissions emphasise that, due to the major legal, political and cultural sensitivities involved, it would be very difficult, if not impossible, for Member States to reach agreement on a text. The SPTL describes it as a 'Herculean task,' the Law Society suggests it would cause 'immense difficulties' and many other contributors express similar views, some pointing out that the tension within Europe between the common law and civil law approaches would give rise to particular complications. In his response to the 2001 Communication, Professor Sir Roy Goode argues cogently against the replacement of existing national law, giving, inter alia, the following reason:

> I can see no prospect of agreement among Member States of the Union. Contract law is a major part of the law of obligations. In any given country it is shaped not merely by scientific considerations but by the structure and philosophy of that country's entire legal system, its culture, its language and its tradition. The divergences among European states are so great that it is difficult to see how any Member State could accept the imposition of a uniform contract law. What is acceptable in a non-binding set of rules may be quite different if imposed on a national legal system. In the case of the [Principles of European Contract Law] I was quite happy, for example, to accept a rule making specific performance the primary remedy and prepared, though rather less willingly, to live with a rule that did not allow the court a general discretion. It would be quite another thing to have this as a rule of English law, which in my opinion proceeds on the correct assumption that, in commercial transactions at least, what businessmen are primarily interested in is money, not specific performance. Again, it is hard to see the English law rule against penalties finding acceptance in France, where the imposition of contractual penalties is considered an entirely legitimate stipulation.[56]

The CBI points out that not only would it be difficult to achieve consensus, but the adoption of a text would have to be followed by a common approach

---

[55] See above p 21.
[56] Response to COM(2001), para 11.

to interpretation, and this, they claim, would be even more difficult to achieve.[57] It has also been argued that an instrument which attempted harmonisation but was incomplete—that is to say, it did not encompass every commercial aspect of a contract, including its interpretation—could be more damaging than no instrument at all:

> Action by the Commission could . . . be a trap for the unwary and mislead business and consumers into believing that the situation would be the same throughout the EU when this would not in fact be the case.[58]

The conclusion of many contributors is that the harmonisation project would be a formidable task, and one which would probably prove unsuccessful.

4. The Virtue of Diversity

The arguments outlined in the previous section are, broadly speaking, negative ones; they focus on the disadvantages of adopting an instrument at EC level. In contrast, the following argument is essentially positive; it maintains that the current system has one key advantage, which it is worth fighting to preserve. The Bar Council expresses the argument as follows. Under the current system, through the mechanism of choice of law clauses, parties to cross-border transactions can negotiate for a system of law within the framework of which they are content to do business.[59] For larger business transactions, the Bar Council argues, this creates little hardship: either the parties will stipulate for a system of law with which they are already familiar and comfortable or they will agree to a foreign system of law, but on terms (eg as to price, limitations of liability, insurance). The crux of the argument is that:

> Far from stifling competition, the wide range of national legal systems currently available promotes the range of choice available to these cross-border suppliers. Furthermore, this competition between the different systems of private law has much to commend it. As noted by K Zweigert and H Kötz in their *Introduction to Comparative Law*,[60] when considering the comparable position in the USA:

---

[57] But it is not impossible. As has been pointed out above (pp 16–17) a case can be made out for the harmonisation of the principles or rules of contract interpretation on the ground that there is a great need for a common approach to the interpretation of contracts. It may well be worth the time and effort involved in order to overcome these difficulties. The Principles of European Contract Law contain principles to be applied in the interpretation of contracts and these could form the basis for a common approach to interpretation.

[58] Response to COM(2001), para 13.

[59] See more generally, on the value of diversity, E McKendrick, 'Traditional Concepts and Contemporary Values' (2002) 10 *European Review of Private Law* 95, especially 103–6.

[60] Translated by Tony Weir (2nd edn, Oxford, Clarendon Press, 1992) 258.

'Thus the United States can be seen as a gigantic laboratory for legal policy in which any state can move forward in any direction by legislation or judicial decision and thus gain experience and reach views which enrich the debates on legal policy and may serve as an encouraging or horrifying example to other states.'

That choice should be preserved, and not done away with by the introduction of a common mandatory code, with which no one would initially be familiar.[61]

The point is made more concisely by Goode, who, under the heading 'The value of diversity', argues:

Within the field of mandatory law harmonisation may be essential to the proper functioning of the Common Market. But in the realm of general dispositive law there is much to be said for retaining the rich diversity of national legal systems, so that contracting parties have a wide range of choice and select their own law or that of another legal system with which they feel comfortable. European legal culture would be greatly impoverished if, at the level of fundamental principle and dispositive law, a single set of rules were to be imposed on Member States.[62]

There are a number of issues in contract law which are difficult to resolve. When should a breach of contract entitle the other party to terminate further performance of the contract? When should a change of circumstances entitle a court to adapt or to terminate the contract between the parties? What should be the role of good faith within contract law and what meaning is to be given to the phrase 'good faith'? These are difficult questions and they can be answered in different ways by reasonable, informed individuals. Given that this is so, should we persist in our quest for a uniform solution to these (and other) problems? Would it not be better to celebrate our diversity rather than continue the quest for (a dull) uniformity?

IV. THE FUTURE

The future course of the harmonisation of European contract law is difficult, if not impossible, to predict. The likelihood is that the calls for further harmonisation of national contract laws will increase in future years. But, as this chapter has sought to demonstrate, the arguments are not all one way. There are serious obstacles to be overcome on the road to further harmonisation and proponents of the view that there ought to be further harmonisation would do well to take them seriously.

The tenor of this chapter will doubtless strike many as being unduly sceptical of the merits of the case for further harmonisation of European contract law. But let us suppose that we do take the merits of harmonisation

---

[61] Response to COM(2001), para 17.
[62] Response to COM(2001), para 11.

seriously. On this view, a further question arises. If we do believe in the virtues of harmonisation, why insist on harmonisation at a European level? Why not go a stage further and advocate harmonisation at a global level? The (alleged) difficulties caused by differences in national legal systems can be said to be an international issue, rather than a specifically European one. As the SPTL response to the Commission Communication emphasises, 'international trade is increasingly global in nature' and the problems associated with differences between national laws are 'not confined to the EU.' This argument is best illustrated, perhaps, by the CISG. Given that the CISG is now well recognised internationally, why would one want to create a European law of sales which is separate and distinct from the CISG? Is the CISG not appropriate for contracts of sale concluded between Member States of the EU? A similar question can be posed in relation to the PECL. Why make use of the PECL when we have a global equivalent, the UNIDROIT Principles of International Commercial Contracts? In the modern world it is becoming increasingly difficult to discern the level at which matters are most appropriately regulated. Some matters which were previously the domain of the Nation State have been devolved down to regional assemblies. Others have gone up a level to what may be termed the transnational regional level (eg Europe), while others have gone further to a truly international stage. It is unlikely that contract law will in the future be regulated at the level of a regional assembly. The most likely battleground (at least in Europe) is whether regulation should be at the level of the Nation State, or at a European or international level. As matters stand, it would appear that the Nation State has the most to lose as calls for greater harmonisation increase. But, as the responses to the various Commission Communications demonstrate, those who wish to preserve national contract laws can be expected to fight their case in vigorous terms. It is far too early to write the obituary for national contract laws in Europe. The debate still has a long way to go.

3

English Law Reform and the Impact of European Private Law

HUGH BEALE[*]

The interaction between European private law and law reform in England and Wales must be considered at two levels: the impact of Community law, in other words of Community legislation and the jurisprudence of the European Court of Justice, and the impact of the laws of the other Members States, whether directly or mediated through 'soft law' instruments such as the Principles of European Contract Law.

I. THE IMPACT OF COMMUNITY LAW

The impact of Community legislation on English law, and similarly on its law reform, has been relatively slight for two reasons. The first is a form of institutional failure; the second, a pragmatism among the leaders of the English legal establishment that leads to an innate conservatism.

Institutional failure is exemplified by when European directives are implemented by 'copy-out', so that new legislation is superimposed on the existing law rather than by adjusting English law to 'fit' the requirements of the directive. Sometimes the implementing legislation is completely separate. This was the case with implementation of the Directive on Unfair Terms in Consumer Contracts:[1] the Unfair Terms in Consumer Contracts Regulations 1994[2] and the 1999 regulations of the same name[3] that replace them do not purport to amend the Unfair Contract terms Act 1977 but are simply superimposed. On other occasions the implementing legislation does amend the existing legislation, but does so merely by adding additional sections. Thus, in order

---

[*] The views expressed here are purely personal.

[1] Council Directive 93/13/EEC of 5 April 1993 on unfair terms in consumer contracts [1993] OJ L95/29.

[2] SI 1994/3159.

[3] SI 1999/2083, amended by Unfair Terms in Consumer Contracts (Amendment) Regulations 2001, SI 2001/1186.

to implement the Directive on Consumer Sales,[4] the Sale and Supply of Goods to Consumers Regulations 2002[5] have amended the Sale of Goods Act 1979 primarily by adding new sections.

Implementing a directive by copying out its words directly into domestic legislation is entirely defensible when the directive covers ground on which there is no existing domestic legislation or directly relevant caselaw. For example, the Products Liability Directive[6] purported to create a form of 'strict liability'[7] on producers for injury caused by defective products which had no direct counterpart in English law. It is sensible that the Consumer Protection Act 1987 follows the wording of the directive fairly closely.[8] It is also justified where the existing English law is closely similar to the directive, as with the Directive on Consumer Credit.[9] However, it is not justified where a new directive overlaps with existing law or where it uses significantly different concepts or terminology.

This was certainly the case with the Unfair Terms in Consumer Contracts Directive. I will give just two examples.[10] Under the Unfair Terms Act 1977 some exclusion or limitation of liability clauses in consumer contracts are simply of no effect[11]; others may be valid if they are fair and reasonable.[12] The latter includes any term that would entitle the business to perform in a way that is substantially different to what the consumer reasonably expected. The Unfair Terms in Consumer Contracts Regulations require that any clause that is not a 'core term'[13] not be 'unfair'. The terms of a consumer contract are subject to both sets of controls. The resulting law is incoherent and quite unnecessarily complex. Businesses and consumers (or more realistically, consumer advisers) have to be familiar with both sets of rules and the meaning of both 'fair and reasonable' under the Act and 'fair' under the

---

[4] Directive 1999/44/EC of the European Parliament and of the Council of 25 May 1999 on certain aspects of the sale of consumer goods and associated guarantees [1999] OJ L171/12.

[5] SI 2002/3045.

[6] Council Directive 85/374/EEC of 25 July 1985 on the approximation of the laws, regulations and administrative provisions of the Member States concerning liability for defective products [1985] OJ L210/29.

[7] In fact, the strictness of the liability is heavily qualified, eg by the need to show that the product was 'defective' and by the 'development risk' defence in Art 7(e), transposed by s 4(1)(e) of the Act.

[8] But not precisely: see Case C–300/95 *Commission v United Kingdom* [1997] ECR I–2649 on how s 4(1)(e) must be interpreted so as to conform to the Directive.

[9] Council Directive 87/102/EEC of 22 December 1986 for the approximation of the laws, regulations and administrative provisions of the Member States concerning consumer credit [1987] OJ L42/48.

[10] For a full study of the differences, see Law Commissions, 'Unfair Terms in Contracts, a Joint Consultation Paper' (Law Com Consultation Paper No 166, Scot Law Com Discussion Paper No 119, 2002), available at www.lawcom.gov.uk.

[11] Eg a clause limiting liability when the goods are not of satisfactory quality under the Sale of Goods Act 1979, s 14: see Unfair Contract Terms Act, s 6(2).

[12] Unfair Contract Terms Act, s 3.

[13] The main definition of the subject matter of the adequacy of the price, provided they are in plain intelligible language: Unfair Terms in Consumer Contracts Regulations, reg 6(2).

Regulations—if they are different. Not only was there complaint from academics; businesses and consumers complained, and the Department of Trade and Industry had to ask the Law Commissions to produce a unified and more accessible regime for unfair terms in contracts. This they have done.[14] Whether the government will accept the Report and implement it remains to be seen.

Although the Sale and Supply of Goods to Consumers Regulations 2002[15] implemented the Consumer Sales Directive primarily by amending the Sale of Goods Act 1979, the net result is much the same. The principal change is that the Regulations add new sections to the Act, giving consumers additional rights to repair and replacement of goods that do not conform to the contract. However, consumers' existing rights to reject the goods or to claim damages appear not to be affected. Thus again there are overlapping provisions that result in great complexity. Discussions between Law Commission staff and newly trained consumer advisers suggest that the advisers find the law overwhelmingly difficult. There is now a strong case for a consumer supply of goods and services Act. The amendments also leave the general law of sales incoherent. Why is the right to demand repair or replacement of non-conforming goods available only to consumers? It seems to be a rule that would be suitable for many commercial sales,[16] and in my experience many sales contracts contain express provisions to a similar effect.

There are reasons for copy-out. First, it is quicker and easier. Frequently directives have to be implemented in a relatively short time by Departments whose resources are already stretched. Secondly, it reduces the risk that the directive will not be implemented correctly. Thirdly, most directives are somewhat ephemeral in two senses: they affect only consumer law and they are subject to review after a relatively short period.[17]

However, none of these reasons is persuasive. When copy-out takes the form it has in the case of unfair terms, it saves no time at all in the long

---

[14] See their Joint Report, 'Unfair Terms in Contracts' (Law Com No 292, Scot Law Com No 199, 2005), also available at www.lawcom.gov.uk.

[15] SI 2002/3045, above n 5.

[16] It would probably not be suitable for commodity sales. On this, see further below.

[17] Thus Art 9 of the Unfair Terms in Consumer Contracts Directive requires the Commission to report to the European Council and Parliament on its application after five years. The European Commission issued a Report: Report from the Commission on the Implementation of Council Directive 93/13/EEC of 5 April 1993 on unfair terms in consumer contracts, COM(2000) 248 final (27 April 2000). In turn, the Department of Trade and Industry issued a consultation paper: Commission Review of Directive 93/13/EEC on unfair terms in consumer contracts (July 2000, URN 00/1033); see also Law Commission Consultation Paper No 166, above n 10, para 2.16. The Directive will now be caught up in the review of eight directives announced by the Commission as part of its Action Plan: see its 'Action Plan on a More Coherent European Contract Law', COM(2003) 68 final, [2003] OJ C63/1, and 'European Contract Law and the revision of the *acquis*: the way forward', COM(2004) 651 final (11 October 2004).

run. Moreover, there need not be a rush if work begins early enough.[18] In most cases the likely shape of the directive will become apparent long before it is approved and, even though the work might be wasted if the draft is not approved, I believe that serious thought should be given to how we might implement the draft directive as soon as the matter has reached the Council of Ministers, if not before. After all, that work might lead us to try to obtain alterations to the language of the directive to make it an easier 'fit' with English law.

As to the risk of non-implementation, I accept that there is a risk but I think it is easy to exaggerate it. First, at present most consumer directives are minimum harmonisation directives. Member States may give consumers greater rights. This means that any uncertainty in the meaning of the directive can be resolved by 'erring', if error it be, in favour of the consumer without risk of implementing the directive incorrectly. Secondly, while it might be embarrassing for the government to be found not to have implemented a directive correctly, the nature of most consumer directives is such that it is hardly likely to pose a financial threat. Even if the necessary criteria for an action for non-implementation were satisfied,[19] the amount of money at stake would normally be so low that there would be no real threat.[20] In any event, I think the slight risk that a directive will not be implemented correctly has to be set against the importance of ensuring that domestic legislation, particularly legislation that has direct effects on consumers and businesses, is as clear and as accessible to them as possible.[21]

The same point meets the argument that directives are 'ephemeral'. Consumer law may be peripheral to many practising lawyers and academics, but it of enormous importance; and even directives that are subject to review after five years or so will in practice have a much longer life. The process of revising the consumer *acquis* that the European Commission has announced will not result in any changes before 2008 at the earliest, so that the Unfair Terms Directive will be in force for at least 15 years.

I suspect the real reason for our failure to do a better job of implementing directives is because of the division of responsibility between the Department of Trade and Industry (DTI), which is responsible for consumer law, the Department of Constitutional Affairs (DCA), which has responsibility for civil law generally, and the Law Commission.

The Law Commission can only take on projects that are approved as part of its programme by the Lord Chancellor, or that are referred to it by other

---

[18] For details of the consultation documents issued by the Department of Trade and Industry on implementation of the Consumer Sales Directive, see Law Commission Consultation Paper No 166, above n 10, para 3.2 note 5.

[19] See Case C–690 *Francovich v Italy* [1991] ECR I–5357.

[20] Compare the risk posed by non-implementation of a directive like that on Financial Collateral Arrangements: see Law Commission, 'Company Security Interests' (Law Com No 296, 2005), para 5.59.

[21] See Law Commission Consultation Paper No 166, above n 10, paras 4.12–4.13.

ministers.[22] In practice, in recent years matters of implementing European directives seem to have been referred to it only after the event. It is perfectly appropriate that directives on technical matters such as food colouring that have no impact on English private law generally should be dealt with solely by the DTI. However, when a draft directive is likely to have an impact on civil law, as with the two examples I have mentioned, it seems to me that not only should the DCA take an interest but that the two Departments should consider referring the matter to the Law Commission.

It is only fair to say that there has been some improvement in recent years. I have mentioned that the DTI invited the Law Commission to review the law of unfair terms in order to produce a unified and more coherent scheme. When we have spoken to officials about the defects of the law on consumer sales, we have at least had a sympathetic hearing, and it may be that when the DTI has finished the considerable task of implementing the Unfair Commercial Practices Directive, we may be able to work on a consumer sales Act. I suspect, however, that it may also have to wait until any revision of the Consumer Sales Directive by the European Commission has taken place. It would have been good to have a clear and up-to-date statement of domestic law that could be offered to the European Commission as a model for revision of the European law, but it is probably too late for that now.

The Law Commissions should not be brought in to clear up the mess after directives have been implemented hurriedly, but at the start of the implementation process. Better still, they could hold a 'watching brief' over the draft as it progresses through the European institutions. The Law Commission has recently been encouraged by the DCA to seek a larger role in relation to European legislation, and we are embarking on a project which is something of a first in this respect. We are to examine the law relating to property rights in indirectly held-investment securities, a project urged on us by the Financial Markets Law Committee.[23] The aim is not in the first instance to produce domestic legislation; the European Commission's Legal Certainty Group is working in that field,[24] and our role is to provide information and advice to assist the Treasury to respond to any proposals made by the European Commission. Only if little or no progress is made at the European level will we consider producing a report with draft legislation for England and Wales.[25] I think it would be good if the Law Commissions could play a similar

---

[22] Law Commissions Act 1965, s 3.

[23] See Financial Markets Law Committee, 'Property Interests in Investment Securities', issue 3 (July 2004).

[24] Communication from the Commission to the Council and the European Parliament, 'Clearing and Settlement in the European Union—The Way Forward', COM(2004) 312 final (28 April 2002) 25. This follows concern expressed by the second report by the Giovanni Group at insufficiencies in the legal framework for clearing and securities settlement systems.

[25] See Law Commission, 'Ninth Programme of Law Reform' (Law Com No 293, 2005), paras 3.31–3.38.

role with consumer and other directives that are likely to have any significant impact on general principles of contract or other areas of private law.

More careful examination of how European legislation will fit with existing domestic legislation will become even more important if the recent Unfair Commercial Practices Directive[26] sets a precedent that future consumer directives will be 'full harmonisation' directives. This appears to be the Commission's intention.[27] It will be more important for two reasons. First, the impact on domestic law is likely to be greater. Thus the Unfair Commercial Practices Directive may require significant amendments to the Trade Descriptions Act 1968. Secondly, it will no longer be possible to smooth over 'awkwardness of fit' by providing that consumers will have better rights than are required by the relevant directive. At the same time, consumer directives are likely to become more contentious at the EU level, since Member States that currently give their consumers more rights than are required by the existing *acquis* may not wish to reduce those rights, while those which do not may demand a 'levelling down'.

I doubt whether in England we would ever see the kind of reaction to a European directive that we have just witnessed in Germany, where the Consumer Sales Directive acted as a catalyst for wholesale reforms of the *Schuldrecht*.[28] The case law system encourages English lawyers to be pragmatic, and their pragmatism extends to law reform by statute: 'if it ain't broke, don't fix it.' Parliament—or, more accurately, Ministers and Departments that effectively control the legislative programme—take a not dissimilar attitude. They are reluctant to agree to devote large amounts of Parliamentary time to projects that might make the law more coherent, clearer and more accessible but which would not solve some pressing problem. Witness the demise of the project for a commercial code proposed by Professor Sir Roy Goode.[29] The DTI showed initial enthusiasm, holding a seminar on it in May 2000; but the idea was dropped, apparently when it was pointed out how much Parliamentary time, and Departmental effort in setting up a major Bill team, would be involved.

Part of the explanation for the reluctance of so many leading practitioners to see the law changed is a fear that the new law will be uncertain in its effect. This is a wholly understandable concern. What is not clear is whether certainty is to be so highly prized when we are dealing with the rather small

[26] Parliament and Council Directive 2005/29/EC of 11 May 2005 concerning unfair business-to-consumer commercial practices in the internal market and amending Council Directive 84/450/EEC, Directives 97/7/EC, 98/27/EC and 2002/65/EC of the European Parliament and of the Council and Regulation (EC) No 2006/2004 of the European Parliament and of the Council [2005] OJ L149/22.

[27] See the discussion in COM(2004) 651 final, above n 17, para 2.1.1.

[28] Cf the contribution of R Zimmermann, 'Contract Law Reform: The German Experience' ch 5 in this volume.

[29] In his Fullagar Memorial Lecture, which is reprinted in (1988) 14 *Monash Law Review* 135. He produced a further paper for the DTI's seminar but it has not been published.

transactions entered by consumers and small businesses, most of which leading practitioners will very seldom see.

II. THE IMPACT OF DOMESTIC EUROPEAN LAWS

European private law in the sense of the domestic laws of other Member States need have no impact on English law, and indeed it is hard to find many instances in which it has done so. True, continental law has sometimes been cited in the courts, perhaps most famously when Lord Goff referred to German law in the 'disappointed beneficiary' case, *White v Jones*.[30] However, the solution adopted was not that of German law. The same is true of European law as mediated through 'soft law', such as the Principles of European Contract Law. The Principles were cited by the House of Lords in *Director-General of Fair Trading v First National Bank plc*,[31] but it not obvious that their Lordships' decisions were in fact influenced by the Principles.

This may be seen as advantageous. It enables English law to retain the distinctive characteristics that are claimed to make it the law of choice for so many international transactions. The understandable reluctance to alter those characteristics, along with a pragmatic attitude, may explain in part why continental (and equally North American) law seems to have had so little influence on our private law.

It is, however, vital that these attitudes do not prevent English law from being kept up-to-date in substance and accessible in form, particularly when it faces competition from other, recently revised, laws, from international conventions such as the Convention on Contracts for the International Sale of Goods and possibly from the optional instrument envisioned as a possibility by the European Commission's Action Plan.[32]

As to keeping the law up-to-date, the Law Commission has indicated what is also my personal view: when there are significant differences in substance between English contract law and that of its European competitors, we need to enquire whether these differences are desirable.[33] We should ask whether our rules do in fact meet modern needs or are, for instance, merely historical anomalies. That approach is in no way inconsistent with maintaining English law as the most suitable system for international commercial transactions.

It is my firm belief that we also need to make English contract and commercial law more accessible. We constantly hear that it is the law of

---

[30] [1995] 2 AC 207 (HL).

[31] [2001] UKHL 52, [2002] 1 AC 481, at [36] and [45].

[32] See COM(2003) 68 final, above n 17, para 4.3; and COM(2004) 651 final, above n 17, para 2.3.

[33] Law Commission, 'Ninth Programme of Law Reform', above n 25, para 4.12.

choice for international transactions; but at international gatherings I am also told very frequently that it would be chosen more often were it not so hard to find out what the English law is. Sometimes this may be the result of a civilian lawyer feeling lost whenever he or she cannot point to an article of a civil code, and not being content with a statement of law in a case or textbook, however clear and incontestable the statement. Sometimes, however, it is a genuine complaint that the relevant cases and statutes are hard to identify and can be, and are, explained in different ways by different authorities, so that the law is unnecessarily complicated and confused.

A single example will suffice to illustrate both the question of substance and the problem of accessibility. The law governing mistake and misrepresentation is very complex and hard to state in a coherent way, and it may have defects in substance. The Court of Appeal in *The Great Peace* suggested that in cases of common mistake the court has little scope for making adjustments when the contract is void.[34] More fundamentally, the narrow scope of the doctrine of mistake and the absence of any general duty of non-disclosure or sanction for 'fraud by silence' mean that English law reaches markedly different results to those that would be reached under many continental laws or in the United States.

Like the Law Commission, I think that if English contract law differs from that of its competitors, it should do so for a good reason. There may be excellent reasons for the differences, but an investigation is called for. I very much regret that the proposed Law Commission project on mistake, misrepresentation and non-disclosure has had to be deferred in favour of more urgent work.[35] I hope that the Commission will be able to carry out the project as part of its next programme of work. We do not need to copy domestic European private law or the rules of soft law like the Principles of European Contract Law, but we should look carefully to see whether we can learn from them.

---

[34] *Great Peace Shipping Ltd v Tsavliris Salvage (International) Ltd* [2002] EWCA Civ 1407, [2003] QB 679, at [161].
[35] Law Commission, 'Ninth Programme of Law Reform', above n 25, para 4.22.

4

The Ideal of Codification and the Dynamics of Europeanisation: The Dutch Experience

MARTIJN W HESSELINK

I. THE NEW DUTCH CIVIL CODE

1. Recodification, not Reform

In 1947 the Dutch government asked Professor Meijers to draft a new civil code. The reason for the recodification was that the 1838 Code was thought to be out of date.[1] During the first half of the twentieth century private law had changed quite dramatically, but most of the new developments had taken place outside the code, in specific statutes and in case law. However, although the aim was to modernise the code, this did not mean that the law also had to be modernised. The idea was that the recodification should be essentially 'technical': the existing private law should be brought into the code. This would restore the coherence of private law. Moreover, it would reaffirm (as far as the codification of case law was concerned) the primacy of the legislator. Such a recodification should not be the occasion to (re)open the debate on such highly political issues as the legal capacity of married women and divorce. In other words, the aim of the project was recodification, not law reform.[2]

---

[1] In 1938, upon the centenary of the civil code, Professor Meijers had appealed for a new code (EM Meijers, 'Wijzigingen en aanvullingen van het Burgerlijk wetboek na 1838' in P Scholten and EM Meijers (eds), *Gedenkboek Burgerlijk Wetboek 1838–1938* (Zwolle, Tjeenk Willink, 1938) 33. However, this idea was rejected by Paul Scholten, the other leading scholar at the time (P Scholten, 'De codificatie-gedachte vóór honderd jaar en thans', *ibid*, 1).

[2] This aim fitted well with Meijers's political ideals. In his view a recodification could contribute to bridging the gap between the law and the people. See CJH Jansen, 'De idealen van E.M. Meijers (1880–1954) ten aanzien van de herziening van het burgerlijk wetboek' in SCJJ Kortmann and others (eds), *Onderneming en 10 jaar Nieuw Burgerlijk Wetboek* (Deventer, Kluwer, 2002) 3–26.

The recodification took far longer than was initially expected.[3] Although Professor Meijers had taken up his task very swiftly and presented a first draft in 1954, he died unexpectedly a few months later. He was succeeded by a team of three who were all individually brilliant but who found collaboration to be no easy matter, and this led to delays. They were succeeded in turn by others and there were further delays. The main part of the recodification, on patrimonial law, finally came into force in 1992.[4] Today, after more than 50 years, the task has still not been completed.[5]

2. Substantive Innovations

In spite of the initially very limited aim of a 'technical reform', several decades of drafting have led to many substantive innovations. Indeed, the new Burgerlijk Wetboek (BW) introduced a number of changes which constituted innovations with regard to both the previous code and, in many instances, established case law.[6]

The innovation with probably the broadest scope was the abolition of the distinction between civil law and commercial law: the BW is a code of private law (regardless of its title).[7] A second fundamental innovation has been the acceptance of a general action in the case of unjustified enrichment (6:212 BW). Some of the other prominent novelties include the introduction of a fourth type of 'defect of consent', ie 'abuse of circumstances' (3:44(4) BW), a rule on change of circumstances (6:258 BW), and the possibility of adaptation (instead of annulment) in cases of abuse of circumstances and mistake (3:54 and 6:230 BW). Perhaps the most significant innovation has been the omnipresence of the concept of good faith throughout the new code.

---

[3] For a detailed account, see EOHP Florijn, *Ontstaan en ontwikkeling van het nieuwe Burgerlijk Wetboek* (Maastricht, Universitaire Pers Maastricht, 1995).

[4] Book 3 on patrimonial law in general, Book 5 on property law, Book 6 on the law of obligations and title 7.1 on sale and exchange.

[5] Book 1 on persons and the family came into effect in 1970, Book 2 on legal persons in 1976, Book 8 on transport in 1991 and Book 4 on succession in 2003. Still to come are several titles of Book 7 on specific contracts, Book 9 on intellectual property rights and Book 10 on private international law.

[6] However, from a comparative perspective, these innovations were not really all that new. In fact, most were already present in the Italian civil code of 1942.

[7] The distinction has been reintroduced through the transposition of the late payment directive. The new Art 6:119a only applies to 'commercial contracts'; these are defined in that same article.

3. The Main Characteristics of the New BW

What are the main characteristics of the new Dutch civil code compared with the old code?[8] First, the new code is much more systematic. It contains many layers of abstraction. For example, the rules which may be applicable to a consumer sales contract are located on six different levels of abstraction:

1. Juristic acts: Book 3 (general part of patrimonial law), title 2 (juristic acts): eg the rules on formation and validity;
2. Obligations: Book 6 (general part of the law of obligations), title 1 (obligations in general): eg the rules on performance, non-performance and damages;
3. Contracts: Book 6, title 5 (contracts in general): eg the rules on standard terms;
4. Synallagmatic contracts: Book 6, title 5, section 5 (synallagmatic contracts): eg the rules on termination and change of circumstances;
5. Sales: Book 7 (specific contracts), title 1 (sale and exchange): eg the rules on non-conformity and on risk;
6. Consumer sales: Articles 7:2 and 7:6, and other specific provisions relating to consumer sales: eg the rules relating to the consumer sale of a home.

Secondly, the new code is more conceptual. It contains many well-defined concepts, which are often rather abstract. On several occasions, the wording of the old code was substituted with terms which, in the view of the drafters, better fitted the concept, eg (famously) *goederen* instead of *zaken* (for things, *biens, Sachen*), *redelijkheid en billijkheid* instead of *goede trouw* (for objective good faith) and *toerekenbare tekortkoming* instead of *wanprestatie* (for breach).

Thirdly, the new code is much more nuanced than the old code. Many 'all or nothing' rules on subjects like validity, termination, damages and penalty clauses have been replaced by rules which allow for many intermediate solutions.

A fourth and striking characteristic of the new code is the frequent use of general clauses and open norms, especially in the law of obligations. Not only is good faith omnipresent, tort liability and unjustified enrichment are also based on general clauses.

From a comparative perspective it is probably right to say that the new code is more 'Germanic' than the previous code, which was heavily inspired by the French Code civil.[9]

---

[8] On the characteristics of the new Code see, eg AS Hartkamp, 'Civil Code Revision in the Netherlands 1947–1992' in PPC Haanappel and E Mackaay (eds), *New Netherlands Civil Code: Patrimonial Law* (Deventer, Kluwer Law and Taxation, 1990) xiii.

[9] See D Tallon, 'The new Dutch Civil Code in a Comparative Perspective—French View-point' (1993) 1 *European Review of Private Law* 189. In the same sense, see also E Hondius, 'Das neue

II. THE HARMONISATION OF CONTRACT LAW

1. Directives and the New Code

In 1992, with the enactment of Books 3, 5 and 6 on 'patrimonial law', the aim of recodifying private law seemed to have been achieved: except for a few specific subjects which were still delayed, all private law was once again contained in a single, well-balanced and coherent code. The system and concepts had been developed during a 45-year debate between the legislator and scholars. Dutch private law seemed to be ready for the twenty-first century. Then came the directives.

The directives on doorstep selling,[10] product liability[11] and commercial agency[12] could still be taken into account in the final stage of the drafting process. However, after the enactment of Books 3, 5 and 6 of the new BW the EC issued a host of new directives in the area of 'patrimonial law', especially contract law. After January 1992 the transposition of the following directives on contract law became due:

— Directive 90/314/EEC on package travel, package holidays and package tours
— Directive 93/13/EEC on unfair terms in consumer contracts
— Directive 94/47/EC on the protection of purchasers in respect of certain aspects of contracts relating to the purchase of the right to use immovable properties on a timeshare basis
— Directive 97/7/EC on the protection of consumers in respect of distance contracts
— Directive 1999/44/EC on certain aspects of the sale of consumer goods and associated guarantees
— Directive 2000/31/EC on certain legal aspects of information society services, in particular electronic commerce, in the internal market (Directive on electronic commerce)

Niederländische Zivilgesetzbuch' (1991) 191 *Archiv für die civilistische Praxis* 378, 394; E Hondius, 'Le Code civil et les néerlandais' in *Le Code civil 1804–2004: Livre du Bicentenaire* (Paris, Dalloz, 2004) 613, 615; and D Dankers-Hagenaars, 'Le nouveau code civil néerlandais: un cousin lointain dans la famille du droit français' in J-P Dunand and B Winiger (eds), *Le code civil français dans le droit européen* (Brussels, Bruylant, 2005) 179, 181.

[10] Council Directive 85/577/EEC of 20 December 1985 to protect the consumer in respect of contracts negotiated away from business premises [1985] OJ L372/31.
[11] Council Directive 85/374/EEC of 25 July 1985 on the approximation of the laws, regulations and administrative provisions of the Member States concerning liability for defective products [1985] OJ L210/29.
[12] Council Directive 86/653/EEC of 18 December 1986 on the coordination of the laws of the Member States relating to self-employed commercial agents [1986] OJ L382/17.

— Directive 2000/35/EC on combating late payment in commercial transactions
— Directive 2002/65/EC concerning the distance marketing of consumer
financial services

How did the Dutch legislator respond to this somewhat unexpected challenge? It acted completely in the spirit of codification. Indeed, all these
directives have been integrated into the system of the code.[13] In order to
achieve this result, it was often necessary to dissect directives into several
pieces which were then spread over several levels of abstraction. Moreover,
on many occasions the terminology had to be adapted. In other cases the
Dutch legislator deemed its new code to be already up to standard and
thought it could remain inactive. This rather defensive strategy was inspired
by the desire to preserve the system of the new code which had been prepared
meticulously over half a century. Indeed, the aim of this approach towards
implementation was to maintain the 'systematic purity' of the new BW.[14]
Three examples may illustrate this approach.

2. Example 1: Standard Terms

One of the innovations in the new Dutch civil code was the section on
standard terms (section 6.5.3). The old code did not contain any specific
rules on either standard terms or unfair terms. Under the old law unfair
terms, especially exclusion clauses, were policed by the courts on the basis
of the general good faith clause (Article 1374(3) of the old BW).[15] The
section in the 1992 code was inspired by the German law on the subject.[16]
However, unlike German law, where standard terms were regulated in a
separate statute that was outside the code (AGBG)[17] but completely in line
with the codification ideal, the Dutch legislators had included these rules
in the new civil code.[18] Their place in the system is: section 3 (General

---

[13] The same applies to most other directives in the area of private law. According to JM Smits,
'Europa en het Nederlandse privaatrecht' [2004] *Nederlands Tijdschrift voor Burgerlijk Recht*
490, 493, today 10% of the provisions in the BW are the result of the transposition of directives.

[14] Cf (sceptical) Smits, *ibid*, 496.

[15] HR 19 May 1967 (Saladin/HBU) *NJ* 1967, 261, note GJ Scholten, (1966/1967) 16 *Ars Aequi*
214, note Stein; HR 20 February 1976 (Pseudo-Vogelpest) *NJ* 1976, 486, note GJ Scholten,
(1976) 25 *Ars Aequi* 467, note Van der Grinten.

[16] Cf AS Hartkamp, *Mr C Asser's handleiding tot de beoefening van het Nederlands burgerlijk
recht; Verbintenissenrecht; Vol II Algemene leer der overeenkomsten* (12th edn, Deventer, Tjeenk
Willink, 2005) 345.

[17] This has changed since then. One of the politically most significant (symbolic) changes of the
Schuldrechtsreform of 2002 was the inclusion of 'special private law' in the civil BGB.

[18] This is not only an ideal, but also a constitutional obligation (which, however, allows for
exceptions). See Art 107(1) of the 2002 *Grondwet* of the Netherlands.

conditions) of title 5 (Contracts in general) of Book 6 (General Part of the Law of Obligations).

Dutch legal practice was just getting used to these new rules—all businesses had their standard terms checked and, where necessary, revised by lawyers—when the European Community published Directive 93/13/EEC on unfair terms in consumer contracts. The object and the scope of the directive was different from the relevant section in the brand new Dutch code: the directive was concerned with 'unfair terms', not standard terms, and with 'consumer contracts', not all contracts. However, there were also many similarities: like the Dutch code, the directive policed terms through a general clause and the sanction was (or, rather, seemed to be) invalidity. Moreover, the directive contained an annex which looked very similar to the grey and black lists (Articles 6:237 and 6:236 BW) in the new Dutch code.

What should be done? The Dutch government examined the Directive thoroughly and came to the conclusion that Dutch law was completely up to standard.[19] However, the European Commission (hereafter 'Commission') did not agree. There followed an exchange of letters between the Commission and the Dutch government. In this correspondence the Dutch legislator referred to a case where the Hoge Raad (the Supreme Court) had explicitly stated that the Dutch rules on standard terms must always be interpreted in such a way as to provide at least as much consumer protection as the Directive.[20] However, the Commission insisted on formal implementation and ultimately delivered a 'reasoned opinion' under Article 169 (now 226) EC.

Eventually, the Dutch legislator enacted minor textual adaptations to two articles. When sending the proposal to Parliament the government explicitly stated that the proposed bill did not envisage any substantive change in Dutch law, but was 'merely a textual clarification in order to comply with [the Commission's] reasoned opinion.'[21] In the meantime, however, while the bill was still pending for debate in Parliament, the Commission had brought the matter before the European Court of Justice (ECJ) under 169 (now 226) (2) EC. The ECJ found in favour of the Commission. It rejected the Dutch government's argument that the aims sought by the Directive could be attained by applying Dutch law as it stood. It said:[22]

> even where the settled case-law of a Member State interprets the provisions of national law in a manner deemed to satisfy the requirements of a directive, that cannot achieve the clarity and precision needed to meet the requirement of legal certainty. That, moreover, is particularly true in the field of consumer protection.

---

[19] In the past the ECJ had ruled that 'the implementation of a directive does not necessarily require legislative action in each Member State' (Case 29/84 *Commission v Germany* [1985] ECR 1661).

[20] HR 19 September 1997, *NJ* 1998, 6.

[21] *Kamerstukken II*, 1998–99, 26 470, no 5, 3.

[22] C–144/99, at [21].

At the end of the day, the transposition of the directive into Dutch law has led to the situation where all but two of the 17 articles in section 6.5.3 (Articles 6:231–6:247) have remained untouched. Moreover, their link with European law is in no way apparent.[23]

3. Example 2: Time-sharing

The transposition into Dutch law of the time-sharing directive was an entirely different story.[24] The new BW did not contain any specific rules concerning the purchase of timeshares. Therefore, the Dutch government concluded that Dutch law as it stood was incompatible with the directive; it had to be adapted.[25] There was no doubt that the proper place for such new rules was the civil code, for the simple reason, as the Minister of Justice put it, that the directive dealt with contract law (codification principle).[26] Interestingly enough, on this occasion the Minister was of the opinion that, with a view to achieving clarity in legislation, it was preferable to place all the provisions which are based on the same directive together in one place in the code.[27] Hence, a new section was created, section 10A of title 7.1 on Sale and exchange, which is dedicated entirely to the directive.

Nevertheless, the directive was not transposed lock, stock and barrel: the terminology was adapted to the terminology of the BW (with a view to consistency), the number of provisions was reduced and their order was changed (with a view to simplicity), and the annex was placed in a separate royal decree (because detailed rules were considered to be unsuitable for a civil code).[28]

4. Example 3: Consumer Sales

In 1999 the European Parliament and the Council of the European Union adopted the Consumer Sales Directive.[29] The German legislator concluded that many of the rules contained in the Consumer Sales Directive had to be implemented through rules with a broader scope and decided to embark

[23] Dutch publishers of the civil code do not even refer to the directive in a footnote.
[24] Directive 94/47/EC of the European Parliament and of the Council of 26 October 1994 on the protection of purchasers in respect of certain aspects of contracts relating to the purchase of the right to use immovable properties on a timeshare basis [1994] OJ L280/83.
[25] *Kamerstukken II*, 1995–96, 24 449, no 3, 2.
[26] *Ibid.*
[27] *Ibid.*
[28] *Ibid.* Jac. Hijma, *Mr C Asser's handleiding tot de beoefening van het Nederlands burgerlijk recht; Bijzondere overeenkomsten; Vol I Koop en ruil* (6th edn, Deventer, Tjeenk Willink, 2001) 150b.
[29] Directive 1999/44/EC of the European Parliament and of the Council of 25 May 1999 on certain aspects of the sale of consumer goods and associated guarantees [1999] OJ L171/12.

upon a general reform of the law of obligations, the largest reform of the law of obligations since the BGB entered into force in 1900.[30]

In contrast, the Dutch legislator reached a very different conclusion. After having remarked that, in order 'correctly' to fit the directive into the code, a precise comparison between the directive and Dutch law was necessary,[31] and after a close examination of the definitions contained in Article 1 Directive, the Dutch government concluded:[32]

> the directive only deals with what Art 7:5 BW defines as a consumer sale. The BW contains, in Title 1 of Book 7, a separate regulation of consumer sales. Hence this directive only requires adaptation and supplementation of that particular regulation.

The Dutch legislator emphasised that the aim of the directive was to provide a Europe-wide minimum of consumer protection with regard to sales contracts.[33] As a result, the focus of the legislator was entirely on consumer protection: with regard to each article in the directive, the government enquired whether the directive provided further-reaching protection to consumers than Dutch law as it stood. If so, then the rules on consumer sales in the Dutch code had to be adapted or supplemented. If not, then the code could remain as it was.

With regard to most provisions in the Directive, the government concluded that Dutch law was up to standard. This conclusion was made easy by the fact that the new sales law of 1992 (title 7.1 BW) was strongly inspired by the United Nations Convention on Contracts for the International Sale of Goods (CISG) (Vienna, 1980). Unlike many older civil codes in Europe—including, in particular, the German BGB before the reform—the central notion in Dutch sales law was already 'non-conformity' (Article 7:17 BW), exactly that concept which lies at the heart in the Directive (see Article 2).

Moreover, the Dutch legislator chose not to implement the two-year term limitation period in Article 5(1) Directive, thus continuing to provide the consumer with further-reaching protection than that required by the Directive (minimum harmonisation). As a result, again unlike in Germany, the question whether the whole law of prescription had to be revised did not

---

[30] On the reform, see the contribution of Zimmermann in this volume; see also S Grundmann, 'Germany and the *Schuldrechtsmodernisierung* 2002' (2005) 1 *European Review of Contract Law* 129, with further references.

[31] Transposition in a separate statute was not even considered as an option: a very strong expression of the codification idea.

[32] *Kamerstukken II*, 2001–2, 27 809, no 3, 2–3. The translation is mine.

[33] *Kamerstukken II*, 2001–2, 27 809, no 3, 1. See also *Kamerstukken I*, 2001–2, 27 809, no 323b, 4. The Italian legislator adopted the same approach. Cf V Roppo, 'Italy' (2005) 1 *European Review of Contract Law* 273, 274.

arise.[34] Indeed, only on very few occasions did Dutch law extend the scope of a provision in the Directive beyond consumer sales.[35] Obviously, the Dutch style of implementing has led to great complexity: many cases which to most observers seem rather similar are dealt with differently.

For one aspect of the implementation of the directive the legislator had to rely on another level of abstraction. Article 7(1) (binding nature) of the Directive says that any waiver or restriction of the rights resulting from the directive 'is not binding on the consumer.' The Dutch code already contained a similar provision (Article 7:6 BW). However, through Article 3:40(2) BW this provision renders such clauses 'annullable': the latter article declares that contractual clauses which violate a rule that protects the interests of only one party are annullable (in contrast to contracts which violate a rule that is in the general interest; they are null and void). It is doubtful whether that is sufficient in the light of the decisions of the ECJ in the *Océano* and *Cofidis* cases.[36] The government raised the issue, but decided to leave Article 7:6 and to consider Articles 3:40(2) and 7:6 combined as a sufficient implementation of Article 7(1) Directive, saying that Article 3:40(2) leaves the courts with sufficient freedom, where necessary, to declare contractual clauses void of their own motion.[37] It is doubtful whether the ECJ would share this view.[38]

The whole style of the official comment on the government's proposal is very defensive: the dogmatic structure of the code has to be preserved at all costs in a heroic defence (for which the government is applauded by Parliament[39]) against the destructive forces from Brussels. One example suffices to illustrate the tone in The Hague. Article 3(2)(5) of the Directive requires that, in the case of a lack of conformity, the consumer is entitled to an appropriate price reduction. However, that particular remedy had just been abolished as such (ie as a specific remedy in sales law) with the introduction of the new code in 1992.[40] The Dutch government was of the opinion that the directive did not require explicit reintroduction; the application of Article 6:270 BW, the provision on partial termination in the general law of synallagmatic contracts, would lead to the same result. It took the arguments, pressure and

---

[34] For a comparison see MBM Loos, *Consumentenkoop* (Mon NBW 65b) (Deventer, Kluwer, 2004) 7 and 32.

[35] The main examples are Art 2(2) Directive, a provision which *limits* the protection of the buyer (Art 7:17(5) BW); Art 3(2) Directive, the 'free of charge' requirement; and Art 2(2)(d) Directive, which makes pre-contractual statements binding, thus *extending* in the latter two cases the protection to professional buyers (Arts 7:21(2) and 7:17(2) BW respectively).

[36] Joined cases C–240/98 to C–244/98 *Océano Grupo Editorial SA v Rocio Murciano Quintero (and others)* [2000] ECR I–4941; Case C–473/00 *Cofidis SA v Jean-Louis Fredout* [2002] ECR I–10875.

[37] *Kamerstukken II*, 2001–2, 27 809, no 3, 12. In the same sense Loos, above n 34, 3.

[38] Cf S Stijns and W van Gerven, 'Article 7: Binding Nature', in MC Bianca and S Grundmann (eds), *EU Sales Directive Commentary* (Antwerp, Intersentia, 2002) para 62, according to whom 'The only safe way to avoid . . . inconsistency [with Art 7 of the directive] is to *take over the sanction, literally*, as it appears in the Directive' (emphasis in the original).

[39] See *Kamerstukken II*, 2001–2, 27 809, 5.

[40] The old code contained the *actio quanti minoris* in Art 1543.

lobbying from the Raad van State (Conseil d'Etat),[41] the Consumentenbond (the main consumer group), scholars[42] and the main coalition parties (socialist and liberal–conservative) to persuade the Minister of Justice to adapt his proposal and explicitly to (re)introduce price reduction as a remedy in Article 7:22(1)(b) BW. Even then, the Minister remained convinced that the directive did not require him to do so,[43] and that, as he said in the Senate, the new remedy dogmatically was still a specific application of the general remedy of partial termination.[44]

III. CODIFICATION AND HARMONISATION

The idea behind directives as a legislative instrument (especially in contrast to regulations) is that they are not 'parachuted' into the legal systems of the Member States just as they are. Instead, they leave to the national authorities the choice of form and methods of their implementation (249 EC), in order to take account of the fact that Member States have differing legal systems.[45] In the words of Stephen Weatherill, they act as a bridge between Community and national law:[46] 'They allow the objectives of the Community legal order to be harnessed to the established patterns of national law.'

Still, the Dutch experience shows that codification and harmonisation do not easily match. The experience in other codified systems is similar.[47] The reason for this is that national codification and European harmonisation of

[41] *Kamerstukken II*, 2000–1, 27 809 B.

[42] Notably JM Smits, 'De voorgenomen implementatie van de richtlijn consumentenkoop: een gebrekkig wetsvoorstel' (2001) *Weekblad voor Privaatrecht Notariaat en Registratie* no 6470, 1047.

[43] *Kamerstukken II*, 2001–2, 27 809, no 8, 3.

[44] *Kamerstukken I*, 2001–2, 27 809, no 323b, 2. Cf EH Hondius, 'Introduction' in Bianca and Grundmann, above n 38, 154, who rightly speaks of 'the obstinacy of the Dutch government.'

[45] P Craig and G de Búrca, *EU Law: Text, Cases and Materials* (3rd edn, Oxford University Press, 2003) 115.

[46] S Weatherill, *Law and Integration in the European Union* (Oxford, Clarendon Press, 2005) 82.

[47] See eg W-H Roth, 'Transposing "Pointillist" EC Guidelines into Systematic Codes—Problems and Consequences' (2002) 10 *European Review of Private Law* 761. In non-codified systems some of the problems may seem less acute. However, those systems also experience problems with 'legal irritants' like the concept of good faith (see G Teubner, 'Legal Irritants: Good Faith in British Law or How Unifying Law Ends Up in New Divergences' (1998) 61 *MLR* 11). Moreover, common lawyers care more for system and coherence than some scholars (notably Pierre Legrand, 'European Legal Systems Are Not Converging' (1996) 45 *International and Comparative Law Quarterly* 52) want us to believe. See, for example, the recent proposal by the Law Commissions of England and Wales and of Scotland to bring some order into the several statutes (including one which implemented the EC directive) relating to unfair terms: The Law Commission and The Scottish Law Commission's 'Unfair Terms in Contracts' (Law Com No 292, Scot Law Com No 199, February 2005) and Unfair Contract Terms Bill. This question, which is beyond the scope of this article, will not be further pursued here.

private law each have distinct characteristics, most of which are radically opposed (see Table 1).

First, codification is comprehensive. This means that it aims to include all private law in one single code. It also means that the code is supposed to provide an answer to any single question that may emerge in a dispute between private parties. This latter aim is attained by the inclusion of some very general (or abstract) rules which apply, for example, to any contract, obligation or juristic act.

In contrast, harmonisation is necessarily partial. Each specific harmonisation measure requires a sufficient legal basis; no 'horizontal' measures can be taken on the European level. The reason is that harmonisation measures cannot go further than that which is necessary (not merely desirable) with a view to the proper functioning of the internal market (Articles 94, 95 EC). They 'must genuinely have as [their] object the improvement of the conditions for the establishment and functioning of the internal market'; 'a mere finding of disparities between national rules and of the abstract risk of obstacles to the exercise of fundamental freedoms or of distortions of competition liable to result therefrom' is insufficient to justify Article 95 EC as a legal basis.[48] Even if there is a sufficient legal basis, the Community is allowed to

Table 1: Codification and Harmonisation

Codification	Harmonisation
Comprehensive	Partial
All private law in one code	Legal basis
Code answers all questions	Subsidiarity
Systematic	Unsystematic
General rules	Sector-specific
Several levels of abstraction	No abstraction
Coherent (presumably)	Incoherent
One level of governance	Two levels of governance
National	National and European
One legislator	No Kompetenz-Kompetenz
One court system	Harmonious interpretation
Static	Dynamic
Non-instrumental (at most: justice)	Instrumental (Internal Market)
(Can be changed)	Aims at change

[48] See Case C–376/98 *Germany v European Parliament and Council* [2000] ECR I–8419, at [83].

take legislative action only insofar as the objectives of the proposed action cannot be sufficiently achieved by the Member States (the principle of subsidiarity) whereas any action taken cannot go beyond what is necessary to achieve the objectives of the Treaty—here, creating a functioning internal market—(the principle of proportionality) (Article 5). As a result, EC contract law is necessarily fragmentary.

Secondly, codification is also systematic. It contains general rules, usually on several layers of abstraction, eg specific contracts, synallagmatic contracts, general contract law, general law of obligations, and sometimes even a general part of civil law (in Germany) or patrimonial law (in the Netherlands). Moreover, a code is coherent (or rather, it is presumed to be so): there is no contradiction between the rules contained therein. Indeed, during the drafting process great care is taken to avoid internal inconsistencies and to treat like cases alike. Moreover, application and interpretation are based on the idea that the coherent system of the code provides one single (right) answer to a legal question.

In contrast, harmonisation is unsystematic. Internal consistency between directives is difficult to achieve as they are often prepared in different branches of the Commission, eg in D-G Sanco and in DG Markt. Directives do not focus on, or contain a comprehensive regulation of, say, the entire law of juristic acts, the law of obligations, general contract law or the law of synallagmatic contracts, or of one specific contract, such as sales, nor on entire branches of the law of contract, such as formation, interpretation, validity, or non-performance and remedies; indeed, they do not even entirely and generally regulate specific doctrines like fraud, causa or privity. They always regulate only some very specific issues (eg information to be provided before the conclusion of a contract), and they regulate them only for this particular contract (eg a timeshare contract) and for these particular types of parties (eg a consumer and a professional). Different 'sector-specific' directives often use different concepts. Directives are also completely flat: in a directive all rules are located on the same level of abstraction.

Codification takes place on one level of governance, ie the national level. Indeed, many codifications were the crowning glory of national unity. As a consequence, only one legislator (ie the national legislator) is responsible for the whole system of private law and will guard over its internal coherence. Similarly, there is only one court system, which is pyramidal. The Supreme Court (Cour de cassation, BGH, Hoge Raad, etc) alone has final responsibility for the coherent application (and further development) of the law by the courts.

In contrast, harmonisation takes place on two different levels of governance, ie the European and the national levels. The European and the national legislators share legislative responsibilities; neither body has final responsibility for the whole. Nor is there a superior authority (eg a constitution or a constitutional court) which has the final say on who is responsible for what (Kompetenz-Kompetenz). The same applies to the court system. National courts apply the national law as it stands after the transposition of a directive. They have to interpret national rules which are meant to transpose a directive in conformity with that directive.[49] However, the parties have no right to appeal to the ECJ; the national courts are free to decide whether or not to ask the ECJ for a preliminary ruling. Moreover, in its rulings, the ECJ does not determine the merits of the particular case (nor does it have the power to invalidate national legislation[50]); its jurisdiction is limited to questions relating to the interpretation of the Treaty and on the validity and interpretation of the relevant directive (Article 234 EC).

Finally, codification is static. It is meant to state the law as it stands in a clear and coherent way. Of course, a code can be changed, but the code itself does not aim at change. Even a recodification, as in the Netherlands (see above), does not aim at reform but rather at restating, in a clear and coherent way, the law as it is.

In contrast, harmonisation is dynamic. Directives are instrumental. They aim at change. In particular, they aim at improving the conditions for the establishment and functioning of the internal market. The objective is to establish the internal market, an area without internal frontiers where the free movement of goods, persons, services and capital is ensured (Articles 3(1)(c) and 14 EC).[51]

In view of these structural differences between the logic of national codification and the logic of European harmonisation, it is not at all surprising that the European harmonisation of private law through directives has led to many frictions in codified systems. This, in turn, has led to irritation, hostility and sometimes despair. Directives have often been perceived, especially by legal scholars, as attacks from Brussels on monuments of national pride.

---

[49] Settled case law. See Case C–106/89 *Marleasing v La Comercial Internacional de Alimentación* [1990] ECR I–4135; Case C–334/92 *Wagner Miret v Fondo de Garantía Salarial* [1993] ECR I–691; Case C–91/92 *Faccini Dori v Recreb* [1994] ECR I–3325; and Case 240/98 *Océano Grupo Editorial v Murciano Quintero* [2000] ECR I–4941.

[50] See the ECJ in Cases 10–22/97 *Ministero delle Finanze v IN.CO.GE'90* [1998] ECR I–6307, at [2]: 'The incompatibility with Community law of a subsequently adopted rule of national law does not have the effect of rendering that rule of national law non-existent.'

[51] Very critical of the instrumental character of European private law (from different angles) are MJ Schermaier, 'Rechtsangleichung und Rechtswissenschaft im kaufrechtlichen Sachmängelrecht' in MJ Schermaier (ed), *Verbraucherkauf in Europa* (Munich, Sellier, 2003) 3, 23 ('Wird Gesetzgebung im Privatrecht instrumentalisiert, um politische Vorgaben zu erfüllen, degradiert sie sich selbst zur Anlaßgesetzgebung. Seit der römischen Kaiserzeit wissen wir daß solche Gesetzgebung bestehende Systeme nicht weiterbildet, sondern zersetzt') and CU Schmid, 'The Instrumentalist Conception of the Acquis Communautaire in Consumer Law and its Implications on a European Contract Law Code' (2005) 1 *European Review of Contract Law* 211, 227 ('a European code might terminate once and for all the current tendency of downgrading private law to a mere integration tool—a slave of the *effet utile* so to speak'). Contrast H Collins, 'A Workers' Civil Code? Principles of European Contract Law Evolving in EU Social and Economic Policy' in MW Hesselink (ed), *The Politics of a European Civil Code* (The Hague, Kluwer Law International, 2006) 75, who sees an opportunity to seize the European private law project for a more social agenda.

There were many complaints: this had to stop; the Commission had to do something about it. And in fact it did.

IV. THE CFR AS CODIFICATION

1. The EC's Action Plan; the Way Forward

In 2003 the European Commission published an Action Plan on European contract law.[52] The Commission identifies problems concerning the uniform application of EC contract law and the smooth functioning of the internal market. The Action Plan suggests a mix of non-regulatory and regulatory measures in order to solve those problems. The main aim of the plan seems to be a more coherent European contract law.[53] In particular, the Commission envisages revising and improving the *acquis communautaire* in the area of contract law while continuing its sector-specific approach. However, the Commission will also consider non-sector-specific measures like an optional code.

All these measures will be based on what the Commission calls a 'common frame of reference' (CFR), which will be drafted by researchers. This CFR will be a publicly accessible document which should help the Community institutions to ensure the greater coherence of existing and future *acquis* in the area of European contract law.[54] It will provide clear definitions of legal terms, fundamental principles and coherent model rules of contract law.[55]

In a follow-up communication (*The Way Forward*), published a year later, the Commission underlined that it does not envisage proposing a European civil code.[56] One should not be ingenuous. As Jo Shaw notes, a notable feature of EU 'soft law' has been its progressive nature:

---

[52] Communication from the Commission to the European Parliament and the Council 'A More Coherent European Contract Law: an Action Plan' COM(2003) 68 final (12 February 2003) OJ 2003/C63/01 (hereafter 'Action Plan'). Two years earlier the Commission had started a consultation with its Communication from the Commission to the Council and the European Parliament on European contract law: COM(2001) 398 final (11 July 2001) OJ 2001/C 255/01.

[53] See, eg the title of the Action Plan.

[54] Action Plan, above n 52, para 59. The Commission seems to rely here on what has been called 'a prospective notion of coherence': 'The idea of coherence is thereby understood as a device for uniformly developing a system of laws, rather than a strategy with which to acknowledge the authority of past rules and decisions' (S Bertea, 'Looking for Coherence within the European Community' (2005) 11 *European Law Journal* 154, 169).

[55] See the Communication from the Commission to the European Parliament and the Council on European Contract Law and the Revision of the *Acquis*: The Way Forward, COM(2004) 651, 4 (hereafter 'The Way Forward').

[56] The Way Forward, *ibid*, 9.

Where a policy field lies at the margins of Community competence, the evolution of a common Community policy may well shift from the soft to the hard over a period of time, with non-binding measures . . . forming a useful prelude to the adoption of more rigorous measures.[57]

Indeed, it seems likely that the CFR process will eventually lead to a European Code of Contracts, eg one or more optional codes that the parties can choose. [58]

Still, there is no reason to think that the Commission has an elaborate plan, well hidden in a drawer in Brussels, for enacting a European civil code which will replace the national private laws of the Member States.[59] This does not mean, however, that the CFR will not lead to a radical change in the Europeanisation of private law.

2. Codification in a Substantive Sense

Even though the Commission is not now proposing a European civil code in a formal sense, the CFR process will effectively lead to a European private law codification in a substantive sense. In order to grasp this point, it suffices to examine the Commission's communications: the CFR will have all the main characteristics of a codification (see Table 2).

The CFR will be comprehensive. It will deal with the whole of contract law in the very broad and functional sense in which the Commission understands it, ie the law that applies to disputes between the parties to an economic transaction. The main goal of the CFR is to serve as a toolbox for the Commission when preparing proposals for reviewing the existing *acquis* and for new instruments.[60] For that purpose the Commission envisages a document that

---

[57] J Shaw, *Law of the European Union* (3rd edn, Basingstoke, Palgrave, 2000) 248. Compare Craig and de Búrca, above n 45, 167. For objections against the soft law character of the CFR from a constitutional perspective (especially democracy), see MW Hesselink, 'The European Commission's Action Plan: Towards a More Coherent European Contract Law?' (2004) 12 *European Review of Private Law* 397. See, in general terms, also Craig and de Búrca, above n 45, 117: 'Recourse to informal law may also prevent the Council and EP from having effective input into the content of the resulting norms.'

[58] See Hesselink, above n 57 ('a European civil code in disguise'); E Hondius, 'Towards a European Civil Code' in AS Hartkamp, MW Hesselink, EH Hondius, CA Joustra, CE du Perron and M Veldman (eds), *Towards a European Civil Code* (3rd edn, The Hague, Kluwer Law International, 2004) 13 ('a "pre-code"'); H Collins, 'The "Common Frame of Reference" for EC Contract Law: a Common Lawyer's Perspective' in M Meli and MR Maugeri (eds), *L'armonizzazione del diritto privato europeo* (Milan, Giuffrè, 2004) 107 ('Let's just call it a Code'); House of Lords (European Union Committee), *European Contract Law—The Way Forward?* (London, The Stationery Office Limited, 2005) 115 ('Once the CFR has been agreed it would not be a major task to convert or adapt it into an optional instrument. [T]he CFR may turn out to be something of a Trojan Horse').

[59] In the same sense, see House of Lords, above n 58, 99.

[60] The Way Forward, above n 55, 4. This emphasis is also reflected in the title of the communication. Cf D Staudenmayer, 'The Way Forward in European Contract Law' (2005) 13 *European Review of Private Law* 95, 96.

Table 2: The CFR as Codification

Comprehensive

    All subjects of contract law in one code

    Answers all general questions

Systematic

    General rules

    Several levels of abstraction

    Coherent (presumably)

One level of governance

    One, European CFR

Static

    Non-instrumental

    (Can be changed)

---

will contain fundamental principles of contract law: definitions of the main relevant abstract legal terms and model rules of contract law on all subjects of general contract law, specific contracts, and related subjects like (some parts of) property law (transfer of property; securities in moveables) and tort law.[61]

Of course, an ideal toolbox would be one that would provide answers to all important questions of contract law. The traditional way in which codes assure an answer to all questions is by offering general (or abstract) rules: the more general the rule, the more cases are covered. Indeed, the CFR will include and, in particular, define several abstract rules and concepts: [62]

> The common frame of reference should provide . . . common terminology and rules, i.e. the definition of fundamental concepts and abstract terms like 'contract' or 'damage' and of the rules that apply for example in the case of non-performance of contracts.

The CFR will certainly be systematic. Indeed, one of the principal aims of the Action Plan is a more coherent contract law.[63] In particular, the main purpose

---

[61] The Way Forward, above n 55, 4. Cf also Staudenmayer, above n 60, 103, who expects that the CFR will have a broad scope because the Commission has explicitly left open the question as to the desirability of one or more optional codes. 'The fact that this remains an open question is an argument for giving a broader scope to the CFR, in order to have the necessary material available for the possible development of one or more optional instruments.'

[62] Action Plan, above n 52, para 3.

[63] See 'First Annual Progress Report on European Contract Law and the Acquis Review' COM(2005) 456 final (23 September 2005) (First Annual Progress Report) 5.

of the CFR is to make the existing and future *acquis* more coherent.[64] Not only does the title of the Action Plan explicitly focus on the coherence of European contract law, the plan also includes measures which are explicitly meant to increase the coherence of the EC *acquis* in the area of contract law:[65]

> The objective is to achieve an European contract law acquis which has a high degree of consistency in its drafting as well as implementation and application . . . it should avoid similar situations being treated differently without relevant justification for such different treatment. It should also avoid conflicting results and should define abstract legal terms in a consistent manner allowing the use of the same abstract term with the same meaning for the purposes of several directives.[66]

For that purpose, the CFR will contain general principles, definitions and rules. Moreover, unlike directives, the CFR will almost certainly have several layers of abstraction. In the annex to the 2004 communication the Commission published a 'possible structure of the CFR'.[67] Chapter III (Model rules) of that structure is based on several distinctions between more general and more specific rules, eg general contract law[68] and 'specific rules' for sales and insurance contracts, 'remedies in general' and 'particular remedies,' whereas Chapter I (Principles), which contains 'some common fundamental principles of European contract law and exceptions for some of these principles,' displays some similarity with the general part of some civil codes in Europe (notably those in the Germanic tradition).

Both the content and the scope of the CFR will be determined by systematic considerations, in particular the concern for coherence: [69]

---

[64] The Action Plan is an expression of the Commission's more general policy towards improving European governance: one of the five principles of good governance in its white paper is 'coherence'. See 'European Governance—A White Paper' COM(2001) 428 final (12 October 2001) OJ 287/1.

[65] Action Plan, above n 52, para 3.

[66] Action Plan, paras 56–57. Compare R Zimmermann, 'Codification: History and Present Significance of an Idea' (1995) 3 *European Review of Private Law* 95, 110, 120: 'a codification constitutes an intellectual effort to look at private law as a systematic entity'; R Sacco, 'Codificare: modo superato di legiferare?' (1983) *Rivista di diritto civile* 117, 119: 'Codificare significa rinnegare il particolarismo giuridico'; J Basedow, 'Das BGB im künftigen europäischen Privatrecht: Der hybride Kodex; Systemsuche zwischen nationaler Kodifikation und Rechtsangleichung' (2000) 200 *Archiv für die civilistische Praxis* 445, 471: 'Schließlich gilt die Kodifikation auf dem europäischen Kontinent vielen als "Ausdruck und Garant [des] Systemdenkens".'

[67] The Way Forward, above n 55, annex I.

[68] In most civil codes some of the subjects would be placed on an additional level of abstraction: the general law of obligations. So far, the Commission has avoided broadening the scope of its plans that far. (See, however, the Dutch-language version of the Action Plan, which consistently speaks of *verbintenissenrecht*—the law of obligations).

[69] The Way Forward, above n 55, 12. See also Action Plan, above n 52, para 64: 'the objectives of the common frame of reference determine its content. The first objective is to allow the existing *acquis* to be improved and simplified and to ensure the coherence of the future *acquis*.'

The primary criterion for determining which areas are covered [by the CFR] should be the usefulness in terms of increasing the coherence of the acquis.

In *The Way Forward* the Commission discusses the specific example of the consumer *acquis*. The Commission will examine, among other things, whether there are any 'significant gaps, inconsistencies or overlaps between the eight directives,' whether 'the scope of the directives [is] correct' and whether there is 'scope for merging some of the directives to reduce inconsistencies between them.'[70]

Like national codes, but unlike harmonisation through directives (see above), the CFR process will be situated exclusively on one level of governance, ie the European level. It will be a European CFR; there is no obligation for the Member States to implement it, as such, into their national laws.[71] In other words, with regard to contract law the Commission is moving from a 'vertical' to a 'horizontal' approach, thus responding to a demand from the Council:

the Council report would seem to favour a more horizontal approach to harmonisation, aiming at the creation of a European common core of private law if a need for harmonisation is revealed.[72]

Finally, the CFR will be static. Unlike directives, it will not aim, as such, at changing the law. In contrast, the Commission regards the CFR process as being part of a broader policy towards 'Consolidation, codification and recasting,'[73] where codification is defined as

the adoption of a new legal instrument which brings together in a single text, but without changing the substance, a previous instrument and its successive amendments, with the new instrument replacing the old one and repealing it.

The fact that the CFR does not aim at change does not, of course, mean that it cannot itself be changed: like any national code, the CFR can be changed at any time.

In sum, even if the CFR process will never lead to a formally enacted (optional) European Code of Contracts, Europe will soon have a substantive codification of contract law (and some other parts of private law) in the shape of a 'common frame of reference'. This raises the question of what will be the consequences for the national codifications of private law in Europe.

---

[70] Quoted by the Commission in The Way Forward, above n 55, 5.
[71] On the implications of the CFR for national private laws, see below, p 58.
[72] Action Plan, above n 52, para 28.
[73] Action Plan, above n 52, para 77. See also COM(2001) 398 final, above n 52, 58. The Commission refers to the Interim Report from the Commission to the Stockholm European Council 'Improving and Simplifying the Regulatory Environment' COM(2001) 130 (7 March 2001) 10.

3. National Coherence v European Coherence

The adoption of the CFR by the Commission is foreseen for 2009.[74] Once the CFR is in place, the Commission will use it for making the *acquis* more coherent. The Commission will revise the existing *acquis* and will enact new directives in the light of the coherent system of general principles, definitions and model rules of the CFR. In other words, the Commission will re-enact the *acquis* and will gradually add elements to it which (presumably) are all perfectly coherent (among each other and) with the general principles, definitions and model rules which are contained in the CFR but which will not be formally enacted (due to the lack of a legal basis or to a lack of urgency).[75] The enacted part (ie the *acquis*) and the not (yet) enacted part of the CFR will be fully complementary: together they will form a complete and coherent system, based on a European conception of (social) justice.[76] However, it may be difficult to understand fully the meaning of the enacted part without knowing the part which has remained soft law.

National courts must interpret national law, as far as possible, in the light of the wording and purpose of relevant directives.[77] When trying to determine the proper meaning of a directive, courts will often be inclined to consult the full CFR.[78] Indeed, they may even be under an obligation to do so.[79] The ECJ has held that EU soft law measures may have to be taken into account when interpreting national law, especially when they are capable of clarifying other provisions of national or EU law.[80] In Grimaldi the Court remarked (with regard to recommendations):[81]

> in the light of the fifth paragraph of Art 189 of the EEC Treaty [now Art 249 EC], [Commission Recommendations] cannot in themselves confer rights on individuals upon which the latter may rely before national courts. However, national courts are bound to take those recommendations into consideration in order to decide

---

[74] The Way Forward, above n 55, 14.

[75] The Council emphasises that the CFR will not be a binding document. See Council Resolution on 'A More Coherent European Contract Law' [2003] OJ C 246/01: 'This Common Frame of Reference would not be a legally binding instrument.'

[76] See Study Group on Social Justice in European Private Law, 'Social Justice in European Contract Law: a Manifesto' (2004) 10 *European Law Journal* 653; MW Hesselink, 'The Politics of a European Civil Code' (2004) 10 *European Law Journal* 675.

[77] Settled case law. See above n 49.

[78] Indeed, the Commission seems to expect that the Member States will do so when implementing directives. See *First Annual Progress Report*, above n 63, 5.

[79] This will mean a major change from the present situation. In *Leitner* (C–168/00) the ECJ refused to interpret the concept of damage in Art 5 of the package travel directive (90/314/EC) in the light of the meaning of that same concept in Art 9 of the Directive on product liability (85/374/ECC) (as was suggested by the Austrian and the French governments, and which had been followed by Advocate General Tizzano). That bar to a coherence-friendly interpretation or *favor cohaerentiae* has certainly contributed to the sense of fragmentation in the Member States as a result of harmonisation through directives.

[80] Shaw, above n 57, 247, 449.

[81] Case 322/88 *Grimaldi v Fonds des Maladies Professionnelles* [1989] ECR 4407.

disputes submitted to them, in particular where they are capable of casting light on the interpretation of other provisions of national or Community law.

It is to be expected that the CFR will contribute to making European contract law more coherent. However, at the same time it will lead to (strong) tensions and incoherences of a new kind in the national legal systems. As we have seen above (sections 2 and 3), so far there has been tension between the coherence-oriented logic of national codifications and the sector-specific and instrumental logic of European harmonisation. Once the CFR is 'in force'—ie once it is the Commission's starting point for revising the *acquis* and for preparing new directives—this tension will be between the national codification with its coherent system and the CFR with its own coherent system. In other words, after the familiar tension between systematic codification and instrumental harmonisation, there will be a new tension between two different systematic codifications, ie the formal civil codes in the Member States and the substantive codification of contract law at the Community level, eg between the Dutch BW and the European CFR.

So far (in the Netherlands), only the BW contains general definitions of abstract terms, general rules on the formation, validity, interpretation, performance and non-performance of contracts, general rules of sales law, etc. From 2009 onwards there will also be European definitions of the same concepts and rules on the same subjects. It is very unlikely that these definitions will completely coincide with the Dutch definitions and rules simply because, today, they are different from eg the French, German and English rules and definitions. For example, the rules on damage (the main example in the Action Plan) differ considerably among the Member States. The Commission acknowledges this; indeed, it is one of the justifications for the CFR.

V. THE WAY FORWARD FOR NATIONAL LEGISLATORS: THREE CODIFICATION STRATEGIES

The indirect effect of the CFR raises many questions on the European level. The European constitutional dimension will be that the CFR, despite not being formally enacted due to the lack of a legal basis,[82] may have a substantive effect similar to a formal code. This raises many constitutional questions relating to sovereignty, the rule of law and democracy.[83]

However, the question which concerns us here is how the national legislator should react. What should a legislator which continues to be inspired by

---

[82] In the words of the Commission, it will be 'adopted' (The Way Forward, above n 55, 14).

[83] See further on this substantive effect (*Geltung*) Hesselink, above nn 57 and 76. See also MT Bouwes, 'Harmonisatie van het burgerlijk recht door de achterdeur; Een Common Frame of Reference' [2005] *Nederlands Juristenblad* 944, who speaks of 'harmonisation through the backdoor,' and House of Lords, above n 58, 669, which emphasises that 'the detailed content of the CFR is going to involve political choices and decisions.'

the codification ideal (eg the Dutch legislator) actually do? In the light of this new tension between two codes, a national and a European one, each with its own distinct coherent system, what is the best strategy for maintaining a coherent system of private law?[84]

A national legislator that continues to be inspired by the codification ideal can react in at least three different ways to the adoption by the Commission of a Common Frame of Reference. In the belligerent terms in which 'foreign' influence is often experienced the national legislator can decide to resist, to segregate or to surrender to the influence of the CFR.

1. Resistance

The first possible strategy towards the harmonisation of private law through directives is to try to integrate them, as much as possible, into the national civil code, and to do so in such a way that upsets the domestic system as little as possible. This approach implies a faithful transposition, but nothing further: in particular, no broadening of the scope of directives. It also means adapting the harmonisation measure as much as possible to the terminology and structure of the domestic national system. As a result, one directive will often be transposed into different parts of the code, on different levels of abstraction. Moreover, it means that very often, especially in the case of minimum harmonisation, the national legislator will conclude that its legal system is already up to standard, ie that the result at which the directive aims has already been achieved under the code as it stands. In other words, in this model the legislator stretches the possibilities provided by Article 249(3) EC to the very limits.

As we have seen, this strategy has been adopted by the Dutch legislator in the area of private law. The legislator has consistently tried to preserve national coherence by 'translating' the new measures, as much as possible, into the concepts and system of the new BW, and to limit their impact to the absolute minimum. This is not a surprising reaction from a legislator which has striven for half a century to create a perfect system.

Will it be possible to maintain this strategy once the CFR is in place? Of course, the Dutch legislator could continue to transpose any new directives as much as possible into the system of the national civil code (BW). This strategy would be completely in line with the nature of harmonisation through directives (Article 249 EC).

---

[84] Here, and throughout this paper, I understand 'coherence' as 'perceived coherence', ie as something that the relevant players experience as being there. I will not go into the question whether any legal system is ever 'actually' coherent or whether one system is 'objectively' more coherent than another. See further on this phenomenological approach D Kennedy, *A Critique of Adjudication {fin de siècle}* (Cambridge, MA, Harvard University Press, 1997) ch 7. For various different notions of coherence in relation to Community law see Bertea, above n 54.

What would be the likely consequences of maintaining this strategy? It would mean continued friction within the code, between the parts of national origin and the parts of European origin. However, with the CFR in place the nature of the friction will be different. Whereas, so far, directives have often lacked internal coherence because they were not based on a general idea about the whole of contract law, the new directives (the new *acquis*) will be internally coherent: they will be the formally binding parts of a complete system which is internally coherent, albeit not formally binding in its totality. These new directives will be consistently based on the same definitions of general concepts like 'consumer', 'contract' and 'damage', and will contain specific remedies which will be formulated consistently against the background of the general 'rules' on defects of consent, interpretation, non-performance of contracts, etc in the CFR. These definitions, principles and rules will usually be very different from the ones contained in the national code.

The friction may become very acute once the Commission comes to revise the present *acquis*, eg in the area of consumer contract law,[85] and enact the revised *acquis* in one coherent (framework) directive, as seems to be envisaged.[86] The revision will be entirely based on the CFR.[87] (Remember that the revision of the *acquis* is the main purpose of the CFR.[88]) Notably, the concepts, principles, rules and structure will be consistently based on the CFR. Moreover, such (an) *acquis* directive(s) will probably contain full harmonisation.[89] This raises the question of whether it will be at all possible to transpose the revised *acquis* directive(s) into the system of the BW in the same way as the Dutch legislator has done so far, ie by dissecting it into

---

[85] Cf Staudenmayer, above n 60, 97.

[86] If the Commission were to opt for a regulation, which has direct applicability, the situation would be even more dramatic. The national legislators would probably have to remove from their codes the rules which implemented the directives as they will lack effect (as a result of the direct applicability of the new regulation), at least for those cases falling under the scope of the (consumer) *acquis* regulation, and will have to decide what to do with those rules which were meant to broaden the scope of the directives but may have become inappropriate in the light of the revised (!) *acquis*. This horror scenario (think, for example, of the consequences for the German *Schuldrechtsreform*) seemed unlikely until recently because the Protocol on the application of the principles of subsidiarity and proportionality to the Treaty of Amsterdam, (OJ C340 of 10 November 1997) says (under 6): 'Other things being equal, directives should be preferred to regulations and framework directives to detailed measures.' See also the proportionality principle, Art 5(3) EC, which was introduced by that same Treaty. However, in its recent 'Communication of the Commission to the European Parliament, the Council, the European Economic and Social Committee and the Committee of the Regions; Implementing the Community Lisbon Programme: A Strategy for the Simplification of the Regulatory Environment' COM(2005) 535 final, 8, the Commission announces that it 'intends to further exploit, on a case by case basis, the potential for simplification (*sic!*) through substituting directives with regulations.'

[87] The Way Forward, above n 55, 3.

[88] Action Plan, above n 52, para 59.

[89] Cf the Commission's 'Consumer Policy Strategy 2002–2006' COM(2002) 208 final 12: 'There is also a need to review and reform existing EU consumer protection directives, to bring them up to date and progressively adapt them from minimum harmonisation to "full harmonisation" measures.'

segments, placing the rules on different levels of abstraction and by adapting the terminology to the national terminology.

In its recent Progress Report the Commission describes two possible options between which it can choose for the revision of the *acquis*, a vertical approach consisting of the individual revision of existing directives or the regulation of specific sectors (eg a directive on tourism) or a more horizontal approach, adopting one or more framework instruments to regulate common features of the *acquis*.[90] The Commission only elaborates on the second option, which it seems to favour. It says that under the horizontal approach it could, for example, prepare a directive on consumer contracts for the sale of goods. Such a directive would consistently regulate the contractual aspects of sale, which are currently scattered among several directives, eg the directives on the sale of consumer goods, unfair contract terms, distance selling and doorstep selling. In the view of the Commission, such an instrument 'would rationalise the regulatory framework considerably since all the relevant provisions of the relevant existing directives would be systematised into the new directive.'

It will be a formidable task, if it is at all feasible, to faithfully transpose such a directive into the code without completely upsetting the system of the code. Where should this new coherent European consumer sales law be placed?[91] As we saw in the Dutch BW, today unfair contract terms are regulated, generally for all contracts, in Book 6, whereas sales law is regulated specifically in Book 7. It is not excluded that the *corpus extraneus* will eventually be rejected and that the Dutch legislator will have to opt for an alternative method of transposing directives in the area of private law. However, as we will see, the alternatives also have their drawbacks.

Even if the Dutch legislator manages to adapt the revised *acquis* to the system of the Dutch code without failing to fulfil its obligations under the EC Treaty (Article 249), the trouble will not be over. On the contrary, with every new sector-specific measure which contains concepts, principles and rules based on the same coherent European system (ie the CFR) the 'attack' on the system, concepts and structure of the BW will continue.

Moreover, as said, national law has to be interpreted in conformity with directives (indirect effect).[92] What will this mean once the revised and the new *acquis* is based on the CFR? It will mean that a whole set of provisions in the (presumably) coherent Dutch system of private law will have to be interpreted in the light of a directive which is part of another, now (presumably)

[90] First Annual Progress Report, above n 63, 8–9.

[91] Compare Basedow, above n 66 (in relation to the question whether a European code of contract law could be enacted through a directive): 'Eine europäische Kodifikation läßt sich nicht in präexistente und heterogene nationale Rechtssysteme einfügen. Sie verträgt keine Anpassung an ein fremdes System, in dem dann vielleicht einzelne Vorschriften der europäischen Kodifikation ihren Standort in ganz verschiedenen nationalen Gesetzen fänden, der systematische Zusammenhang also auseinandergerissen würde. Die Kodifikation ist vielmehr denknotwendig der Dreh- und Angelpunkt eines größeren Rechtsgebietes, das seinerseits an die Begriffe und Systematik der Kodifikation anzupassen ist.'

[92] See p 51.

equally coherent, set of rules. It seems that the CFR, although not a formally enacted codification, will have some strong effect (Geltung) through the indirect effect of directives based thereon.[93] (Obviously, if the ECJ was ever to come back on its formalist distinction between regulations and directives and was to accept the direct horizontal effect of directives, this would mean the final blow to the Dutch approach to implementation.[94]) Moreover, its effect may be even more explicit. As we have seen, the ECJ has held that EU soft law measures may have to be taken into account when interpreting national law, especially when they are capable of clarifying other provisions of national or EU law.[95]

With a view to the obligation for national courts of harmonious interpretation, the Dutch way of implementing raises the additional problem that the Community origin of the rules remains completely unrecognisable.[96] The larger the proportion of rules of EC origin within the code, the more this will become problematic in practice.

It should also be noted that, in spite of all the efforts, the hope that the codification ideal will be completely fulfilled is in vain. It will never be possible to include all the rules of private law which are applicable in the Netherlands in one coherent system (ie the system of the BW). The reason for this is that European and international rules with direct application will necessarily remain outside the code. These include, for example, the CISG, the air passengers regulation 2004[97] and Article 81 EC on the invalidity of agreements which distort competition within the internal market. In other words, we will have to live with the idea that the private law which is applicable in the Netherlands will be increasingly fragmented; it is an inevitable consequence of multilevel governance.[98]

Finally, an important drawback of this rather formal approach, which mainly concentrates on the concepts and structure of the code, is that it does not solve the substantive problem of normative coherence. In contrast to the German model (see below), in this Dutch approach, where the legislator

---

[93] Weatherill, above n 46, 126, has said that through indirect effect Community directives are 'absorbed into the national legal order.' With regard to directives based on the CFR, one could say that through the indirect effect of such directives the CFR will be absorbed into the national legal order. In the view of F De Ly, *Europese Gemeenschap en privaatrecht* (Zwolle, Tjeenk Willink, 1993) 51, directives merely give the Member States the illusion of maintaining some of their sovereignty.

[94] The direct horizontal effect of directives was explicitly rejected by the ECJ in *Faccini Dori*, above n 49, in spite of strong pleas by three of its Advocates-General and by many academic commentators. On the debate, see Craig and de Búrca, above n 45, 202; Shaw, above n 57, 441.

[95] See the ECJ in *Grimaldi* (discussed above, pp 57–58).

[96] In the same sense, see Roth, above n 47, 773; JM Smits, above n 13, 490.

[97] Regulation 261/2004/EC of the European Parliament and of the Council of 11 February 2004 establishing common rules on compensation and assistance to passengers in the event of denied boarding and of the cancellation or long delay of flights OJ L46/1.

[98] See Christian Joerges, 'The Impact of European Integration on Private Law: Reductionist Perceptions, True Conflicts and a New Constitutional Perspective' (1997) 3 *European Law Journal* 378. There are also autonomous decodification tendencies, eg the development of functional fields of the law like labour, consumer, environmental, information, transport, and building law. See further p 63.

consistently refuses to broaden the scope of directives, cases that may be regarded as similar will not be treated alike.[99] This problem is not the Dutch legislator's fault; it is immanent to the sector-specific approach which characterises European market integration. However, a national legislator that wishes to see normative coherence might well opt for an approach where like cases are treated alike, at least as far as possible. The Dutch legislator seems to focus exclusively on initial coherence and desperately tries to limit the impact of disturbing directives. The defensive and formalistic Dutch approach has therefore been rejected by commentators.[100] The German legislator, in contrast, tries to create a new coherence, extending the scope of several directives.[101] However, as we will see, once the CFR is in place, then adopting such an alternative approach may have far-reaching consequences.

In sum, it is very doubtful whether this approach, legitimate as it may be in the light of the constitutional principles on which the Union is based, will prove to be practicable in the long run.[102] Resistance against the invasion of definitions, principles and rules of CFR may become untenable. Indeed, Tjeenk Willink, the president of the Dutch Raad van State (Conseil d'Etat), warns, in more general terms, that the Dutch government is often too attached to the concepts and structure of its own national system, and this leads to a minimalist approach to harmonisation that, when it has to be given up, leaves legal practice completely unprepared for a major law reform.[103]

2. Segregation

A second way of transposing directives into the national legal system is simply

---

[99] Obviously the question whether cases actually *are* similar (and *have to* be treated alike) is a normative question. See P Scholten, *Mr C Asser's handleiding tot de beoefening van het Nederlands burgerlijk recht; Algemeen Deel* (3rd edn, Zwolle, WEJ Tjeenk Willink, 1974).

[100] See, eg Smits, above n 13, 500 ('De Nederlandse wetgever moet niet proberen om die fragmentatie weg te poetsen door richtlijnen zoveel mogelijk in te passen in de systematiek van het Burgerlijk Wetboek. Dat is tot mislukken gedoemd.') Contrast J Hijma, 'Bedenktijd in het contractenrecht' in J Hijma and WL Valk, *Wettelijke bedenktijd* (Deventer, Kluwer, 2004) 1, 6 ('Het siert de Nederlandse wetgever dat hij zich wél over die inpassing pleegt te buigen en uit te spreken') and EH Hondius, *Nieuwe methoden van privaatrechtelijke rechtsvinding en rechtsvorming in een Verenigd Europa* (Amsterdam, KNAW, 2001) 40 ('Voordeel van integratie is dat de wederzijdse kruisbestuiving gemakkelijker zal verlopen. Om deze reden heb ik zelf een voorkeur voor integratie in het Burgerlijk Wetboek, zoals dat in Nederland geschiedt').

[101] Cf Roth, above n 47, 767: 'To state the obvious: There is no Community obligation to extend consumer protection beyond the scope of the relevant directives, and to flatten out the somewhat arbitrary differentiations in Community law. However, any legal order which cares for coherence and consistency will have to give a satisfactory explanation for a limited (and even arbitrary) scope of consumer rights. The fact that it is the directive which itself claims only a limited scope of application is certainly not a sufficient answer if the solution found violates basic notions of coherence and consistency.'

[102] In the same sense JM Smits, above n 13, 490, 497.

[103] HD Tjeenk Willink, 'Toetsing van wetsvoorstellen aan EU-regelgeving' in GJM Corstens, WJM Davids and MI Veldt-Foglia (eds), *Europeanisering van het Nederlands Recht* (Deventer, Kluwer, 2004) 74, 80.

to reproduce them verbatim in national statutes while the code remains unaffected; it continues to exist as it was. In this strategy no attempt is made to integrate the new rules into the system of the national code. In its most extreme form, directives are transposed as literally as possible: the terminology is not adapted nor is the scope of any of the rules extended. The codification ideal may even make the legislator decide to place all the statutes which implement directives together, without structuring them any further, into a national '*acquis* code'. This idea could also be limited to the directives which have something in common, eg all the directives on consumer law.

The style of directives is increasingly well suited for this approach. In theory, they still address the Member States, but their drafting often allows for direct effect. The Consumer Sales Directive, for example, reads like a statute.[104] Instead of telling the Member States what to do, they say what the seller must do.[105]

This segregation strategy has been adopted with regard to many directives in several Member States.[106] For example, in Germany it was the standard procedure until the law reform of 2002. Thus, the rules of European origin were segregated from the national rules and the purity of the national code was preserved.[107]

This approach solves (or avoids) several problems which occur under the first approach ('resistance'). First, transposition is much easier. Instead of studying each directive meticulously and cutting it into pieces which are then placed in the code, on those levels of abstraction and with those general concepts which seem most appropriate, the directive can be 'transplanted' whole into one or more national statutes.[108] Moreover, in this second approach the EC origin of the relevant national rules remains clearly recognisable. As said, this is very helpful with a view to the obligation of harmonious interpretation. Finally, the differences and tensions between the original national law and the new rules of European origin are out in the open.[109] Indeed, the national legal order will contain two

---

[104] Contrast eg the style of the commercial agency directive (86/653/EEC).

[105] See, eg Art 2(1): 'The seller must deliver goods to the consumer which are in conformity with the contract of sale.'

[106] Eg in Italy for all directives in the field of contract law except the ones on unfair terms and consumer sales. Cf Roppo, above n 33, 274.

[107] In Germany this policy was part of a broader policy to preserve the purity of the BGB.

[108] In the common law system of the United Kingdom literal transposition into secondary legislation (regulations), based on Art 2(2) European Communities Act 1972, has long been the ordinary style of implementation. This has led to criticism. See, eg M Bridge, 'Introduction' in Bianca and Grundmann, above n 38, 131: 'the product of a union between primary legislation and secondary legislation transposing a European Directive is . . . difficult to rationalise and understand in its entirety.'

[109] EH Hondius, 'Produktenaansprakelijkheid: de voordelen van een dualistische rechtsorde' (1996) 45 *Ars Aequi* 38, argues, with reference to the experience that several legal orders have had with internal tensions within one legal system (*ius civile* v *ius honorarium*; common law v civil law; Roman-Dutch law v common law), that a 'dualistic' character may actually be beneficial for the development of a legal system.

complementary systems of private law, each with its own system (and with its own code).

This second strategy also has its problems. The first is that directives address states and not citizens and may therefore not be well suited for literal transposition. They sometimes tell the Member States that they must attain aims without telling them how to do so. Such provisions are inappropriate for direct invocation by citizens. Secondly, some directives provide the national legislator with an option.[110] Finally, the approach does not seem to fit well with the recent case law of the ECJ, which leaves much discretion to the national system. In *Freiburger Kommunalbauten*[111] the Court held that it was for the national court to decide whether the contractual term at issue satisfied the requirements for it to be regarded as unfair under Article 3(1) of the unfair terms directive.[112] The consequences of the term under the law applicable to the contract must be taken into account. This requires that consideration be given to the national law. This approach seems to point to an interpretation which is in conformity with national coherence. Such an interpretation by the courts is not made any easier by a segregationist approach to implementation.

This approach will also not solve the problem of direct application. EC and international rules with direct effect application necessarily remain outside a national *acquis* code. As a result, if, for example, the Netherlands were to adopt this approach, then the private law applicable in the Netherlands would be fragmented into the civil code, the national *acquis* code, and the European and international provisions with direct application.

Finally, of course, the main drawback is that no attempt is made to solve, or even to mitigate, the conflicts between the two sets of rules, as far as either form (concepts, structure) or substance (normative coherence) is concerned.

How will this strategy work out once the CFR will be adopted? Once the CFR is in place the national *acquis* code will probably become increasingly internally coherent, the rules contained therein (old and new *acquis*) will consistently use the same concepts, will be based on the same principles and will represent elements taken from the same complete set of rules of contract law. With the further growth of the *acquis* in the area of contract law the relative importance of the *acquis* code will gradually increase compared with the importance of the old civil code. In this approach it would make sense, when applying rules contained in the *acquis* code, to interpret them, as much as possible, in conformity with the CFR, even though the CFR is not law in a

---

[110] This problem has been solved in Great Britain, in the case of the commercial agency directive, by passing the option on to the citizens.

[111] Case C–237/02 *Freiburger Kommunalbauten* [2004] ECR I–3403.

[112] Contrast I Klauer, 'General Clauses in European Private Law and 'Stricter' National Standards: the Unfair Terms Directive' (2000) 8 *European Review of Private Law* 187, who argued that it is up to the Court of Justice to give a common, European interpretation of Art 3 of the unfair terms directive and of similar general clauses.

formal sense. In other words, when interpreting rules of European origin one would always interpret them with a view to the internal coherence of the *acquis*, whereas in the first ('Dutch') approach the courts are more likely to interpret the *acquis*, as far as possible (see above), with a view to the coherence of the national civil code.

A 'revised consumer *acquis* directive', especially if it aims at full harmonisation, is likely to solve or diminish some of the problems related to this strategy. Even though such a directive will formally address the Member States, it will probably be formulated in such a way that literal transposition will not lead to many problems. It will probably contain (model) rules which effectively address citizens and it will probably not contain any options. That is what the Commission seems to have in mind when it considers the possibility of a comprehensive directive on consumer sales contracts.[113] On the other hand, however, with such an *acquis* directive the problem of the lack of normative and conceptual coherence in the whole private law applicable in the Member State will only become more acute. Private law will increasingly be segregated, consisting of two complementary parts, each with its own underlying principles, concepts and rules. In codified systems it could lead to a system with two complementary codes, the civil code and the *acquis* code.

Moreover, the situation may become even more complex since this process of fragmentation would overlap only partly with another fragmentation process, ie the development towards functional fields of law like labour, consumer, environmental, information, transport and building law, which typically are a mix of private and public law.[114] In some Member States this latter fragmentation process has contributed to the decodification of the law.[115] However, in other countries, notably in France, it has led to functional codes like the Code de la Consommation.[116] Naturally, a consumer code and an *acquis* code would not have entirely the same scope, whereas a consumer *acquis* code would lead to the result that neither the whole consumer law nor the whole private or contract law *acquis* would be codified.

---

[113] See First Annual Progress Report, above n 63, 9.

[114] See further MW Hesselink, *The New European Private Law* (The Hague, Kluwer, 2002) ch 8.

[115] Cf N Irti, *L'età della decodificazione* (Milan, Giuffrè, 1986) and B Oppetit, *Essai sur la codification* (Paris, PUF, 1998) 41: 'la décodification' (with regard to French commercial law). Against 'codification pessimism', see Zimmermann, above n 66, 105. See also Basedow, above n 66, 490.

[116] Critical of such fragmentation, on normative grounds, is EH Hondius, 'Consumer Law and Private Law: the Case for Integration' in W Heusel (ed), *New European Contract Law and Consumer Protection* (Bundesanzeiger, Trier, 1999) 19, 22: 'The advantage of this [ie including protective rules in the civil code, like the Dutch legislator has done] is that the protection of employees, tenants, patients and consumers has become such a major element that it has changed the paradigm of civil law. No longer freedom of contract can be regarded as the only prevailing value of contract law; protection of the weaker party, including the weaker professional, now is on equal footing.'

Obviously, this prospect of fragmentation is far from ideal from a coherence perspective. The segregationist approach does not lead to the same problems as resistance, but it has its own drawbacks. What does the third approach have to offer?

3. Surrender

A third possible approach to transposing directives into private law is to broaden their scope in all cases where, in the eyes of the national legislator, cases that are not covered by the directive should be dealt with in the same way. Such an approach is inspired by a concern for normative (or, in some cases, conceptual) coherence. Where a directive requires the national legislator to change, for a subset of cases (eg for consumer sales contracts), a national rule with a broader scope (eg all sales contracts), the national legislator chooses to use its legislative autonomy (with regard to the cases which are not covered by the directive) in such a way as to avoid creating incoherencies. In other words, rather than treating similar cases differently, as would happen in a minimalist approach (the Dutch model), the legislator opts for a maximalist approach. Since the national legislator is bound by the directive and cannot change the policies contained therein for the cases covered by it, it decides to surrender and give up its deviating national policy entirely (ie for all cases) rather than to create normative incoherence.

The approach of broadening the scope of rules contained in directives has been adopted in several member states on several occasions.[117] By far the most dramatic example of this approach is the recent German reform of the law of obligations. The German legislator decided to broaden the scope of a number of directives considerably, notably the Consumer Sales Directive,[118] and, as a consequence, to overhaul fully its law of obligations (thus reviving a reform plan from the 1980s which had become stalled).

The ECJ has decided that it has jurisdiction under Article 234 EC where the situation in question is not governed directly by Community law but the national legislature, in transposing the provisions of a directive into domestic law, has chosen to apply the same treatment for purely internal situations and those governed by the directive, so that it has aligned its domestic legislation

---

[117] MH Wissink, *Richtlijnconforme interpretatie van burgerlijk recht* (Deventer, Kluwer, 2001) 256; MH Wissink, 'De invloed van Europese richtlijnen op het Nederlandse privaatrecht' [1999] *Nederlands Tijdschrift voor Burgerlijk Recht* 1, 6, speaks of '*intern doorharmoniseren*': ie to bring other parts of national law into harmony with the new rules which are based on European harmonisation. See also HB Krans, 'Europa en ons contractenrecht' [2004] *Nederlands Tijdschrift voor Burgerlijk Recht* 501, 508. But see Smits, above n 13, 497.

[118] Compare also German observers who conclude that the directive effectively deals with the general law of obligations. See eg Roth, above n 47, 764; MJ Schermaier, above n 51, 3; S Grundmann, 'European Contract Law(s) of What Colour' (2005) 1 *European Review of Contract Law* 184, 201, 210.

with Community law. This may happen, for example, when the national legislator extends the scope of a concept contained in a directive to cases which are not covered by that directive.[119] This case law seems to imply that German courts can now submit preliminary questions to the ECJ with regard to most subjects covered by the reform of the law of obligations, eg in non-consumer sales cases.[120]

The implication, with regard to the CFR, of this approach in its purest form would be voluntarily, without any obligation, to broaden the scope of the formally binding *acquis* and to formally enact the non-binding CFR, thus replacing the relevant national law in its entirety.[121] As a result there would no longer be any tension between the rules of national origin and those of European origin in this particular area.[122] Obviously, this approach is highly satisfactory from the perspective of normative coherence. However, this approach comes at a price.

First, it would mean a major reform of national private law, the second within two decades for the Netherlands (1992) (and only one decade for Germany, which underwent a major reform in 2002). Today, few countries' MPs would be eager to spend their valuable time on such a massive legislative enterprise: normative coherence in private law does not seem to yield instant electoral gain.

Moreover, broad as the scope of the CFR may be, it will still not cover the whole of private law. Therefore, the original national private law relating to some subjects will remain in effect. Hence, there will continue to be issues of normative incoherence. This would also hold true, in the Netherlands, for much of the general part of patrimonial law (and in other systems, such as German law, for the general part of civil law), which will continue to exist as many of its concepts (eg juristic act) and rules (eg on validity) 'serve' other branches of the law, such as the law of succession. In other words, as long as the national and European legal orders do not fully coincide there will always

---

[119] Cases C–28/95 *Leur-Bloem* [1997] ECR I–4161 (on directives); C–130/95 *Giloy* [1997] ECR I–4291.

[120] In this sense Roth, above n 47, 764. Cf S Grundmann, 'Introduction' in Bianca and Grundmann, above n 38, 39. It is unclear whether this case law also applies to the (reverse) case where the national legislator translates the directive into a pre-existing national concept with a broader scope (eg in the Netherlands 'nietigheid' in 3:40 BW; see p 47). If so, this ECJ case law would have equally dramatic consequences for the member states, like the Netherlands, which have adopted the second strategy (resistance) (see p 59).

[121] LAD Keus, 'De Europeanisering van het vermogensrecht, in het bijzonder van het contractenrecht' in GJM Corstens et al (eds), above n 103, 194, 201, expects that if, in the future, a non-optional European code is adopted for cross-border transactions (a hypothesis that the Commission does not exclude in its Action Plan) there will be a certain pressure on the national legislators to voluntarily adopt the same code also for purely internal transactions.

[122] Cf with regard to (a formally binding) European codification of the law of obligations Basedow, above n 66, 491: 'Die vorhandenen Schuldrechtsregelungen der Mitgliedstaaten würden durch die europäische Kodifikation weitgehend verdrängt; die Mitgliedstaaten müßten die Restbestände ihrer Zivilgesetzbücher in begrifflicher und systematischer Hinsicht an das europäische Obligationenrecht anpassen.'

be borderlines and tensions between two different coherent systems with different concepts, principles, etc.

Moreover, similar problems may occur in the opposite case, where the Commission formally re-enacts revised parts of the *acquis*.[123] As we have seen above, the Commission is currently considering the possibility of adopting a 'horizontal' approach towards the revision of the *acquis*.[124] Such an approach would consist of adopting one or more framework directives, eg a Consumer Sales Directive which 'would regulate consistently the contractual aspects of sale, which are currently scattered in several directives (eg Directives on the Sale of Consumer Goods, Unfair Contract Terms, Distance Selling and Door-step Selling).' However, what if the national legislator, looking at the broader horizon, has in the meantime extended the scope of some of these directives to issues other than sales contracts and has therefore regulated the issue on another level of abstraction (eg general contract law or the general law of obligations)?

The most important cost of this approach would be the loss of national legal culture and, in the case of the Netherlands, the loss of all the energy that has gone into 60 years' work on the new BW and its implementation.[125] It would also clearly be in contrast with at least the idea underlying the principle of subsidiarity.

VI. FINAL REMARKS

Half a century ago the aim of the Dutch legislator was to codify all the existing private law into one coherent national code. In 1992, when the core

---

[123] Critical of this idea is GP Callies, 'Coherence and Consistency in European Consumer Contract Law: a Progress Report' (2003) 4 *German Law Journal* 333: 'Harmonising the patchwork acquis by means of harmonisation directives amounts to a strategy of replacing one evil with another.'

[124] See above, p 59.

[125] In a (controversial) report which was submitted to Parliament a few years before the introduction of Books 3, 5 and 6 (on patrimonial law) two professors and a member of the Senate argued that the introduction of the (remainder of) the new BW would be too expensive; JM van Dunné, EAA Luyten and PA Stein, *Kosten en tekortkomingen van het Nieuw Burgerlijk Wetboek (boeken 3, 5 en 6)* (Arnhem, Gouda Quint, 1990). They distinguished: (a) preparation costs (for the drafting process); (b) implementation costs (mainly courses for judges and practitioners and the adaptation of contracts etc); (c) costs related to the application of transition rules; and (d) structural costs (due to the 'deficient' and 'complicated' character of the new code). They estimated these costs to be as follows: some €250 million for the State and some €700 million for business. These are not net costs, as (surprisingly) benefits are not calculated. Indeed, many of the costs for some parties concerned directly led to gains for others. For example, more than one Dutch academic could buy a summer house in France from the revenues of 'nieuw BW' courses they taught in law firms. Whatever the desirability of this distributional consequence, the point is that most of the 'costs' presented in the report were not net social costs. See also H Drion, 'Het doorzettingsvermogen van Prof Van Dunné' [1989] *Nederlands Juristenblad* 137, who points to the possibility that having a better and clearer law may be a benefit in itself and will subsequently save costs.

part of the new civil code came into effect, that aim finally seemed to have been almost achieved.

During the 1990s the European Commission issued a stream of directives in the area of contract law. The obligation to transpose these instrumental and impressionistic directives into a coherent and comprehensive code led to tensions in the Netherlands and other Member States with codified systems of private law.

In response to the growing incoherence of European contract law, the Commission is now planning to adopt a 'common frame of reference' in 2009. That CFR will effectively constitute a codification in a substantive sense. As a result, in codified systems like the Netherlands there will be a shift from the familiar tension between impressionistic harmonisation and systematic codification to a new tension, that between the system of the national civil code and the system of the substantive European code.

Therefore, once the CFR is adopted by the Commission as a tool for revising the *acquis* and for drafting new directives, national legislators inspired by the codification ideal will have to reconsider their strategies towards the implementation of directives in the area of private law. Three such strategies were considered here. Each of them has advantages and disadvantages. None of them solves the tension between national codification and Europeanisation.

It seems unlikely that private law will ever again be contained exclusively in one comprehensive code, on either the national or European level. The CFR will make a comprehensive national codification increasingly difficult to achieve, whereas a comprehensive European civil code which replaces national private law will lack both a legal basis and political support. The Commission does not even want this. Therefore, it seems, we will have to live with a two(or multi)-level system of private law. As a result, the Dutch and other national legislators will have to revise their codification ideals.

The British House of Lords has expressed its concern that the CFR might be a Trojan horse which might lead to a European civil code.[126] This would pose a great threat to the common-law tradition of non-codification. Ironically, however, the CFR, proposed with a view to (substantive) codification, will also contribute to the further decodification and fragmentation of private law in civil law Member States. A real Trojan horse, one might say!

---

[126] House of Lords (European Union Committee), above n 58, 62.

5

Contract Law Reform: The German Experience

REINHARD ZIMMERMANN

I have been asked by the organisers of the conference, the contributions to which are contained in this volume, to present an overview and critical evaluation of the so-called 'modernisation' of the German law of obligations. The story that I have to tell is of a kind that has two sides to it. For while a number of very positive aspects can be identified, the reform cannot, unfortunately, be hailed as a great triumph in the art of legal drafting, or as a model of conceptual perfection.[1]

I. THE MODERNISATION OF THE LAW OF OBLIGATIONS ACT

On 1 January 2002 the most sweeping individual reform ever to have affected the German Civil Code (or BGB) came into force: the Modernisation of the Law of Obligations Act.[2] It had been triggered by the necessity of implementing the Consumer Sales Directive.[3] But it went far beyond what was required by the European Community. The then Minister of Justice had decided to use the tailwind from Brussels finally to implement an ambitious reform project that had been shelved for a number of years. The title of that

---

[1] The present paper is based on R Zimmermann, *The New German Law of Obligations: Historical and Comparative Perspectives* (Oxford University Press, 2005). That book attempts to provide a detailed analysis and assessment of the German law of obligations after the reform of 2002. It also contains full references to the pertinent legal literature. For a general introduction to German legal culture (including types of legal literature and quotation conventions), see R Zimmermann, 'Characteristic Aspects of German Legal Culture' in J Zekoll and M Reimann (eds), *Introduction to German Law* (2nd edn, The Hague, Kluwer Law International, 2005) 1.

[2] *Gesetz zur Modernisierung des Schuldrechts* of 26 November 2001, *Bundesgesetzblatt* 2001 I, 3138. As a result, the BGB was re-promulgated on 2 January 2002: *Bundesgesetzblatt* 2002 I, 42.

[3] Directive 1999/44/EC of the European Parliament and of the Council of 25 May 1999 on certain aspects of the sale of consumer goods and associated guarantees [1999] OJ L171/12; easily accessible in O Radley-Gardner et al, *Fundamental Texts on European Private Law* (Oxford, Hart, 2003) 107.

reform project, and of the legislation based on it (Modernisation of the Law of Obligations Act), is curiously misleading. For it is not the entire law of obligations that has been revised. With one exception, the reform has been confined to the law of contract, or more precisely, certain (though centrally important) aspects of the law of contract. The one exception is the law of (liberative) prescription (or limitation of claims).[4] Even in this respect, however, the title of the Act is imprecise, for the scope of application of the rules on prescription in Germany extends far beyond the law of obligations; it also covers, for example, claims arising under property law, family law and the law of succession.[5] This is why prescription finds its systematic place in the general part (Book I) of the BGB rather than in the general part of the Law of Obligations (Book II).

What are the key areas affected by the reform? Doctrinally, the most remarkable feature of the revised BGB is the new regime concerning liability for breach of duty in general, and for non-conformity in sales law in particular. The most important aspect of the Act of 2002, from the point of view of legal practice, is the fundamental revision of the German law of prescription. More than by any other component of the reform process, however, the face of the BGB has been changed by the incorporation of a number of special statutes aimed at the protection of consumers. The present paper will confine its attention to these four issues.[6]

The 'modernisation of the law of obligations' has divided the German private law professoriate in an unprecedented manner. Resolutions have been passed and published; symposia have been organised with a view to influencing, perhaps even aborting, the reform process; and sometimes the controversy has even descended to the level of personal invectives. On the one hand, it was maintained that a monument of German legal culture (the BGB) was about to be destroyed. On the other hand, the reform was seen to

---

[4] On the terminology, see R Zimmermann, *Comparative Foundations of a European Law of Set-Off and Prescription* (Cambridge University Press, 2002) 75. The Principles of European Contract Law, ch 14, refer to 'prescription', the UNIDROIT Principles of International Commercial Contracts 2004, ch 10, use the term 'limitation periods'.

[5] For details, see H-P Mansel and C Budzikiewicz in *Anwaltkommentar BGB* I (Bonn, Deutscher Anwalt Verlag, 2005) s 195, notes 4ff.

[6] Other aspects of the reform include a revision of the notoriously difficult rules dealing with the restitution of benefits after termination for breach of contract—on which, see R Zimmermann, 'Restitution after Termination for Breach of Contract: German Law after the Reform of 2002' in A Burrows and A Rodger (eds), *Mapping the Law: Essays in Memory of Peter Birks* (forthcoming)—and the incorporation into the text of the BGB of a number of doctrines that had previously come to be recognised *praeter legem*: *culpa in contrahendo* (section 311 II BGB); change of circumstances (*Störung der Geschäftsgrundlage*: section 313 BGB); the possibility of terminating, for good reason, contracts for the performance of a recurring obligation (section 314 BGB); the concept of an obligation as requiring each party to have regard to the other party's rights and interests (section 241 II BGB); and the existence, in some cases, of such duties vis-à-vis third parties (section 311 III BGB). The German government wanted the living law to be reflected in the code; for a critical assessment of this intention, see B Dauner-Lieb, 'Kodifikation von Richterrecht' in W Ernst and R Zimmermann (eds), *Zivilrechtswissenschaft und Schuldrechtsreform* (Tübingen, Mohr Siebeck, 2001) 305.

bring German law up to date, to make it compatible with the international development of contract law and to secure for it a leading position on the way towards a Europeanisation of private law, or perhaps even a European civil code.[7] These were the two extreme positions. The truth appears to lie somewhere in between. In principle, a reform of German contract law was to be welcomed. But the way in which it has been carried out leaves much to be desired. As a result, the reform legislation is open to considerable criticism both of form and of substance.

Why is this so? Was not enough time taken to prepare the reform? Again, there are two sides to the answer. The origins of the reform project date back to the late 1970s. What was then envisaged was indeed a revision of large parts of the law of obligations, including delict, strict liability, unjustified enrichment and *negotiorum gestio*. A great number of expert opinions by a wide variety of German law professors was requested by the Minster of Justice and published in three large volumes in 1981.[8] In 1984 a high-level Commission (including Professors Diederichsen, Kötz, Medicus and Schlechtriem) was appointed which duly prepared a report as well as draft legislation.[9] The scope of the project had, by now, been considerably restricted. The German Lawyers' Association (*Deutscher Juristentag*) debated that report in 1994, but then the discussion petered out. The impression gained ground that the reform was no longer going to happen. This is why the publication of a 630-page 'Discussion Draft' of a Modernisation of the German Law of Obligations Act in September 2000[10] caused so much surprise. It was well known that the Consumer Sales Directive had to be implemented. That could, however, have been done by way of effecting a number of comparatively minor adjustments to the existing code.[11] Thus, it was not widely suspected that the Department of Justice was about to use the opportunity to resurrect the earlier reform project. One problem became immediately visible: the Discussion Draft deviated, in some respects substantially, from the recommendations of the earlier Commission. Vehement criticism was raised, particularly forcefully at a symposium of German private law professors in Regensburg.[12] This criticism induced the government to

---

[7] H Däubler-Gmelin, 'Die Entscheidung für die so genannte Große Lösung bei der Schuldrechtsreform' [2001] *Neue Juristische Wochenschrift* 2281.

[8] Bundesminister der Justiz (ed), *Gutachten und Vorschläge zur Überarbeitung des Schuldrechts* (Cologne, Bundesanzeiger Verlag, vol I, 1981; vol II, 1981; vol III, 1983).

[9] Bundesminister der Justiz (ed), *Abschlußbericht der Kommission zur Überarbeitung des Schuldrechts* (Cologne, Bundesanzeiger Verlag, 1992).

[10] The Discussion Draft is easily accessible in C-W Canaris (ed), *Schuldrechtsmodernisierung 2002* (Munich, CH Beck, 2002) 3.

[11] W Ernst and B Gsell, 'Kaufrechtsrichtlinie und BGB: Gesetzentwurf für eine "kleine" Lösung bei der Umsetzung der EU-Kaufrechtsrichtlinie' [2000] *Zeitschrift für Wirtschaftsrecht* 1410.

[12] W Ernst and R Zimmermann, above n 6; the symposium took place in November 2000. A revised version of the Discussion Draft became the subject of discussion at a special meeting of the Association of German Professors of Private Law on 30–31 March in Berlin. The lectures delivered at that meeting have been published in [2001] *Juristenzeitung* 473ff.

establish two working groups charged with the task of critically examining and revising the Discussion Draft.[13] However, these two working groups had only about two months in which to deliberate. Nonetheless, even within that brief period, they effected fundamental changes, particularly in the fields of liability for breach of duty and prescription. While, therefore, it may be said that the entire reform process took 24 years, it would be equally true to say that the decisive stage of it took little more than a year. In the end, the Government Draft was rushed through Parliament by an accelerated procedure. Again, a great number of last minute changes were made. It is hardly surprising, under these circumstances, that many details and ramifications could not be examined properly. The reform legislation was promulgated on 26 November 2001; less than six weeks later, it entered into force. More than three years had been allowed between the promulgation and entry into force of the original BGB.

II. REMEDIES FOR BREACH OF DUTY

Liability for breach of contract under the old law was an issue of great doctrinal complexity, and it was very different, structurally, from the respective regulation in other European countries and from the Convention on Contracts for the International Sale of Goods (CISG).[14] In particular, it was structured by specific types of breach (impossibility, delay, positive malperformance, latent defects, etc) rather than by the remedies available. The new law has moved considerably closer to the dominant European pattern of regulation, as it has been restated particularly clearly in the Principles of European Contract Law (PECL).[15] (i) The conceptual cornerstone is now a uniform notion of breach of duty[16]—the term 'breach of duty' (*Pflichtverletzung*) having unfortunately been chosen in preference to the term 'non-performance' in the Principles.[17] (ii) The new system is largely remedy-oriented; it is structured, in the first place, according to the legal remedy available (most importantly: specific performance, damages, termination). (iii) The availability of termination no longer depends on fault.[18]

---

[13] For details, see C-W Canaris, above n 10, ix.

[14] K Zweigert and H Kötz, *An Introduction to Comparative Law* (trans T Weir, 3rd edn, Oxford University Press, 1998) 486ff; R Zimmermann, *The Law of Obligations: Roman Foundations of the Civilian Tradition* (Oxford, Clarendon Press, 1996) 806ff.

[15] O Lando and H Beale (eds), *Principles of European Contract Law* I and II (The Hague, Kluwer Law International, 2000) chs 8 and 9. Cf also UNIDROIT (International Institute for the Unification of Private Law) (ed), *UNIDROIT Principles of International Commercial Contracts* (Rome, UNIDROIT, 2004), ch 7.

[16] Section 280 BGB.

[17] U Huber, 'Das geplante Recht der Leistungsstörungen' in W Ernst and R Zimmermann (eds), *Zivilrechtswissenschaft und Schuldrechtsreform* (Tübingen, Mohr Siebeck, 2001) 31, 98.

[18] Section 323 BGB.

(iv) Damages and termination can be cumulated.[19] (v) A contract is no longer to be regarded as void because it is impossible to render the performance that has been promised.[20] In all these respects, the new German law differs from the old and has acquired a more modern, European face.

However, in a number of other respects, German law still retains its own characteristic features, setting it apart from a model regulation such as that contained in the Principles. (i) Damages remain a fault-based remedy.[21] (ii) Crucial for triggering the right to termination is not the notion of a fundamental breach but the granting of an extra period which has to have lapsed to no avail.[22] (iii) The different types of breach have, in the final stages of the reform process, been reintroduced as significant elements for determining the debtor's liability, albeit under the umbrella concept of a breach of duty.[23]

In addition, German law continues to be characterised by a number of doctrinal distinctions which are likely to create problems. Here are three examples. (iv) The right to claim specific performance is excluded, as far as such performance is (factually) impossible (section 275 I BGB). The debtor is granted a right to refuse to perform as far as such performance is practically impossible (section 275 II BGB). Whether, and to what extent, relief is granted to a debtor in cases of economic impossibility is to be determined according to the rules on change of circumstances (*Störung der Geschäftsgrundlage*: section 313 BGB). These three situations are not easy to distinguish, yet they have to be distinguished because of the differences in legal consequences.[24]

(v) In one respect, the remedy-orientation of the new law has been carried to an extreme not found in other legal systems. If a creditor claims damages, it has to be determined whether he claims damages in lieu of performance, damages for delay of performance or 'simple' damages.[25] Damages in lieu of performance are what are usually referred to as the positive interest: the creditor has to be placed, by way of damages, in the position he would have been in had the debtor performed properly. They can only be claimed after an extra period has been granted to the debtor and has lapsed to no avail, and provided we are dealing with a case of impossibility (section 283 BGB), delay of performance or deficient performance (section 281 BGB), or infringement of ancillary duties which do not affect the performance as such

---

[19] Section 325 BGB.
[20] Section 311 a I BGB. For the contrary rule, as contained in section 306 BGB (old version), and ostensibly based on the Roman *impossibilium nulla est obligatio*, see Zweigert and Kötz, above n 14, 488ff; Zimmermann, above n 14, 686ff.
[21] Section 280 I 2 BGB.
[22] Section 323 BGB.
[23] Sections 280ff BGB.
[24] C-W Canaris, 'Die Reform des Rechts der Leistungsstörungen' [2001] *Juristenzeitung* 499; S Meier, 'Neues Leistungsstörungsrecht' [2002] *Juristische Ausbildung* 118, 128; W Ernst, in *Münchener Kommentar zum Bürgerlichen Gesetzbuch* 2a (4th edn, Munich, CH Beck, 2003) s 275, note 1.
[25] Sections 280 III, 281, 282, 283 BGB.

(section 282 BGB). Damages for delay of performance comprise the loss resulting from the fact that the debtor has performed late, and they are available if the traditional requirements of *mora debitoris* have been met (section 286 BGB). 'Simple' damages (section 280 I BGB) are supposed to cover the loss suffered by the creditor as a result of a breach of duty with respect to his other objects of legal protection; they thus safeguard the creditor's integrity interest. The delimitation between these different types of damages can be very difficult:[26] hardly easier, at any rate, than the notorious distinction between *Mangelschäden* and *Mangelfolgeschäden* under the old law.[27] And yet, every investigation into a damages claim has to start with it. A simple example may illustrate these difficulties. A defective machine has been delivered. It cannot be used until it has been repaired or replaced by another one. The result is a loss of production. Even today, ie only three years after the reform has entered into force, no less than four different solutions have been proposed in the pertinent legal literature:

— application of the rules on damages in lieu of performance;[28]
— application of the rule on 'simple' damages;[29]
— a distinction depending on when the loss has occurred (whether at a time when the seller could still have corrected the defective performance or not);[30] and
— application of the rules on damages for delay of performance (reason: the loss has not arisen because the seller has delivered a defective machine but because he has failed to deliver a machine that was not defective).[31]

(vi) The damages rules sketched so far only apply to situations where the breach of duty has occurred after the conclusion of the contract (ie to subsequent impediments). The BGB provides a different liability regime for cases of initial impediments.[32] Why was that thought necessary? The answer lies in the fact that the point of reference for the attribution of fault is different in these situations. If a painting that has been sold is stolen or destroyed after the

---

[26] F Faust, in P Huber and F Faust, *Schuldrechtsmodernisierung* (Munich, CH Beck, 2002) 65, 100, 137; Ernst, above n 24, before s 281, note 7 and s 281, note 108; HC Grigoleit and T Riehm, 'Die Kategorien des Schadensersatzes im Leistungsstörungsrecht' (2003) 203 *Archiv für die civilistische Praxis* 727.

[27] D Medicus, *Bürgerliches Recht* (18th edn, Cologne, Carl Heymanns Verlag, 1999) notes 351ff.

[28] P Huber, in P Huber and F Faust, *Schuldrechtsmodernisierung* (Munich, CH Beck, 2002) 351.

[29] C-W Canaris, 'Die Neuregelung des Leistungsstörungs- und des Kaufrechts: Grundstrukturen und Problemschwerpunkte' in E Lorenz (ed), *Karlsruher Forum 2002: Schuldrechtsmodernisierung* (Karlsruhe, VVW, 2003) 37.

[30] F Faust, in G Bamberger and H Roth, *Kommentar zum Bürgerlichen Gesetzbuch* I (Munich, CH Beck, 2003) s 437, note 53.

[31] Grigoleit and Riehm, above n 26, 754.

[32] Section 311 a II BGB.

conclusion of the contract, the seller can be blamed for not properly looking after it. Before the contract has come into existence, on the other hand, the seller can hardly be made responsible for lack of diligence vis-à-vis the purchaser. What he can be blamed for is merely the fact that, at the time the contract was concluded, he knew, or could have known, that the painting had been stolen or destroyed.[33]

(vii) Finally, an example of poor legal drafting. According to section 275 I BGB, the debtor is relieved from his duty to perform in cases of factual impossibility. Yet, at the same time, under sections 280 I, III and 283 BGB he is liable to pay damages in lieu of performance provided he can be blamed for the performance having become impossible. The reason is that he has been responsible for a breach of a duty. However, a debtor can hardly be said to have been acting in breach of a duty of which the law has specifically relieved him. This difficulty could have been avoided by focusing on non-performance rather than on breach of duty.[34]

German law, in this area, is still characterised by a very considerable degree of complexity which is bound to cause problems: already a number of defects have become apparent and have given rise to dispute.[35] Foreign lawyers will continue to be baffled by the new regime.[36] The way in which the new rules have been drafted and structured has not done much to render German law more easily accessible or comprehensible.[37] A comparison with chapters 8 and 9 of the PECL is particularly instructive in this respect. At the same time, however, German law contains a number of ideas which may be used to refine the rules contained in that instrument. For while these rules are clearly structured and easily comprehensible, they are also very general and will have to be specified for various types of situations should they ever come to be applied in practice. They will have to be subject to a considerable degree of doctrinal refinement. The experiences gathered in Germany will then be valuable, on the positive as much as on the negative side.

---

[33] Canaris, above n 24, 505; and see now C-W Canaris, 'Grundlagen und Rechtsfolgen der Haftung für anfängliche Unmöglichkeit nach § 311 a Abs. 2 BGB' in S Lorenz et al (eds), *Festschrift für Andreas Heldrich* (Munich, CH Beck, 2005) 11.

[34] Faust, in Huber and Faust, above n 26, 113–14.

[35] See the evaluation by Ernst, above n 24, before s 275, notes 11, 25.

[36] See O Lando, 'Das neue Schuldrecht des Bürgerlichen Gesetzbuchs und die Grundregeln des europäischen Vertragsrechts' (2003) 67 *Rabels Zeitschrift für ausländisches und internationales Privatrecht* 231, who expresses regret that the reform has led to 'such a labyrinth of rules.'

[37] This begins with the fact, irritating for neophytes in German law, that the pertinent rules can be found in two different systematic places: book 2, section 1 (Content of Obligations) (sections 275ff BGB) and book 2, section 3, title 2 (Synallagmatic Contracts) (sections 320ff BGB). This reflects the traditional desire, as far as possible, to provide rules covering all types of obligations, including unilaterally binding, and imperfectly bilateral, contracts. Sections 275ff BGB essentially deal with the transition from the claim to specific performance to a damages claim and are not, therefore, confined to synallagmatic contracts. Sections 320ff BGB, on the other hand, deal with the impact of one party's failure to perform, or to perform properly, on the other party's obligation. This has the consequence of obscuring the parallelism of the claim for damages and the right of termination.

III. LIABILITY FOR NON-CONFORMITY IN THE LAW OF SALE

Liability for non-conformity in sales law has always been, and continues to be, a special type of liability for breach of contract. There is an added level of complexity in that the new regime is based on the Consumer Sales Directive. Certain inconsistencies flow from the approach adopted by the draftsmen of that Directive. Thus, for example, according to section 439 II BGB (following recital 10 of the Directive), it is the purchaser who may choose between repair and the delivery of substitute goods, even though it is usually the seller who can more easily assess the chances, and determine the effectiveness, of these two forms of supplementary performance, and even though the BGB decides this question differently as far as contracts for work are concerned.[38] Also, in assessing the new German sales law it must always be asked whether its draftsmen have correctly implemented the requirements of the Directive. This is doubtful, for instance, with regard to section 323 I BGB, according to which the purchaser may terminate the contract, 'if he has fixed, to no avail, an additional period of time for performance.' Article 3 (5) of the Directive, on the other hand, states that the consumer can have the contract rescinded 'if the seller has not completed the remedy within a reasonable time.' Here German law requires more of the purchaser than the Directive since even after the lapse of a reasonable period he cannot simply terminate the contract unless he has previously fixed such a period.[39] To some extent, the greater complexity of the legal rules governing liability for non-conformity is also due to the additional remedy of supplementary performance. It constitutes a continuation, in a modified form, of the purchaser's original right to specific performance.[40] At the same time, it is the purchaser's primary right. All his other rights, particularly termination, price reduction and damages, are only available on a secondary level. Effectively this means that the seller is granted a right to correct the defective performance; he has a second chance to comply with his contractual obligations.[41]

One of the two main features characterising the reform of German sales law is a determined effort to extend the requirements of the Consumer Sales Directive to all types of sale, including commercial sales.[42] This leads to a methodological problem insofar as it has to be asked whether the rules of German sales law have to be interpreted in accordance with the provisions of

[38] Section 635 I BGB. See D Zimmer, 'Das geplante Kaufrecht' in W Ernst and R Zimmermann (eds), *Zivilrechtswissenschaft und Schuldrechtsreform* (Tübingen, Mohr Siebeck, 2001) 199.

[39] Faust, above n 30, s 437, note 17.

[40] Canaris, above n 29, 77.

[41] The position of the consumer has, therefore, arguably been weakened by the new approach, for under the old law, he immediately had a very strong and, from the point of view of the seller, inconvenient right at his disposal: the *actio redhibitoria* in its modern statutory version; for details of the development, see Zimmermann, above n 14, 311ff.

[42] Canaris, above n 29, 54.

the Consumer Sales Directive only for consumer sales or also for other types of sale.[43] The former alternative is unsatisfactory in that it leads to the undesirable situation of a split interpretation. The consequence of the latter alternative would be that the interpretation of large parts of the German law relating to breach of contract is ultimately governed by a European Directive.

The second characteristic trait of the reform is the attempt to integrate liability for latent defects, as far as possible, into the general regime governing breach of contract under the revised German law of obligations. This attempt has, however, been only partly successful. For example, the remedy of reduction of the purchase price is still confined to its traditional areas of application, ie the law of sale (section 441 BGB), lease (section 536 BGB) and contracts for work (section 638 BGB). Proposals to generalise this remedy and, more specifically, also to apply it to contracts of service[44] have not been implemented. They would have brought German law into line with Article 9:401 PECL. Much more importantly, the new German sales law perpetuates the tradition of a prescription regime that differs from the general rules.[45] If, however, non-conformity is merely one instance of non-performance (or breach of duty), it is difficult to see why the claim for damages should not also be governed by the same, ie the general, prescription rules. Obviously, a number of the problems which the draftsmen of the new law intended to iron out will continue to be a source of irritation. Liability in cases of *Weiterfresserschäden* provides one example.[46] The same is true with regard to the vexed problem of how to deal with cases where the seller delivers not a defective object but one that is different from that envisaged in the contract. According to section 434 III BGB, delivery by the seller of a different object is equivalent to a defect as to quality. This rule is intended to avoid the necessity of distinguishing between the two types of case.[47] But does this mean that a seller who has procured a painting by Picasso and proceeds, in fulfilment of the contract, to deliver a bag of coal has to be treated as if he had delivered a defective painting of Picasso: with the result that the purchaser would not retain his original claim to specific performance, which is subject to the regular prescription regime, but could only avail himself of the rights listed in section 437 BGB (including supplementary performance), which are governed by the less favourable prescription rule of

---

[43] U Büdenbender, 'Die Bedeutung der Verbrauchsgüterkaufrichtlinie für das deutsche Kaufrecht nach der Schuldrechtsreform' (2004) 12 *Zeitschrift für Europäisches Privatrecht* 36; J Drexl, 'Die gemeinschaftsrechtliche Pflicht zur einheitlichen richtlinienkonformen Auslegung hybrider Rechtsnormen und deren Grenzen' in S Lorenz *et al* (eds), *Festschrift für Andreas Heldrich* (Munich, CH Beck, 2005) 67.

[44] M Lieb, 'Dienstvertrag' in *Gutachten und Vorschläge zur Überarbeitung des Schuldrechts* III, above n 8, 183, 219.

[45] Text to note 61.

[46] Text to notes 62–64.

[47] For the old law, see U Huber, in *Soergel, Bürgerliches Gesetzbuch* III (12th edn, Stuttgart, Kohlhammer, 1991) before s 459, notes 106, 132.

section 438 BGB?[48] Whoever regards this as absurd, or inappropriate,[49] is faced, once again, with problems of delimitation, though on a different level and subject to other criteria than under the old law.

Many of the problems vigorously discussed today in German law (particularly concerning the right of supplementary performance) will also arise in other countries which have had to implement the Consumer Sales Directive. The purchaser of an object which is not in conformity with the contract has the choice between asking for the removal of the defect or supply of another object free from defects.[50] But what is the position if the defect can be removed in one of two different ways: the defective part of an object can either be repaired, or it can be substituted by a new one?[51] Can supplementary performance by way of supply of another object free from defects be demanded in contracts for the sale of a specific object?[52] May the purchaser himself remove the defect? Would that not mean that he makes supplementary performance by the seller impossible and has to be accountable for that?[53] And what is the scope, or extent, of supplementary performance in cases where the defect has spread to other parts of the object sold, or where it has caused damage to other pieces of the purchaser's property?[54] Germany has gone further than most other legal systems in tailoring its general sales law to the new international pattern. Since it is a jurisdiction with a large incidence of litigation and an active academic community, German case law and academic discussion should be also of considerable interest to courts and lawyers outside Germany.

---

[48] This is the view adopted by P Huber, in Huber and Faust, above n 28, 308 (from whom the example is taken; Huber explicitly states that the bag of coal is, so to speak, a defective Picasso); K Tiedtke and M Schmidt, 'Die Falschlieferung durch den Verkäufer' [2004] *Juristenzeitung* 1092. This is in line with the approach adopted by the CISG and the Consumer Sales Directive; see EA Kramer, 'Abschied von der aliud-Lieferung?' in F Harrer, W Portmann and R Zäch (eds) *Besonderes Vertragsrecht—aktuelle Probleme: Festschrift für Heinrich Honsell* (Zürich, Schulthess, 2002) 247.

[49] Canaris, above n 29, 68; A Thier, 'Aliud- und Minus-Lieferung im neuen Kaufrecht des Bürgerlichen Gesetzbuches' (2003) 203 *Archiv für die civilistische Praxis* 399.

[50] Section 439 BGB.

[51] M Jacobs, 'Die kaufrechtliche Nacherfüllung' in B Dauner-Lieb, H Konzen and K Schmidt (eds), *Das neue Schuldrecht in der Praxis* (Cologne, Carl Heymanns Verlag, 2003) 371, 377; but see HP Westermann, in *Münchener Kommentar zum Bürgerlichen Gesetzbuch* III (4th edn, Munich, CH Beck, 2004) s 439, note 4.

[52] OLG Braunschweig, [2003] *Neue Juristische Wochenschrift* 1053; C-W Canaris, 'Die Nacherfüllung durch Lieferung einer mangelfreien Sache beim Stückkauf' [2003] *Juristenzeitung* 831; but see M Jacobs, above n 51, 377; and see the controversy between T Ackermann and C-W Canaris, [2003] *Juristenzeitung* 1154.

[53] S Lorenz, 'Selbstvornahme der Mängelbeseitigung im Kaufrecht' [2003] *Neue Juristische Wochenschrift* 1417; but see J Oechsler, 'Praktische Anwendungsprobleme des Nacherfüllungsanspruchs' [2004] *Neue Juristische Wochenschrift* 1825, 1826–27.

[54] Faust, above n 30, s 439, notes 14ff.

IV. PRESCRIPTION (OR LIMITATION)

There can be no doubt that the German law of prescription was in dire need of reform. The great diversity of prescription periods, as well as the fact that some of them were much too long while others were much too short, had given rise to a great variety of practical problems and doctrinal distortions.[55] The German model of regulation was largely outdated. If we look at the international development of the law of prescription since the days of the enactment of the BGB, we find a number of characteristic trends.[56]

1. There is a clear tendency towards uniform periods of prescription.
2. Such uniform period must neither be particularly short (six months) nor excessively long (thirty years): it has to be fixed between two and five years. A period of three years appears to be regarded as reasonable internationally.
3. The running of this relatively short general period of prescription should not be tied to an objective criterion, such as due date, accrual of the claim, delivery, acceptance, completion (of a building); rather, it should depend on whether the creditor knew (or ought reasonably to have known) of the identity of his debtor and of the facts giving rise to his claim.
4. Prescription must not be deferred indefinitely; at some stage, the parties have to be able to treat an incident as indubitably closed. This is why a relative period (the running of which depends on the discoverability criterion) has to be supplemented by a maximum period ('long stop'), tied to an objective criterion, at the expiry of which a claim must be barred regardless of the creditor's knowledge. For this long stop a period of between 10 and 30 years may be chosen; increasingly, however, the upper end of this range is regarded as reasonable only for personal injury claims.
5. It is internationally widely recognised that prescription should only have a 'weak' effect: once the period of prescription has run out, the creditor's right is not extinguished but the debtor is merely granted a right to refuse performance. Prescription, in other words, constitutes a defence which the debtor may or may not choose to raise.

Both the new German law of prescription[57] and chapter 14 of the PECL reflect these developments; they constitute variations of the same model.[58] In

---

[55] For details, see F Peters and R Zimmermann, 'Verjährungsfristen' in *Gutachten und Vorschläge zur Überarbeitung des Schuldrechts* I, above n 8, 77; for an account in English, see R Zimmermann, 'Extinctive Prescription in German Law' in E Jayme (ed), *German National Reports in Civil Law Matters for the XIVth Congress of Comparative Law in Athens 1994* (Heidelberg, CF Müller, 1994) 153.

[56] R Zimmermann, above n 4, 85.

[57] Sections 194ff BGB.

[58] The same is true of the UNIDROIT Principles of International Commercial Contracts 2004, ch 10. For a comparison of that chapter with ch 14 of the PECL, see R Zimmermann, 'Die

fact, the German regulation has been decisively influenced by the PECL, as the motivation to the Government Draft specifically acknowledges.[59] Unfortunately, however, and contrary to the PECL, German law also retains a number of specific periods of prescription. Thus, for instance, there is a 30-year period for the *rei vindicatio* (and other claims arising in property law). But the *rei vindicatio* is designed to give full effect to the absolute right of ownership. It should not, therefore, be affected by prescription, but should rather perish with the absolute right itself; otherwise we would be faced with the undesirable consequences of *dominium sine re*. Whether, and under which circumstances, the interests of someone who has been in possession of an object for a long time may prevail over those of the owner—whether, and under which circumstances, in other words, the public interest requires acknowledgement of the *status quo*—is a question requiring a uniform answer which the BGB provides, in an entirely satisfactory manner, by means of its rules on *acquisitive* prescription (sections 937ff BGB).[60] Also, as was mentioned earlier, we have a special prescription regime for liability for non-conformity in sales law. This provides for a two- rather than a three-year period which, moreover, commences to run from an objective date, ie the moment of delivery of the object sold.[61] The coexistence of this and the general prescription regime will continue to give rise to problems of delimitation and distortions similar to those which the draftsmen of the reform originally set out to resolve. Where the object sold is damaged or destroyed by a 'functionally separable' part of it that was defective, the German Federal Supreme Court has maintained that a damages claim can be based on the law of delict, for the seller can be seen to have infringed the purchaser's property in terms of section 823 I BGB.[62] This delictual claim is subject to the more generous (from the point of view of the purchaser) general prescription regime. A delictual claim was thus granted, for example, where the purchaser's car had been damaged as a result of a collision caused by a defective accelerator pedal.[63] Effectively, the courts used, and will continue to use, the law of delict to devise an additional remedy for damages arising from latent defects in order to subvert the stricter prescription regime

Unidroit-Grundregeln der internationalen Handelsverträge 2004 in vergleichender Perspektive' (2005) 13 *Zeitschrift für Europäisches Privatrecht* 264, 269.

[61] Bericht des Rechtsausschusses, BT-Drucksache 14/7052, easily accessible in Canaris, above n 10, 1051 (1066); cf also Begründung der Bundesregierung zum Entwurf eines Gesetzes zur Modernisierung des Schuldrechts, BT-Drucksache 6857, in Canaris, above n 10, 569 (600, 612).

[62] Peters and Zimmermann, above n 55, 186, 287; R Zimmermann et al, 'Finis Litium? Zum Verjährungsrecht nach dem Regierungsentwurf eines Schuldrechtsmodernisierungsgesetzes' [2001] *Juristenzeitung* 684, 692–93.

[63] Section 438, as opposed to sections 195, 199 BGB.

[64] BGHZ 67, 359; H Sprau, in *Palandt, Bürgerliches Gesetzbuch* (63th edn, Munich, CH Beck, 2004) s 823, notes 177–78; B Gsell, *Substanzverletzung und Herstellung* (Tübingen, Mohr Siebeck, 2003).

[65] BGHZ 86, 256.

governing claims for non-conformity.[64] This is but one of a number of examples.[65] Other deviations of the German prescription regime from the model set out in the PECL could also be highlighted.[66] Unfortunately the draftsmen of the new German law often failed to provide a reasoned motivation for their choice. By and large, I think, that the draftsmen of the PECL have taken the sounder view. Nonetheless, in view of the fact that the general framework is the same, the differences in detail offer interesting perspectives for comparison.

V. CONSUMER CONTRACT LAW

The incorporation into the BGB of the majority of special statutes concerning consumer contract law has not affected the substance of German private law very much, though it has changed the face of the BGB more than any of the reforms discussed so far. Broadly speaking, three solutions to the problem of the systematic position of consumer contract law within a civilian legal system are imaginable: (i) piecemeal legislation; (ii) the drafting of a code concerning consumer contract law; and (iii) incorporation into the general civil code.[67] The reform of German contract law has brought about a transition from model (i) to model (iii). The tradition of piecemeal legislation, incidentally, goes back quite far. Contrary to widely held opinion, the draftsmen of the BGB did not reject the legitimacy of specific policy concerns militating for special rules of a protective character.[68] But they saw them as special concerns requiring special legislation outside a civil code which was

---

[66] For the new law, see Faust, above n 30, s 437, note 188; Ernst, above n 24, s 280, note 78.

[65] See further D Leenen, 'Die Neuregelung der Verjährung' [2001] *Juristenzeitung* 552; Zimmermann et al, above n 60, 688.

[66] R Zimmermann, 'Das neue deutsche Verjährungsrecht—ein Vorbild für Europa?' in I Koller, H Roth and R Zimmermann (eds), *Schuldrechtsmodernisierungsgesetz 2002* (Munich, CH Beck, 2002) 9. In the meantime the German parliament has enacted another important piece of reform legislation: the Act on the Adjustment of Prescription Periods to the Modernisation of Obligations Act (*Gesetz zur Anpassung von Verjährungsvorschriften an das Gesetz zur Modernisierung des Schuldrechts*) of 9 December 2004, which entered into effect on 15 December 2004. It is designed to tidy up the maze of special prescription rules contained in a wide variety of statutes outside the BGB. See H-P Mansel and C Budzikiewicz, 'Verjährungsanpassungsgesetz: Neue Verjährungsfristen, insbesondere für die Anwaltshaftung und im Gesellschaftsrecht' [2005] *Neue Juristische Wochenschrift* 321.

[67] A consumer code exists in France since 1993; on which see C Witz and G Wolter, 'Das neue französische Verbrauchergesetzbuch' (1995) 3 *Zeitschrift für Europäisches Privatrecht* 35; D Heuer, *Der Code de la consommation: Eine Studie zur Kodifizierung des französischen Verbrauchsrechts* (Frankfurt am Main, P Lang, 2002). Austria has a Consumer Protection Act; it dates from 1979 and is neither comprehensive nor systematic; see H Koziol and R Welser, *Grundriss des bürgerlichen Rechts* II (12th edn, Vienna, Manz, 2001) 372ff. Incorporation into the general civil code has been the path pursued in the Netherlands; see E Hondius, 'European Contract Law: The Contribution of the Dutch' in H-L Weyers (ed), *Europäisches Vertragsrecht* (Baden-Baden, Nomos, 1997) 45, 62.

[68] T Repgen, *Die soziale Aufgabe des Privatrechts* (Tübingen, Mohr Siebeck, 2001).

designed to provide a general framework for parties to regulate their own affairs.[69] This explains why the provisions of the Act concerning Instalment Sales,[70] or the early doorstep legislation contained in the Act concerning Trade and Industry,[71] were not incorporated into the BGB. That tradition was continued in the last quarter of the twentieth century, particularly once the European Community had discovered that the regulation of consumer affairs was a promising field of activity.[72] Thus, by the end of the century, we had a wide variety of special statutes dealing with matters such as distance teaching, doorstep selling, consumer credit, unfair terms of business, timeshare agreements and distance contracts. These statutes provided a patchy and conceptually largely incoherent picture, which was increasingly regarded as unsatisfactory.[73] In spite of this, and the fact that the German government had, on previous occasions, not refrained from amending the BGB (by introducing a set of provisions dealing with package tours[74] or, increasingly, by placing certain doctrinal 'anchors' for the consumer contract statutes into the BGB[75]), the decision to incorporate caused considerable surprise: it was a step neither required by the Consumer Sales Directive nor envisaged by the Reform Commission of the 1980s.

Again, as with the reform of German contract law in general, it has to be said that the decision to incorporate was right in principle.[76] There are a number of arguments supporting it. The most important one lies in the fact that general contract law and consumer contract law are designed to serve the

[69] J Rückert, in M Schmoeckel, J Rückert and R Zimmermann (eds), *Historisch-kritischer Kommentar zum BGB* I (Tübingen, Mohr Siebeck, 2003) before s 1, notes 39ff.

[70] *Abzahlungsgesetz* of 16 May 1894, *Reichsgesetzblatt* 1894, 450. See H-P Benöhr, 'Konsumentenschutz vor 80 Jahren: Zur Entstehung des Abzahlungsgesetzes vom 16. Mai 1894' (1974) 138 *Zeitschrift für das gesamte Handelsrecht und Wirtschaftsrecht* 492.

[71] 'Gewerbeordnung für den Norddeutschen Bund', *Bundesgesetzblatt des Norddeutschen Bundes* 1869, 245. See R Geyer, *Der Gedanke des Verbraucherschutzes im Reichsrecht des Kaiserreichs und der Weimarer Republik (1871—1933)* (Frankfurt am Main, P Lang, 2001) 9.

[72] B Lurger, in R Streinz (ed), *EUV/EGV* (Munich, CH Beck, 2003), Art 153, notes 3ff; O Remien, *Zwingendes Vertragsrecht und Grundfreiheiten des EG-Vertrages* (Tübingen, Mohr Siebeck, 2003) 238; B Heiderhoff, *Grundstrukturen des nationalen und europäischen Verbrauchervertragsrechts* (Munich, Sellier, 2004) 3.

[73] J Basedow, 'Das BGB im künftigen europäischen Privatrecht: der hybride Kodex' (2000) 200 *Archiv für die civilistische Praxis* 445, 449; TMJ Möllers, 'Europäische Richtlinien zum Bürgerlichen Recht' [2002] *Juristenzeitung* 121; Hannes Rösler, *Europäisches Konsumentenvertragsrecht* (Munich, CH Beck, 2004) 218.

[74] Sections 651a–651k BGB.

[75] H Dörner, 'Die Integration des Verbraucherrechts in das BGB' in R Schulze and H Schulte-Nölke, *Die Schuldrechtsreform vor dem Hintergrund des Gemeinschaftsrechts* (Tübingen, Mohr Siebeck, 2001) 177, 181.

[76] F Bydlinski, *System und Prinzipien des Privatrechts* (Vienna, Springer, 1996) 718; WH Roth, 'Europäischer Verbraucherschutz und BGB' [2001] *Juristenzeitung* 475, 484; J Drexl, 'Verbraucherrecht—Allgemeines Privatrecht—Handelsrecht' in P Schlechtriem (ed), *Wandlungen des Schuldrechts* (Baden-Baden, Nomos, 2002) 97, 117; T Duve, in M Schmoeckel, J Rückert and R Zimmermann (eds), *Historisch-kritischer Kommentar zum BGB* I (Tübingen, Mohr Siebeck, 2003) ss 1–14, note 84. To the contrary, most recently, K-U Wiedenmann, *Verbraucherleitbilder und Verbraucherbegriff im deutschen und europäischen Privatrecht* (Frankfurt am Main, P Lang, 2004) 267ff.

same aim. It would be fatal for the integrity of the legal system if general contract law were seen to be the domain of a very formal conception of freedom of contract while consumer contract law would be taken to be informed by loosely defined social concerns. The notion of freedom of contract has to be the lodestar for the entire law of contract; but, at the same time, and in view of the fact that freedom of contract is not an end in itself but a means of promoting the self-determination of those who wish to conclude a contract, a contract can only be accepted by the legal community if it can typically be regarded as reflecting the exercise of both parties' right of self-determination.[77] The legal community, in other words, has to exercise some kind of control in order to preserve, rather than restrict, private autonomy. This consideration can no longer simply be relegated to a special position outside the general system of law but has to (and, in fact, does) permeate contract law as a whole. The process of 'materialising' German contract law, over the past 100 years, has been too pervasive for what then used to be called the accomplishment of the 'social task of private law' to be left to special legislation.[78] It has become a concern of central significance. The way in which the 'general provisions' contained in the BGB, such as the one in section 138 I BGB focusing on the *boni mores*, have come to be interpreted in practice bear testimony to this development. The legitimacy of specific rules of consumer protection has to be assessed in this light.[79] They may be seen as an attempt to sustain private autonomy by providing mechanisms which aim at preventing contracts from coming into existence, or from being enforced, which cannot be regarded as the result of acts of self-determination of both parties to the contract. The main devices used by German law in this context are the imposition of duties of information on the entrepreneur, the granting of a right of revocation to the consumer and the establishment of (unilaterally) mandatory rules of law. They can all be seen as situation-specific reactions to challenges faced by the legal system on a much broader front,[80] and therefore also accommodated by general doctrines such as *culpa in contrahendo*, or by the mandatory rules of law contained in the BGB for more than a century.

If, therefore, the decision to incorporate has to be welcomed in principle, it must also be said that that decision has not been carried out very well. One

---

[77] W Schmidt-Rimpler, 'Grundfragen einer Erneuerung des Vertragsrechts' (1941) 147 *Archiv für die civilistische Praxis* 130; M Habersack, 'Richtigkeitsgewähr notariell beurkundeter Verträge' (1989) 189 *Archiv für die civilistische Praxis* 403; Heiderhoff, above n 72, 300ff; L Fastrich, *Richterliche Inhaltskontrolle im Privatrecht* (Munich, CH Beck, 1992) 29ff, 51ff.

[78] C-W Canaris, 'Wandlungen des Schuldvertragsrechts—Tendenzen zu seiner Materialisierung' (2000) 200 *Archiv für die civilistische Praxis* 273.

[79] A modern theory of consumer protection along these lines has been developed by J Drexl, *Die wirtschaftliche Selbstbestimmung des Verbrauchers* (Tübingen, Mohr Siebeck, 1998).

[80] For duties of information, see H Fleischer, *Informationsasymmetrie im Vertragsrecht* (Munich, CH Beck, 2001); for rights of revocation, P Mankowski, *Beseitigungsrechte* (Tübingen, Mohr Siebeck, 2003) 224ff; for mandatory rules of law, Remien, above n 72.

of the characteristic features of a codification is its systematic nature; it thus promotes the internal coherence of the law and facilitates its comprehensibility. The draftsmen of the reform legislation have attempted to preserve the system of the BGB and to find appropriate systematic niches for the new consumer contract provisions. But they have only partly been successful.[81] The provisions that used to be contained in sections 1–11 of the Standard Terms of Business Act can now be found in sections 305–310 BGB. They deal with a number of different issues. They concern themselves with the question of how standard terms of business can become part of a contract,[82] they include rules of interpretation,[83] they regulate the consequences of non-incorporation and invalidity,[84] and they determine standards for the policing of unfair standard contract terms.[85] Systematically, these issues have to be related to a variety of provisions in different parts of the BGB's first two books. The German government, however, decided to preserve the integrity of what used to be the Standard Terms of Business Act without preserving the Act itself. The provisions were thus shoved, lock, stock and barrel, into one place, and the place chosen for this purpose was the one immediately following the rules on *mora creditoris* (and immediately preceding a section of the code entitled 'contractual obligations': as if standard terms of business were non-contractual obligations). There is no good reason at all to deal with standard terms of business at this specific place; and the only reason that can possibly be advanced is that a convenient space could relatively easily be created by dropping, removing or compressing the rules previously located there. As a result, the new sections 305–310 seem like a piece of pop music tossed into the second movement of a classical symphony: a *corpus alienum* without intellectual connection to its surroundings. The incorporation of the Standard Terms of Business Act into the BGB, in other words, has been a purely formal exercise; it has not lead to anything that could be called an integration into the fabric of the BGB. Another example of an unhappy form of incorporation is provided by section 241 a BGB, ie the rule on unsolicited performances. It sits awkwardly between two of the most fundamental rules within the German law of obligations, and there is no apparent reason for this choice of place—not even, in this case, a *lacuna* in the numbering of the BGB provisions.[86]

There is one argument against the incorporation of consumer contract law into the BGB, the truth of which can hardly be disputed. Consumer law is not yet an area with stable doctrinal structures. It remains unsettled and subject to

[81] See also Wiedenmann, above n 76, 34.
[82] Sections 305, 305 a, 305 c I BGB.
[83] Sections 305 b, 305 c II BGB; cf also s 306 a BGB.
[84] Section 306 BGB.
[85] Sections 307, 308, 309 BGB.
[86] W Flume, 'Vom Beruf unserer Zeit für Gesetzgebung' [2000] *Zeitschrift für Wirtschaftsrecht* 1427, 1428 ('monstrous'); H-P Mansel, in O Jauernig (ed), *Bürgerliches Gesetzbuch* (11th edn, Munich, CH Beck, 2004) s 241 a, n 1 ('unparalleled legislative blunder').

further change and amendment. In view of the European Union's continued activities in this field, and in view of the impending large-scale revision of the existing consumer *acquis* instigated by the European Commission,[87] the decision to incorporate has effectively converted the BGB into a permanent building site.[88] In a sense, this is regrettable. The new BGB will hardly attain the same monumental aura as the old. But a monument can easily become covered by dust and may turn out to be no longer suited to serve the exigencies of real life. On balance, therefore, it may be better to live on a private law building site than in a private law museum.[89]

[87] Communication from the Commission of the European Communities to the European Parliament and the Council 'European Contract Law and the revision of the acquis: the way forward' COM(2004) 651 final (11 October 2004) 3.

[88] WH Roth, 'Europäischer Verbraucherschutz und BGB' [2001] *Juristenzeitung* 475, 488.

[89] Other major amendments, all affecting the first two books of the BGB, include: *Mietrechtsreformgesetz* of 16 June 2001 (concerning the law of lease; for details, see Birgit Grundmann, 'Die Mietrechtsreform—Wesentliche Inhalte und Änderungen gegenüber der bisherigen Rechtslage' [2001] *Neue Juristische Wochenschrift* 2497), *Gesetz zur Anpassung von Formvorschriften des Privatrechts und anderer Vorschriften an den modernen Geschäftsverkehr* of 13 July 2001, *Zweites Gesetz zur Änderung reiserechtlicher Vorschriften* of 23 July 2001 (for details, see Ernst Führich, 'Zweite Novelle des Reisevertragsrechts zur Verbesserung der Insolvenzsicherung und Gastschulaufenthalte' [2001] *Neue Juristische Wochenschrift* 3083), *Gesetz zur Modernisierung des Stiftungsrechts* of 19 July 2002 (concerning the law of foundations; for details, see Ulrich Burgard, 'Das neue Stiftungsprivatrecht' [2002] *Neue Zeitschrift für Gesellschaftsrecht* 697), and *Zweites Gesetz zur Änderung schadensersatzrechtlicher Vorschriften* of 19 July 2002 (concerning the law of damages; for details, see G Wagner, *Das neue Schadensersatzrecht* (Baden-Baden, Nomos, 2002). The introduction of same sex partnerships by means of the *Gesetz zur Beendigung der Diskriminierung gleichgeschlechtlicher Gemeinschaften: Lebenspartnerschaften* of 16 February 2001 (for details, see Nina Dethloff, 'Die eingetragene Lebenspartnerschaft—Ein neues familienrechtliches Institut' [2001] *Neue Juristische Wochenschrift* 2598) has led to more than 30 provisions throughout the BGB to be amended. In addition, the new provisions introduced by the Modernisation of the Law of Obligations Act have repeatedly been amended. All these enactments date from a period of hardly more than one year. For the first hundred years of its existence, on the other hand, the BGB (except for its fourth book on family law) has been remarkably resistant to change; see R Zimmermann, 'Das Bürgerliche Gesetzbuch und die Entwicklung des Bürgerlichen Rechts' in M Schmoeckel, J Rückert and R Zimmermann (eds), *Historisch-kritischer Kommentar zum BGB* I (Tübingen, Mohr Siebeck, 2003) before s 1, notes 20f.

6

Constitutional Issues—How Much is Best Left Unsaid?

STEPHEN WEATHERILL

I. INTRODUCTION

The starting point for this paper is the contention that the European Commission deserves credit for engaging with aspects of the debate about the function of the EU in the field of contract law in a serious and constructive fashion. The three communications on European contract law, released in 2001, 2003 and 2004, have—as a minimum—stimulated a vigorous but tolerably well-focused debate, engaging both national private lawyers and European lawyers. Not before time. What has remained largely hidden in the debate about what the EC *should* do is the question of what is it is *constitutionally competent* to do. The Commission has tended to prefer to address the former issue while leaving the latter concern largely unspoken. This paper first sets out the constitutional fundamentals, then tracks how and why their practical impact has recently increased. It then traces their partially concealed acknowledgement in the three communications of 2001, 2003 and 2004, picking out points where there is at least a serious doubt about available legal competence under the EC Treaty. But it is not the intention to slate the Commission for failure to provide copper-bottomed articulation of why it believes its floated ideas are constitutionally legitimate. Instead, the paper proceeds to identify three reasons why the Commission has been reticent to dig deeply into these matters, at least on the surface—and it finds them, on the whole, to be good reasons. The paper concludes by insisting that the development of a European contract law should not be put on ice for fear that the necessary constitutional foundation is lacking—but that nevertheless the importance of the constitutional ingredient should not be ignored.

II. CONSTITUTIONAL GROUND RULES AND PRACTICAL POLICITICS

Article 5(1) EC provides that 'The Community shall act within the limits of the powers conferred upon it by this Treaty and of the objectives assigned to it therein.' This asserts the constitutionally fundamental principle that the EC can do no more than its Treaty permits. It has only the competence conferred on it by its Member States. And an inspection of the text of the Treaty will reveal that it enjoys no explicit general competence to legislate in the field of contract law.

And yet—famously, notoriously—much has been done. It is the EC's harmonisation programme that supplies the key to understanding the basis for its most prominent interventions into contract law. Insofar as national laws vary, the argument has typically proceeded that the construction of a unified trading space within the EU was hindered. Therefore harmonisation of laws at the EC level was required—'common rules for a common market'. So the strict constitutional purpose of harmonisation was rule-making designed to make an integrated market, but its effect was to allocate to the EC level (albeit, by virtue of the commonly used minimum formula, typically not exclusively) the competence to decide on the substance of the rules in question. So harmonising contract law is not simply a technical process of market-making; it unavoidably means the shaping of a species of European contract law. Article 94 or Article 95—or Article 100 or Article 100a, their predecessors before the renumbering effected by the Amsterdam Treaty—provided a basis for harmonising laws in pursuit of market integration which extended into the field of contract law. The list includes Directive 90/314 on package travel[1]; Directive 93/13 on unfair terms in consumer contracts[2]; Directive 85/577 to protect the consumer in respect of contracts negotiated away from business premises[3]; Directive 87/102 concerning consumer credit, as amended by Directive 90/88 and Directive 98/7[4]; Directive 94/47 on timeshare basis[5]; Directive 97/7 on the protection of consumers in respect

---

[1] Council Directive 90/314/EEC of 13 June 1990 on package travel, package holidays and package tours [1990] OJ L158/59.

[2] Council Directive 93/13/EEC of 5 April 1993 on unfair terms in consumer contracts [1993] OJ L95/29.

[3] Council Directive 85/577/EEC of 20 December 1985 to protect the consumer in respect of contracts negotiated away from business premises [1985] OJ L372/31.

[4] Council Directive 87/102/EEC of 22 December 1986 for the approximation of the laws, regulations and administrative provisions of the Member States concerning consumer credit [1987] OJ L42/48; Council Directive 90/88/EEC of 22 February 1990 [1990] OJ L61/14; Directive 98/7/EC of the European Parliament and of the Council of 16 February 1998 [1998] OJ L101/17.

[5] Directive 94/47/EC of the European Parliament and of the Council of 26 October 1994 on the protection of purchasers in respect of certain aspects of contracts relating to the purchase of the right to use immovable properties on a timeshare basis [1994] OJ L280/83.

of distance contracts[6]; Directive 99/44 on certain aspects of the sale of consumer goods and associated guarantees[7]; and Directive 2002/65 concerning the distance marketing of consumer financial services.[8] This is EC contract law; it is predominantly EC *consumer* contract law and has been analysed as such,[9] although there are modest interventions to be found outside the consumer sphere, such as Directive 2000/35 on late payments in commercial transactions[10] and Directive 86/653 on commercial agents.[11]

In some circumstances the perception that diversity among national contract laws hindered the establishment of a single market may have been genuinely held and justified. In some cases, however, the political reality was that the Member States were committed to the development of an EC consumer policy and, in the absence of any more appropriate legal basis in the Treaty, chose to employ the competence to harmonise laws to put it in place. So, to select a classic example, Directive 85/577 states in its Preamble that the practice of doorstep selling is the subject of different rules in different Member States, and that 'any disparity between such legislation may directly affect the functioning of the common market.' This is hard to believe. Empirical evidence is lacking. The Directive was in fact largely motivated by the prevailing political consensus in favour of EC consumer protection and its Preamble refers more revealingly to the Council Resolutions of 1975 and 1981 on a consumer protection and information policy,[12] adopted in the wake of the commitment made at the Paris Summit of 1972 to broaden the appeal of the EC. The question of whether such consumer contract law-making dressed up in the clothes of harmonisation was truly constitutionally valid was not addressed in any practically significant manner given the unanimous preferences of the Member States to travel down this road.[13] In truth, the background context to much of the harmonisation programme affecting private law is embedded in the sphere of consumer policy. The EC

[6] Directive 97/7/EC of the European Parliament and of the Council of 20 May 1997 on the protection of consumers in respect of distance contracts [1997] OJ L144/19.

[7] Directive 99/44/EC of the European Parliament and of the Council of 25 May 1999 on certain aspects of the sale of consumer goods and associated guarantees [1999] OJ L171/12.

[8] Directive 2002/65/EC of the European Parliament and of the Council of 23 September 2002 concerning the distance marketing of consumer financial services [2002] OJ L271/16.

[9] See eg H Rösler, *Europäisches Konsumentenvertragsrecht* (Munich, CH Beck, 2004); K Riesenhuber, *Europäisches Vertragsrecht* (Berlin, De Gruyter, 2003); S Weatherill, *EU Consumer Law and Policy* (Cheltenham, Elgar, 2005); SA Sánchez Lorenzo, *Derecho Privado Europeo* (Granada, Editorial Comares, 2002).

[10] Directive 2000/35/EC of the European Parliament and of the Council of 29 June 2000 on combating late payment in commercial transactions [2000] OJ L200/35.

[11] Council Directive 86/653/EEC of 18 December 1986 on the coordination of the laws of the Member States relating to self-employed commercial agents [1986] OJ L382/17.

[12] Council Resolution of 14 April 1975 on a preliminary programme of the European Economic Community for a consumer protection and information policy [1975] OJ C92/1; Council Resolution of 19 May 1981 on a second programme of the European Economic Community for a consumer protection and information policy [1981] OJ C133/1.

[13] But see G Close, 'Harmonisation of Laws: Use or Abuse of Powers under the EEC Treaty?' (1978) 3 *EL Rev* 461 for an early appreciation of what was at stake.

lacked any explicit competence in the field of consumer protection until the entry into force of the Maastricht Treaty in 1993, and even today the relevant provision, Article 153 EC, offers only a relatively narrow authorisation to adopt legislation.[14] Harmonisation, today pursuant to Article 95 EC, remains the flagship of the European contract law fleet. The key point of current relevance is that some of the legislative *acquis* affecting contract law was presented as a contribution to improving the process of economic integration in order to cloak the measures with constitutional respectability, while in political reality it was a reflection of the eagerness to shape an EC consumer policy, affecting inter alia private law, particularly contract law.

There is, in short, a constitutional 'dark side' to the pattern of evolution. The allegation is that several Directives have been adopted pursuant to the Treaty-conferred competence to harmonise with no serious expectation that they would advance the process of market integration. And worse—that the legislative *acquis* affecting private law therefore stands an example of the EC legislature surreptitiously 'self-authorising' an extension of its own competence, contrary to the fundamental principle of attribution found in Article 5(1) EC. What is at stake here is what has been labelled 'competence creep'.[15] It is harmful to the EU's legitimacy. It is absolutely no consolation that the laws in question were adopted with the unanimous support of the Member States expressed in Council. It is fundamental that EU Treaty ratification is conducted in each Member State according to local constitutional requirements but performed everywhere on the basis that only a limited grant of power is being made to European level.[16] Legislative excesses condoned by national political élites acting through the Council tend to impoverish democratic structures within national political life.

III. THE RISE OF 'COMPETENCE ANXIETY'

The debate about the importance of achieving a satisfactory balance between the EU's capacity for dynamic growth and its perceived tendency to undermine local autonomy, and diversity is at the centre of current preoccupation with the future of the bloc. The role of harmonisation is also a major element in that debate. In fact, the lurking anxiety that harmonisation had, in short, gone too far—both as a basis for an assertion of centralising Community

---

[14] Weatherill, above n 9, ch 1.

[15] The literature exploring the motors of such creep is vast and, in parts, characterised by disagreement, or at least different points of emphasis. Cf, eg J Weiler, 'The Transformation of Europe' (1991) 100 *Yale Law Journal* 2403; A Moravscik, *The Choice for Europe* (London, UCL Press, 1999); H Wallace and W Wallace, *Policy-Making in the European Union* (5th edn, Oxford University Press, 2005); A Stone Sweet, W Sandholtz and N Fligstein (eds), *The Institutionalisation of Europe* (Oxford University Press, 2001).

[16] Cf, eg S Weatherill, 'Competence Creep and Competence Control' (2004) 23 *Yearbook of European Law* 1; A von Bogdandy and J Bast, 'The European Union's Vertical Order of Competences: the Current Law and Proposals for its Reform' (2002) 39 *CML Rev* 227.

competence and as an incursion into national autonomy—was always likely to force its way to the surface eventually once the voting rule in Council was altered from unanimity to qualified majority voting (QMV). This occurred in 1987 on the entry into force of the Single European Act, which inserted Article 100a, which is now, after amendment, Article 95. Thereafter a Member State opposed to a proposed measure of harmonisation could not simply veto it. It could vote against it, but, if in a small minority in Council, it could find itself outvoted and bound by that legislation.

The temptation to proceed to the Court and argue that the legislation was anyway invalid as an improper exercise of the competence to harmonise laws is obvious. It takes time for such litigation to occur, not least because it remains the case that most measures are supported by unanimity in Council even where this is not formally required. But in 2000 the Court was provided with the opportunity to clarify its view of the scope of legislative harmonisation granted by the Treaty. It did so in the *Tobacco Advertising* judgment,[17] which is of the greatest significance to understanding the permissible reach of Article 95 as a vehicle for advancing, inter alia, contract lawmaking under the cover of the harmonisation programme. Of central importance is that the Court asserted a constitutional reading of the limits of the scope of the Treaty-conferred competence to harmonise laws, notwithstanding past practice, which had placed the matter in the gift of the EC's political institutions, most significantly a unanimity-driven Council.

The Court annulled Directive 98/43 on the advertising of tobacco products on the application of Germany (which had been outvoted in the Council). The measure had been adopted as part of the harmonisation programme.[18] The Court was unimpressed. It insisted that harmonisation measures 'are intended to improve the conditions for the establishment and functioning of the internal market.' The Community legislature enjoys no general power to regulate the internal market.[19] Accordingly, 'curing' legal diversity per se will evidently not do as an adequate basis for legislative intervention founded on Article 95 EC. The EC measure must work harder in the service of market integration. The Directive in question did not cross the required threshold. It prohibited the advertising of tobacco products in circumstances remote from the imperatives of market-making—for example, on ashtrays and parasols used in street cafés. The implication of the Court's judgment is that this was, in effect, public health policy, for which the Community possesses a competence, but the relevant provision, Article 152, expressly forbids harmonisation. In declaring that the Community legislature

---

[17] Case C–376/98 *Germany v Parliament and Council* [2000] ECR I–8419. See, eg T Hervey, 'Community and National Competence in Health after Tobacco Advertising' (2001) 38 *CML Rev* 1421; J Usher, 'Annotation' (2001) 38 *CML Rev* 1519.

[18] Pursuant to Art 100a, now Art 95, and also Arts 57(2) and 66, now Arts 47(2) and 55, governing the services sector.

[19] Para 83 of the ruling.

does not enjoy 'a general power to regulate the internal market' the Court accordingly gave practical force to the constitutionally fundamental principle of attributed competence found in Article 5(1) EC in the particular context of delivering an interpretation of the limits on the use of Article 95.

As a general observation, the pattern of competence allocation established by the EC Treaty is rather ill-defined, even opaque.[20] Above all, there is, as Koen Lenaerts famously remarked, 'no nucleus of sovereignty that the Member States can invoke, as such, against the Community.'[21] But Germany's readiness to convert defeat in Council into a successful challenge to majoritarian centralising preferences before the Court provides a vivid example of how 'state rights' are not wholly neglected in the EC system. This is not subsidiarity in a strictly legal sense, which is contained in Article 5(2) EC, and, since the measure did not comply with Article 5(1) EC, it was logically ignored by the Court in *Tobacco Advertising* and has subsequently been relegated to the margins of judicial review by a Court fearful of incursion into such deep political waters.[22] It is, however, subsidiarity in a general political sense, as an alarm bell sounding for fear of 'creeping' centralisation. It is the EC version of a concern that central authorities may unduly disturb local autonomy which is familiar in many political systems founded on divided power.[23] In conclusion, the main point of *Tobacco Advertising* is not that it reveals that the competence to harmonise is not open-ended—we knew this—but rather that this point of constitutional principle has practical significance and that the Treaty limits will be policed by the Court (if the eccentric patterns of litigation give it a chance). So, although the legal base governing

---

[20] A Dashwood, 'The Relationship between the Member States and the European Union/European Community' (2004) 41 *CML Rev* 355; G De Burca and B de Witte, 'The Delimitation of Powers between the EU and its Member States' in A Arnull and D Wincott (eds), *Accountability and Legitimacy in the European Union* (Oxford University Press, 2002) ch 12; F Mayer, 'Die Drei Dimensionen der Europäischen Kompetenzdebatte' WHI-Paper 2/02 (Walter Hallstein Institut), available at http://www.whi-berlin.de; V Michel, 'Le défi de la repartition des compétences' (2003) 39 *Cahiers de Droit Européen* 17; D Hanf and F Baumé, 'Vers une clarification de la répartition des compétences entre l'Union et ses Etats membres?' (2003) 39 *Cahiers de Droit Européen* 135.

[21] K Lenaerts, 'Constitutionalism and the Many Faces of Federalism' (1990) 38 *American Journal of Comparative Law* 205, 220.

[22] For the Court's deferential approach to the application of the subsidiarity principle, see Case C–491/01 *R v Secretary of State ex parte BAT and Imperial Tobacco* [2002] ECR I–11543, paras 177–85; Case C–103/01 *Commission v Germany* [2003] ECR I–5369, especially para 47; Cases C–154/04 and C–155/04 *Alliance for Natural Health* [2005] ECR I–0000, paras 99–108.

[23] Cf K Nicolaidis and R Howse (eds), *The Federal Vision: Legitimacy and Levels of Governance in the United States and the European Union* (Oxford University Press, 2001) especially ch 3, J Donahue and M Pollack, 'Centralization and its Discontents: The Rhythms of Federalism in the United States and the European Union', and ch 4, D Lazer and V Mayer-Schoenberger, 'Blueprints for Change: Devolution and Subsidiarity in the United States and the European Union'; E Young, 'Protecting Member State Autonomy in the European Union: Some Cautionary Tales from American Federalism' (2002) 77 *New York University Law Review* 1612; L Catá Becker, 'Restraining Power from Below' *Federal Trust Paper* 15/04 (July 2004) available at http://www.fedtrust.co.uk.

harmonisation is functionally broad, it is not limitless and it may be exposed as inadequate to support proposed or adopted legislation.

IV. THE COMMISSION'S COMMUNICATIONS AND QUESTIONS OF LEGAL COMPETENCE

So, the Community legislature does not enjoy 'a general power to regulate the internal market.'

Tobacco Advertising injects 'competence anxiety' into a number of sectors remote from the judgment's particular concern, and it has already become a rich source of speculation about the constitutional validity of existing rules and proposed initiatives.[24] For the particular purposes of this paper, the message of *Tobacco Advertising* is readily transplanted from harmonisation affecting public health to harmonisation affecting consumer contract law. Some Directives are today revealed as vulnerable to potential challenge because they make little visible contribution to market-making. Directive 85/577 on doorstep selling, considered above,[25] would be placed high on any list of candidates.

But what of the future? It is notable that the three documents lately produced by the Commission concerning European contract law are surrounded by a—cautiously and gently expressed—aura of 'competence anxiety'. The Commission's documentation is predominantly directed at the development of a debate about the preferred substance of European contract law. Much of the discussion contained in this volume chews on this rich fare. But the constitutional issues lurk beneath the surface, occasionally breaking through to become visible above it. This paper spotlights them.

In July 2001 the Commission set the ball rolling by issuing its Communication on European Contract Law.[26] This was designed to generate a debate about the proper shape of an EC supplement to existing long-established systems of contract law in the Member States. Four options for future EC action in the field of contract law were aired (though they are not mutually exclusive). The first option was no EC action. The second option centred on the promotion of the development of common contract law principles, leading to greater convergence of national laws. The third option was to improve the quality of legislation already in place. The fourth, most ambitious and most cautiously advanced option was the adoption of new comprehensive legislation at EC level.

---

[24] Eg I Katsirea, 'Why the European Broadcasting Quota should be Abolished' (2003) 28 *EL Rev* 190; N Moloney, 'New Frontiers in EC Capital Markets Law: From Market Construction to Market Regulation' (2003) 40 *CML Rev* 809. See also S Weatherill, 'Why Harmonise?' in P Tridimas and P Nebbia (eds), *European Union Law for the Twenty-First Century: Rethinking the New Legal Order, Volume 2* (Oxford, Hart Publishing, 2004).

[25] See text at n 12.

[26] COM(2001) 398.

The constitutional dimension was addressed only briefly in the Communication. But it is plain that the shadow of the *Tobacco Advertising* ruling has been cast over the Commission's thinking. The Communication calls explicitly for information on whether diversity between national contract laws 'directly or indirectly obstructs the functioning of the internal market, and if so to what extent,' with a view to considering appropriate action by the EC's institutions.[27] The Commission's quest is to identify areas in which the internal market is malfunctioning because of deficiencies in the existing body of harmonised contract law. The Commission wants hard—Court-proof—data to underpin any claim to competence under the Treaty to shape an EC contract law. The Communication addresses these issues predominantly in the language of subsidiarity (Article 5(2) EC) rather than attributed competence (Article 5(1) EC), which is constitutionally misguided,[28] but the general perception that justification for EC intervention must be found and carefully explained holds good. The mood is different from the relatively carefree attitude to competence taken in the consumer contract law Directives adopted in the 1980s. In part this is because, prior to the entry into force of the Single European Act in 1987, the voting rule in Council was unanimity, which meant that the presence of political consensus was the practical be all and end all of the decision whether to legislate. Today the rise of QMV in Council throws up the possibility of outvoted minorities converting political defeat in Council into a constitutional challenge before the Court—precisely as occurred in *Tobacco Advertising* itself. But, of course, one would also hope that the Commission's new painstaking concern to spell out just why it suspects an EC intervention may be required is part of a process of wider and more open-minded dialogue with all interested constituencies.

In February 2003 a follow-up emerged from the Commission. This was the Action Plan on a more coherent European contract law.[29] This revealed the outcome of the process of consultation and the fate of the four options put forward in the 2001 Communication. The Commission, having digested the feedback received, had moved towards a preference for solutions that fall between the extremes of inaction and comprehensive intervention. So the planned way forward was located in a combination of options 2 and 3 from the 2001 menu and the Commission for the first time placed on the agenda the idea of developing a 'common frame of reference' (CFR) for European contract law principles. Once again the constitutional dimension is not explored in depth in the Commission's 2003 communication, but once again it is undoubtedly relevant and once again the Commission nods in its direction. The Action Plan insists on having unearthed 'implications for the

---

[27] Paras 23–33, 72 of the 2001 Communication.
[28] S Weatherill, 'The European Commission's Green Paper on European Contract Law: Context, Content and Constitutionality' (2001) 24 *Journal of Consumer Policy* 339, 361–71.
[29] COM(2003) 68 (12 February 2003).

internal market' arising from legal diversity, drawing a distinction for these purposes between the impact of mandatory and non-mandatory rules of national law.[30]

In October 2004 the Commission, having absorbed feedback on the 2003 Action Plan, issued a third document in the series. This is 'European Contract Law and the Revision of the Acquis: The Way Forward'.[31] It builds on the three measures suggested by the 2003 Action Plan and uses them to map the 'way forward' for European contract law. The starring role of the proposed CFR is confirmed. In the matter of available legal competence, the trend is maintained. The awkward questions of competence lurk beneath the discussion and are visible to the trained eye, but the Commission studiously avoids aggressive engagement with the matter. Issues of competence are merely glimpsed. The goal of eliminating internal market barriers is explicitly associated with review of the consumer-related harmonisation *acquis* (p 3). The question asked is: 'Is the level of harmonisation sufficient to eliminate internal market barriers and distortions of competition for business and consumers?' (p 4). The debate is therefore to be conducted with respect for the 'problem of competence', but the Commission has the question 'should we do this?' much higher up the agenda than the question 'are we competent to do this?'. Similarly, the Communication ends with a very brief remark on the legal base of an 'optional instrument', which is illuminatingly open-ended. Articles 308, 95 and 65 EC are cited, but the Commission observes (pp 21–22) that the question of legal base is tied to those concerning legal form, content and scope. Accordingly, reflection on the question of legal base can be left to addressed 'within a larger debate on the parameters of an optional instrument.'

V. THREE REASONS FOR THE COMMISSION'S RETICENCE

Why does the Commission prefer to set aside detailed inquiry into matters of competence in these communications? There are three reasons, and all three are good ones. One is tactical and for the time being remains persuasive, the second was well-founded but now seems redundant, while the third touches the deep ambiguity of what is constitutionally at stake.

The first reason is that had the Commission include an extended treatment of available legal competence in its 2001 Communication it would doubtless have faced the protest that it was revealing a predilection for those options which most seriously engage the issue of competence, namely option 3 and, most provocatively, option 4. In order to avoid an imbalanced debate the Commission may have acted wisely in striving to maintain an open-minded

---

[30] Part 3.2, paras 25–51; also para 14. The annex to the Communication provides detailed account of responses to the 2001 Communication received by the Commission.
[31] COM(2004) 651.

focus on what is normatively desirable in the field of EC contract law. Only later will it address questions of competence in detail—if that even proves necessary. As the debate has developed it has become apparent that in at least some respects the increased attention given to 'softer' forms of activity in the 2003 and 2004 documents—such as the CFR—has in any event served to take some of the heat out of the debate about available competence.[32] This positive attitude towards the virtue of soft law has close associations with the much broader agenda for change in how the EU operates mapped out by the Commission in its 2001 White Paper on Governance.[33] In the longer term one would expect that the constitutional dimension will and should assume a more prominent place in the debate. A choice to set aside the adoption of binding measures within the meaning of Article 249 EC should not be accompanied by neglect of the demands made by Article 5(1) EC, or else the turn to soft law will simply reinvigorate the corrosion of 'competence creep' in a new guise. Moreover, one must reckon with important questions about the legitimacy of the envisaged process insofar as instruments that carry legal force may be created without recourse to the normal legislative process. This is a concern that attaches to the planned CFR, which the Commission coyly describes as a 'toolbox' which will be non-binding,[34] but it seems plausible that the CFR will come to play more than a merely technical role in improving the operation of the *acquis*.[35] If it does, it will require a political legitimation that goes deeper than that conferred by the current process of consultation and input from experts and stakeholders.[36] Happily, the Commission admits that the matter of the legal status of the CFR may need revisiting.[37] Perhaps, of course, one may wryly suspect that the soft-pedal used by the Commission in addressing these constitutional questions is a ruse to conceal the fact that it already holds a predilection for options at the more ambitious end of the scale mapped out in 2001. However, whatever the underlying reality of Commission preferences, an initially cautious presentation of matters of constitutional weight offers the best chance of promoting an open-minded debate. As long as these issues of competence and legitimacy are not permitted to slip off the agenda, the Commission is, in my judgment, justified in avoiding plunging into them more deeply at this stage in the process.

---

[32] S Weatherill, 'European Contract Law: Taking The Heat out of Questions of Competence' (2004) 15 *European Business Law Review* 23.

[33] European Governance: a White Paper, COM(2001) 428.

[34] COM(2004) 651, 3, 5.

[35] Cf, eg M Hesselink, 'The European Commission's Action Plan: Towards a More Coherent European Contract Law?' (2004) 12 *European Review of Private Law* 397.

[36] For an early insistence on the questions of democracy associated with the Commission's investigation into contract law, see W Van Gerven, 'Codifying European Private Law? Yes, if …!' (2002) 27 *EL Rev* 156.

[37] COM(2004) 651, 5.

The second reason in favour of allowing the competence question to keep a low profile pending attention to substantive concerns arises because of the possibility of Treaty revision. When the Commission launched its inquiry into contract law in 2001 it was perfectly possible that Treaty revision would change the constitutional ground rules. There is a good case to be made in favour of setting to one side concern about constitutional hurdles that might in any event prove temporary. However, it is now apparent that Treaty revision will not change the rules, at least in the medium-term. The Laeken Declaration of 2001 invited reconsideration of the role of just two explicitly listed Treaty provisions, Articles 95 and 308. There were voices raised at the Convention on the Future of Europe in favour of the tighter drafting or even elimination of these provisions as motors of 'competence creep'.[38] However, the majority concluded this would unduly harm the EU's capacity for effective problem-solving. Both provisions were retained in the June 2003 draft agreed by the Convention and both are retained in the text signed in Rome in October 2004. The successor to Article 308 is Article I-18, that to Article 95 is Article III-172. No attempt has been made to alter the wording. The ambiguous status of the scope of the competence to harmonise will remain a hot topic for debate, unchanged by the entry into force of the Treaty establishing a Constitution for Europe (should that occur). Even the Treaty's principal innovation relating to competence control, the monitoring role crafted for national parliaments, extends only to legislative proposals adopted under Article I-18 and not to proposals for the harmonisation of laws advanced under Article III-172 (although the latter could be challenged for perceived violation of the subsidiarity principle). Given Article 95's poor track record in the matter of faithful observance of the limits of EC legislative competence, that exclusion is regrettable.[39] At the very least, the Laeken-inspired twinning of what is now Articles 95 and 308 EC, and will be Articles III-172 and I-18 EU, should have been retained. But it has not been, and on this point the new Treaty, if ratified, would leave much to play for in the quest to control centralisation in Europe, inter alia in the field of contract law. And, a fortiori, if, as seems currently likely, the Treaty establishing a Constitution remains dormant or is even pronounced dead, the debate will continue to focus on the existing and very opaque materials.

The third reason, and probably the major and best reason, for the Commission's preference not to engage deeply with questions of competence is that the answers are very far from being clear. As mentioned above, it is easy

---

[38] Eg CONV 291/02 24 September 2002 (Heathcoat-Amory); WD 14—WG V 7 August 2002 (Heathcoat-Amory, Working Group on Complementary Competencies). On the progress of the debate at the Convention, see S Weatherill, 'Competence Creep and Competence Control' (2004) 23 *Yearbook of European Law* 1; also P Craig 'Competence: Clarity, Conferral, Containment and Consideration' (2004) 29 *EL Rev* 323; J Wuermeling 'Kalamität Kompetenz: Zur Abgrenzung der Zuständigkeiten in dem Verfassungsentwurf des EU-Konvents' [2004] *Europarecht* 216.

[39] S Weatherill, 'Better Competence Monitoring' (2005) 30 *EL Rev* 23.

to identify that the vocabulary used by the Court in *Tobacco Advertising* imperils the validity of some of the older measures harmonising consumer contract law. But that is by no means the end of the story. At the time of their adoption those Directives were not buttressed by constitutionally sophisticated analysis, because there was simply no practical need for such flourishes. Unanimity among the Member States was the guarantee of adoption. It does not follow that, were they to be reconsidered today, they could not be shown to meet the demands of Article 95. It follows only that their proponents would need to work harder. Moreover, it is in any event far from settled just how the scope of Article 95 post-*Tobacco Advertising* should be defined.

There are at least two dimensions to this caveat. First, even on its own terms, the precise dimensions of the shadow cast by the *Tobacco Advertising* judgment cannot yet be known with confidence. The Court's point is that the threshold of a required sufficient contribution to the improvement of the conditions for the establishment and functioning of the internal market must be crossed before the Treaty-conferred competence to harmonise exists, but this offers plenty of scope for detailed argument about the exact height of that threshold. The appearance in the judgment of a jumble of awkwardly imprecise adjectives and adverbs such as 'genuinely', 'likely', 'probable', 'appreciable' and 'remote and indirect' betrays the complexity of the assessment of whether reliance on Article 95 is valid.[40] As a general observation one would expect a degree of judicial restraint in such cases.[41] In this vein, it is striking that in subsequent applications of the threshold test the Court has offered no relief to applicants seeking the annulment of measures in *Netherlands v Parliament and Council*,[42] *R v Secretary of State ex parte BAT and Imperial Tobacco*,[43] *Swedish Match*[44] and *Alliance for Natural Health*[45]—even though at least some of the arguments advanced against these measures seem rather compelling. *Tobacco Advertising* demonstrates that the Court will not permit the EC's political institutions free rein in fixing the scope of the EC's legislative power. False market-making harmonisation is in jeopardy. But it should not be thought that the Court is intent on embarking on a campaign of aggressive curtailment of the scope of harmonisation in circumstances where tolerably plausible explanation accompanies the adopted measure.

There is a second issue that is relevant to the Commission's preference to tread softly in its treatment of the matter of available legal competence. Legislative practice suggests that there is more to Article 95 than simply the

---

[40] Paras 84, 86, 97, 108 and 109 of the judgment (above n 17), respectively.
[41] For a wonderfully illuminating comparison see the decision of the US Supreme Court in *Gonzalez v Raich*, 545 US _ (2005).
[42] Case C–377/98 [2001] ECR I–7079.
[43] Above n 22.
[44] Case C–210/03 [2004] ECR I–11893.
[45] Above n 22.

elimination of obstacles to trade and the removal of appreciable distortions of competition. For example, Directive 99/44 on certain aspects of the sale of consumer goods and associated guarantees, based on (what is now) Article 95 EC, provides in its Preamble that

> Whereas the creation of a common set of minimum rules of consumer law, valid no matter where goods are purchased within the Community, will strengthen consumer confidence and enable consumers to make the most of the internal market . . .[46]

This 'confidence-building' rationale for harmonisation was foreshadowed in the Preamble to Directive 93/13 on unfair terms in consumer contracts.[47] It also connects with broader policy statements about the need to induce consumer confidence in order to make real the integration of the market in reality and not simply on paper. For example, the Report from the Commission on the *Action Plan for Consumer Policy 1999–2001* asserts that

> Ensuring consumers are confident in shopping across borders is as important for making the internal market work as is making it easier for businesses to sell across borders.[48]

This confidence-building perspective has been scattered across many policy documents in recent years.[49] Underpinning this debate is the awkward question of whether a market for Europe can adequately be made by eliminating perceived trade barriers or whether a more aggressive commitment to centralised regulation designed to tackle the uncertainties in the market consequent on trade liberalisation is required. For some, a reading of Article 95 which refuses to extend its use beyond mere reaction to barriers to trade falling within the (post-*Keck*) reach of Article 28 creates the risk of a 'problematic one-sidedness for Community law.'[50] In line with this approach, one plausible view holds that these broader 'confidence-inducing' rationales for harmonising laws represent a dimension to Article 95 that was simply not at stake in *Tobacco Advertising* and which is therefore not ruled out by that

---

[46] Directive 99/44, above n 7.

[47] Directive 93/13, above n 2.

[48] Commission Report on the Action Plan for Consumer Policy of 1999–2001, COM(2001) 486, 11.

[49] See also eg Commission Communication 'Better Monitoring of the Application of Community Law' COM(2002) 725; Commission Communication 'Consumer Policy Strategy 2002–2006' COM(2002) 208, eg para 2.3.3.

[50] A von Bogdandy and J Bast, 'The EU's Vertical Order of Competences: the Current Law and Proposals for its Reform' (2002) 39 *CML Rev* 227, 245; also G Davies, 'Can Selling Arrangements be Harmonised?' (2005) 30 *EL Rev* 370. For a similar metaphor in an adjacent context, see discussion of a 'lop-sided' pattern by the Study Group on Social Justice in European Private Law, 'Social Justice in European Contract Law: a Manifesto' (2004) 10 *European Law Journal* 653, 664.

judgment.[51] An alternative—and, frankly, no less plausible—view is that *Tobacco Advertising* is aimed precisely at suppressing such woolly, open-ended claims to assert legislative competence pursuant to Article 95. Accordingly, examples of legislative practice which rely upon the confidence-building rationale are vulnerable to annulment should a court ever be asked to consider their validity, and the rationale is no basis for future harmonisation initiatives. Adherents to this view might claim that (for good or ill) the Treaty *is* one-sided!

Another way of looking at this is to question whether Articles 28 and 95 are two sides of the same coin. Some national rules of private law fall outwith Article 28.[52] They are not trade barriers. The Member State is not called on to justify them. But can the EC then harmonise these areas pursuant to Article 95? It is simply not clear.

A sub-theme in this debate asks whether it is in any event plausible to regard legislative harmonisation as an effective method in boosting the consumer's confidence in crossing borders to shop. Linguistic variation and impeded access to justice may be much more serious hindrances than the absence of minimum legal rights promised on paper.[53] And should one even take account of different expectations among consumers in different jurisdictions, different cultural milieux? Empirical evidence of the extent to which legal regulation generates confidence in new markets would be useful, though hard to gather.[54] Such data would be potentially germane to an assessment of whether a particular Community initiative crosses the threshold of constitutionality by making an actual contribution to inducing cross-border mobility.

The matter remains deeply ambiguous. It is, however, of central importance in understanding the proper scope of Article 95 EC. Without pretending that the law currently offers sturdy support for this perspective, I would pitch an argument in the following terms. Without a reliable pattern of legal rights 'on paper', the consumer will simply not treat the internal market as trustworthy or viable. He or she will retreat to the relative security of local purchasing. The argument would therefore not be that without harmonised legal protection the internal market will work unfairly; it would instead be

---

[51] S Weatherill 'The Commission's Options for Developing EC Consumer Protection and Contract Law: Assessing the Constitutional Basis' (2002) 13 *European Business Law Review* 497.

[52] Cf. Case C–339/89 *Alsthom Atlantique SA* [1991] ECR I–107; Case C–93/92 *CMC Motorradcenter* [1993] ECR I–5009. Both cases are factually unusual, but may be best read as having partially paved the way to the imminent re-shaping of Art 28 EC effected by the Court in Cases C–267 and 268/91 *Keck and Mithouard* [1993] ECR I–6097.

[53] T Wilhelmsson, 'The Abuse of the Confident Consumer as a Justification for EC Consumer Law' (2004) 27 *Journal of Consumer Policy* 317. Cf also, robustly dismissing the 'confidence-building' perspective, R Goode, 'Contract and Commercial Law: the Logic and Limits of Harmonisation' *Ius Commune Lectures of European Private Law No 8* (Maastricht, METRO, 2003).

[54] Cf in another sector N Moloney, 'Confidence and Competence: the Conundrum of EC Capital Markets Law' (2004) 4(2) *Journal of Corporate Law Studies* 1.

that without harmonised legal protection the internal market will not even come into existence in accordance with the pattern mapped by Article 14 EC. So Article 95 is available only for measures that contribute to the establishment and functioning of the internal market, while wider regulatory ambitions must be pursued under other provisions which are textually more narrowly drawn (such as Article 153(3)(b), concerning consumer protection). But breeding confidence among consumers is essential to the establishment and functioning of the internal market. This can therefore be validly achieved by the creation of harmonised legal protection, albeit that inquiry into the genuine contribution of such legal rules to promoting confidence must be conducted by the legislature. Recourse to the notion of building 'consumer confidence' needs to be securely grounded in each instance in which it is advanced as a justification for legislative action; it should not simply become the new motor of 'competence creep' applied to the harmonisation programme.

VI. CONCLUSION

The Commission's development of European contract law raises some intriguing and, as yet, timidly addressed questions about constitutional propriety. These matters are fundamental to an understanding of the relationship between the power of the Member States and the role of the EU. They are intimately connected to the general debate about the balance that needs to be struck between, on the one hand, centralisation and uniformity in Europe and, on the other, tolerance of diversity and respect for local autonomy. And yet the Commission is right to avoid deep engagement with the constitutional dimension. The complexity and uncertain status of much of the relevant material makes it inappropriate for elaborate examination in the current policy documents. The constitutional questions cannot be ignored—for the EC is not competent to legislate unless its Treaty offers it authorisation and because they touch on wider questions of legitimacy—but they can be left pending while the Commission proceeds with its quest to draw all affected constituencies into the task of determining just what is needed of a European contract law.

7

The European Community's Competence to Pursue the Harmonisation of Contract Law—an Empirical Contribution to the Debate

STEFAN VOGENAUER & STEPHEN WEATHERILL[*]

I. INTRODUCTION

After an extended period in which the European Community merely nibbled at the edges of national contract laws, the bite of a 'European contract law' has lately become more pronounced. In particular, Directive 93/13 on unfair terms in consumer contracts provoked an intensive debate about just *why* the EC might intervene in contractual autonomy, and opinions on the relative virtue and vice of the measure have differed with spectacular ferocity. The Commission has lately attempted to adopt an ostentatiously open-minded attitude to the future shaping of European contract law as part of a quest to generate a constructive debate engaging all relevant constituencies. The purpose of this paper is, first, to outline the development of European contract law over the last two decades, then to sketch the Commission's trio of communications on the way ahead, published in 2001, 2003 and 2004, and finally to report and reflect on the findings of a survey conducted in 2005 of the attitude of European businesses to the advantages and disadvantages of further intervention in this area. Accordingly, this paper seeks to add a dose of empirical evidence to a debate that has hitherto not been conducted with any noticeable emphasis on such material.

[*] This is a revised, up-dated and significantly expanded version of a paper originally published in (2005) 30 *EL Rev* 821.

II. THE QUIET EVOLUTION OF EUROPEAN CONTRACT LAW

Although the debate about European contract law has been slow to come to the boil, the pot has never been empty. The EC Treaty's competition rules have always intimately affected contract law by requiring that contracts which fall foul of its demands be treated as unenforceable.[1] The Treaty rules governing free movement of persons have been interpreted by the European Court of Justice as being capable of direct application to the activities of private parties.[2] Moreover, the gender equality rules and, more recently, the wider equality rules covering, inter alia, race and sexual orientation have exerted an impact on private relations.[3] And, most conspicuously of all, what are today Articles 94 and 95 EC have shaped a legislative *acquis* relevant to contract law as the programme of harmonisation of laws in the service of market-making to which they are dedicated has 'spilled over' even though the relevant Treaty provisions do not explicitly recognise a capacity to affect contract law.

However, these interventions have commonly been treated as peripheral to mainstream contract law. They have been compartmentalised as peculiar to the control of anti-competitive practices or to the regulation of the labour market. Even the bulk of the body of harmonised contract law tackles the special case of formation of particular consumer contracts, such as those concluded 'on the doorstep'[4] and in the field of package travel,[5] with only marginal incursion into commercial contract law.[6] By contrast, more recent measures, such as Directive 93/13 on unfair terms in consumer contracts[7] and Directive 99/44 on consumer sales and guarantees,[8] stand out as much more ambitious. Rather than focusing on formation and information disclosure, they challenge the very notion of contractual autonomy. And, in conformity

---

[1] Art 81(2) EC.

[2] See, eg Case C–415/93 *URBSFA v Bosman* [1995] ECR I–4921; Case C–281/98 *Roman Angonese* [2000] ECR I–4139. For discussion, see S Van den Bogaert, 'Horizontality: the Court Attacks?' in C Barnard and J Scott (eds), *The Law of the Single European Market: Unpacking the Premises* (Oxford, Hart Publishing, 2002) ch 5.

[3] Council Directive 2000/43/EC of 29 June 2000 implementing the principle of equal treatment between persons irrespective of racial or ethnic origin [2000] OJ L180/22, Council Directive 2000/78/EC of 27 November 2000 establishing a general framework for equal treatment in employment and occupation [2000] OJ L303/16.

[4] Council Directive 85/577/EEC of 20 December 1985 to protect the consumer in respect of contracts negotiated away from business premises [1985] OJ L372/31.

[5] Council Directive 90/314/EEC of 13 June 1990 on package travel, package holidays and package tours [1990] OJ L158/59.

[6] Directive 2000/35/EC of the European Parliament and of the Council of 29 June 2000 on combating late payment in commercial transactions [2000] OJ L200/35, Council Directive 86/653/EEC of 18 December 1986 on the coordination of the laws of the Member States relating to self-employed commercial agents [1986] OJ L382/17.

[7] Council Directive 93/13/EEC of 5 April 1993 on unfair terms in consumer contracts [1993] OJ L95/29.

[8] Directive 99/44/EC of the European Parliament and of the Council of 25 May 1999 on certain aspects of the sale of consumer goods and associated guarantees [1999] OJ L171/12.

with the capacity of harmonisation to irritate national legal orders in a manner that escapes its formal bounds,[9] these measures have generated a readiness to reconsider the shape of contract law beyond the consumer sphere.[10] The academic debate about the nature and purpose of European contract law is taking shape.[11]

This is especially so since there is no consensus about the underlying constitutional issues. A number of the Directives which have harmonised national contract laws in the name of promoting the establishment or functioning of the common market or the internal market disguised the political reality that the Member States were committed to the development of an EC consumer policy and, in the absence of any more appropriate legal basis in the Treaty, chose to 'borrow' the competence to harmonise laws to put it in place. So Directive 85/577 states in its preamble that the practice of doorstep selling is the subject of different rules in different Member States, and adds—in deeply unconvincing fashion—that 'any disparity between such legislation may directly affect the functioning of the common market.' The preamble reveals that the Directive was largely motivated by the prevailing political consensus in favour of developing an EC consumer protection programme. So some EC directives that harmonise national consumer contract laws and thereby create a species of European consumer contract law were the product of a political consensus about the desirability of such a development and were not underpinned by a constitutionally pure 'market-driven' pedigree. This was not 'Brussels' imposing unwelcome new rules, though it was often deftly and mendaciously presented as such. This was political élites in the Member States participating cheerfully in exploitation of the EC's lawmaking system as a source of constitutionally questionable intervention. Such legislative practice is troublingly inconsistent with the assertion in Article 5(1) of the Treaty that the EC possesses only the competences attributed to it by its Treaty. The constitutional context and the deep ambiguities that are at stake

---

[9] Cf G Teubner, 'Legal Irritants: Good Faith in British Law or How Unifying Law Ends Up in New Divergences' (1998) 61 *MLR* 11; also P Nebbia, 'Law as Tradition and the Europeanization of Contract Law: a Case Study' (2004) 23 *Yearbook of European Law* 363.

[10] On Directive 99/44 and the reform of sales law in Germany, see H-W Micklitz, 'The New German Sales Law: Changing Patterns in the Regulation of Product Quality' (2002) 25 *Journal of Consumer Policy* 379. On Directive 93/13 and the reform of unfair terms in the UK, see H Beale, 'Unfair Terms in Contracts: Proposals for Reform in the UK' (2004) 27 *Journal of Consumer Policy* 289; and see more recently Law Commissions, 'Unfair Terms in Contracts' (Law Com No 292, Scot Law Com No 199, 2005).

[11] See, eg, but by no means taking the same view, H-W Micklitz, 'Principles of Social Justice in European Private Law' (2000) 19 *Yearbook of European Law* 167; R Schulze and G Ajani (eds), *Gemeinsame Prinzipen des Europäischen Privatrechts* (Baden-Baden, Nomos, 2003); H Rösler, *Europäisches Konsumentenvertragsrecht* (Munich, CH Beck, 2004); K Riesenhuber, *Europäisches Vertragsrecht* (Berlin, De Gruyter, 2003); Sixto A Sánchez Lorenzo, *Derecho Privado Europeo* (Granada, Editorial Comares, 2002); T Wilhelmsson, 'Varieties of Welfarism in European Contract Law' (2004) 10 *European Law Journal* 712; S Grundmann, 'The Structure of European Contract Law' (2001) 9 *European Review of Private Law* 505; S Grundmann, 'European Contract Law(s) of What Colour?' (2005) 1 *European Review of Contract Law* 184.

in this process are explored more fully in the contribution to this volume prepared by Weatherill. For present purposes, one may simply appreciate that it was inevitable that this 'creeping centralisation' would attract discontent, especially as it became ever more visible to surprised national private lawyers. In this vein, Directive 93/13 was a landmark. So too was the European Court of Justice's ruling in *Tobacco Advertising*—more properly, *Germany v Parliament and Council*[12]—which, though not concerned with contract law directly, revealed for the first time a Court willing to annul a directive adopted by a majority in Council in the name of market-making harmonisation, yet which made no adequate contribution to economic objectives and which was by implication condemned as a measure of public health policy for which the EC lacked competence under its Treaty.

'European contract law' can no longer develop in the shadows. Not before time, the Commission has promoted a sober debate about what is really needed of the EC in the field of contract law, against a (sometimes concealed) background assumption that there is in any event a limit to what the EC has constitutional authority to deliver. The Commission has accordingly asked affected parties what they want: this is tracked in the next section. Our survey of business attitudes has revealed further insights: these are elucidated in the section that follows, and they form the core of this paper's contribution to the debate about what the EC can and should deliver in the field of contract law.

III. THE COMMISSION'S TRIO OF COMMUNICATIONS

In July 2001 the Commission issued its first Communication on European Contract Law.[13] The Communication promised a willingness to reflect critically on the desirability of maintaining the hitherto fragmented, patchwork model of lawmaking in the field at the EC level. Four options for future EC action in the field of contract law were floated (though they are not mutually exclusive).

The first option was no EC action. This was based on the perception that markets have a capacity to achieve self-correction without legal intervention. The second option centred on the promotion of the development of common contract law principles, leading to greater convergence of national laws. The third option was to improve the quality of legislation already in place. The current legislative *acquis* is marked by odd inconsistencies, such as the lack of uniform length fixed for 'cooling off' periods in the consumer directives, and by a general absence of common definitions for key phrases. The fourth, most ambitious and most tentatively aired option was the adoption of new comprehensive legislation at EC level, taking the form of a European code

---

[12] Case C–376/98 [2000] ECR I–8419.
[13] COM(2001) 398 [2001] OJ C255/01.

that could either replace national laws or co-exist with them as an optional instrument.

The Commission's Communication served as a focus for a debate that had been brewing for most of the decade since Directive 93/13 on unfair terms ignited a general concern among private lawyers about the impact of the EC. Response to it was vigorous and varied.[14] The main themes of the debate surrounded the key questions that the Commission had astutely placed on the agenda—most of all, just *why* might an EC contribution to contract law be required, and what form might it take? The next task was to determine the benefits and also the costs of EC intervention.

In February 2003 a follow-up was published. This was the Action Plan on a more coherent European contract law.[15] It revealed the outcome of the process of consultation provoked by the 2001 Communication. The Commission had moved towards a preference for solutions falling between the extremes of inaction and comprehensive intervention. So the planned way forward combined options 2 and 3 from the 2001 menu. The sector-specific approach to legislation would be maintained, with additions proposed only where a need is convincingly demonstrated. In addition, a mix of regulatory and non-regulatory measures would be used to increase the coherence of the EC contract law *acquis*. The Action Plan referred to problems associated with the current absence of comprehensive definitions of abstract notions such as 'damage', which may lead to inconsistencies in application at the national level. The Commission aired the idea of developing a 'common frame of reference' for European contract law principles. This would provide a pool of expertise on which jurists could draw in seeking to resolve difficulties and ambiguities in the interpretation of EC measures. The Commission also proposed that the elaboration of EU-wide standard contract law terms should be encouraged. A further (tentatively expressed) idea involved the drawing up of an optional instrument which parties may choose to use in order to facilitate the process of cross-border contracting. It would exist in parallel with national contract law systems.

The debate was truly underway and the Commission, having gone some way to show its hand, did not go short of advice.[16] There was general

---

[14] Eg S Grundmann and J Stuyck (eds), *An Academic Green Paper on European Contract Law* (The Hague, Kluwer, 2002); special issue of *European Review of Private Law* (2002) vol 10 no 1; W Van Gerven, 'Codifying European Private Law? Yes, if . . .!' (2002) 27 *EL Rev* 156; S Weatherill, 'The European Commission's Green Paper on European Contract Law: Context, Content and Constitutionality' (2001) 24 *Journal of Consumer Policy* 339. Cf also D Staudenmayer, 'The Commission Communication on European Contract Law and the Future Prospects' (2002) 51 *ICLQ* 673.

[15] COM(2003) 68 [2003] OJ C63/01.

[16] Eg J Karsten and A Sinai, 'The Action Plan on European Contract Law: Perspectives for the Future' (2003) 26 *Journal of Consumer Policy* 159; C von Bar and S Swann, 'Response to the Action Plan on European Contract Law' (2003) 11 *European Review of Private Law* 595; W Blair and R Brent, 'A Single European Law of Contract?' (2004) 15 *European Business Law*

satisfaction that the Commission had set aside any overt intention to move towards anything akin to a European civil code (although some suspicion was voiced that this reticence was only a tactical holding measure). On the other aspects of the Action Plan there was some lack of certainty about what the Commission had in mind. This was perhaps understandable, since the 2003 Action Plan had been designed to promote further debate rather than to offer immutable solutions.

In October 2004 the Commission, having absorbed feedback on the 2003 Action Plan, issued a third document in the series. This was 'European Contract Law and the Revision of the Acquis: The Way Forward'.[17] It uses the three measures suggested by the 2003 Action Plan to map the way forward for European contract law.

Treatment of the first matter, improving the coherence of the contract law *acquis*, confirms the central role of the proposed common frame of reference (CFR). The Commission's stated aim is to identify 'best solutions', and account will be taken of national practice, the EC *acquis* and relevant international instruments, albeit that the CFR is to be fit for the EC's specific requirements. It would set out common fundamental principles of contract law, including guidance on where exceptions could be required. The principles would be supported by definitions of key concepts and the whole would be followed by model rules which would form the bulk of the CFR.

Although it is envisaged as a non-binding instrument, the CFR is plainly intended to become highly influential in the drafting and interpretation of legislative measures relevant to contract law, both European and national. Of course the European Court of Justice enjoys occasional opportunities to dip into the task of providing a 'Europeanised' interpretation of matters of contract law,[18] but this depends on the random patterns of litigation, and the CFR carries the appealing promise of injecting what one of its principal proponents in the Commission has portrayed as 'a significantly higher degree of coherence in European contract law.'[19]

The CFR is currently being prepared by a pan-European group of academics who receive funding by the Commission under the Sixth Framework Programme for research and technological development. This 'Joint Network on European Private Law' which, for the time being, comprises

---

Review 5. Cf also D Staudenmayer, 'The Commission Action Plan on European Contract Law' (2003) 11 *European Review of Private Law* 11.

[17] COM(2004) 651.
[18] See, eg the treatment of non-material damage under Directive 90/314 in Case C–168/00 *Simone Leitner* [2002] ECR I–2631. Cf, for reflections on the Court's role, O Gerstenberg, 'Private Law and the New European Constitutional Settlement' (2004) 10 *European Law Journal* 766, 782–86.
[19] D Staudenmayer, 'The Place of Consumer Contract Law within the Process on European Contract Law' (2004) 27 *Journal of Consumer Policy* 269, 277. See also J Karsten and G Petri, 'Towards a Handbook on European Contract Law and Beyond' (2005) 28 *Journal of Consumer Policy* 31.

researchers from 60 universities, is supposed to deliver a complete draft CFR by 2007.[20] A number of partial drafts concerning particular areas of contract law have already been produced and discussed with experts nominated by the Member States and the Commission: a first meeting of Member State experts was held in early December 2004. Stakeholders—drawn by the Commission from among business, professional and consumer interests—had their first meeting two weeks later. The process is therefore already underway and the intent is to sustain an intensive dialogue about the shape of the CFR. Drafting such an instrument is self-evidently not a value-free exercise, and those whose input is encouraged doubtless possess their own particular and potentially conflicting aims.[21] It has therefore been made clear that ultimately it is the Commission itself that will be responsible, following a further round of consultation, for choosing the eventual shape and content of the CFR. 2009 is foreseen as a target date for its adoption.

As a second measure, the promotion of the use of EU-wide standard terms and conditions is also promised, in line with the idea floated in the 2003 Action Plan. This would be driven by private parties. The Commission would not prepare the standard terms, but rather would seek merely to act as facilitator, for example by hosting a website on which information could be shared. The focus here is on business-to-business and business-to-government contracts, not the consumer sector.

In respect of the third measure, an optional instrument in European contract law coexisting with national laws, the Commission promises to continue to reflect on 'the opportuneness of such an instrument.' The annex presents 'parameters' of such an instrument. Its possible shape would be assessed in the light of the results of the first two measures and an extended impact assessment is promised. An 'opt-in' model is preferred over 'opt-out', and pursuit of coherence with the conversion of the Rome Convention into a Community instrument is placed on the agenda. Also identified as discussion points are the content of an optional instrument (only at a general level or also sector-specific?) and its scope (only business-to-business transactions or also business-to-consumer transactions?). As a matter of legal form, one may readily detect a preference for a Regulation, which would be directly applicable within the legal orders of the Member States, but the Commission prefers to avoid pinning down what it regards as the appropriate legal base in the Treaty. Most prominent of all is the intended clear connection between the CFR and the optional instrument.

In September 2005 the Commission released its 'First Annual Report on

---

[20] Contract No CIT3—513351; cf European Commission, *Citizens and Governance in a Knowledge-Based Society: Synopses of projects funded as a result of the First Call—Draft* 153–57, available at http://europa.eu.int/comm/employment_social/socio_economic_research/docs/FP6_synopsis_en.pdf.

[21] Cf M Hesselink, 'The Politics of a European Civil Code' (2004) 10 *European Law Journal* 675.

European Contract Law and the Acquis Review'.[22] This reports that the 'CFR-net', the network of stakeholder experts now comprising 177 members, is at work on the draft CFR, which is due by the end of 2007. We learn that since March 2005 workshops have been held on services contracts; franchise, agency and distribution; personal security rights; benevolent intervention; unjust enrichment; notion and functions of contract; and the notions of consumer and professional. The network of Member State experts also held a workshop on 31 May 2005, to follow up their inaugural meeting in December 2004. Furthermore we learn that the review of the consumer acquis 'is still in the diagnostic phase,'[23] examining in particular the practice of transposition and application in the Member States. The Commission reveals that, if revision or completion of the *acquis* is required, it could 'theoretically'[24] choose between a vertical approach, adjusting each Directive as it sees fit, or a more horizontal (and, one may observe, more ambitious) approach, involving the adoption of framework measures to regulate common features of the *acquis*. The Commission concludes by disclosing that it has abandoned the notion of hosting a website on which private parties could promote EU-wide standards terms and conditions, and by observing that the opportuneness of an optional instrument, now labelled a '26th regime',[25] is being addressed in particular in the area of financial services, though no amplification of the nature of this dimension of the overall project is provided.

The Commission's concern is conspicuously to move away from orthodox notions of legislative harmonisation. Moreover, the 2004 Communication asserts explicitly that the Commission does not intend to propose a European civil code, although this assertion is made in the context of the 'optional instrument', not the 'common frame of reference'. For all the Commission's evident concern to persuade that the CFR is simply a device for improving the quality of the regulatory environment, others have been more sceptical of the mild presentation of what is at stake. For some critics it is the CFR which may sow the seeds of a code which would challenge the diversity of legal culture in Europe. Moreover, some among that body of sceptics identify a risk that the emphasis may be on the contribution of the CFR to economic growth in preference to wider distributional concerns.[26] One may choose to disagree with the assessment of the gravity of this risk, but this body of critics is plainly correct to perceive that as a minimum the parameters of the debate should include such anxieties.

---

[22] COM(2005) 456 (23 September 2005).

[23] *Ibid*, 6.

[24] *Ibid*, 9.

[25] There are 25 Member States in the EU, but, because of the conditions of the 1707 Act of Union between England and Scotland, there are already 26 distinct legal systems, so one may question the Commission's counting.

[26] Cf Study Group on Social Justice in European Private Law, 'Social Justice in European Contract Law: a Manifesto' (2004) 10 *European Law Journal* 653.

IV. ESTABLISHING COMPETENCE: THE PERCEIVED VIEWS OF EUROPEAN BUSINESS

The Commission is provoking a deeply significant debate ranging over culture, economics and constitutional legitimacy. It is particularly aware of the need to establish competence under the EC Treaty. The most convincing basis for a Community competence to enact a comprehensive European contract law going beyond the current, fragmentary approach to legislation would seem to be Article 95 EC.[27] In order to establish this competence, two requirements would have to be met. First, as noted above, the Commission would be required to show that further steps in the area of contract law must actually contribute to eliminating obstacles to the free movement of goods or the freedom to provide services, or to removing appreciable distortions of competition.[28] Secondly, the enactment of a comprehensive Community contract law would have to be proportionate, as per Article 5(3) EC, ie it would have to be appropriate for attaining the removal of such obstacles and distortions, it must not go beyond what is necessary to achieve these objectives, and the disadvantages caused must not be disproportionate to the aims pursued—in particular, when there is a choice between several appropriate measures, recourse must be had to the least onerous.

This is why the consultation exercise set in motion by the Commission's 2001 Communication can essentially be narrowed down to three questions:[29] first, do the divergences in contract laws across the Member States result in obstacles to trade in goods and services, such as increasing the costs of cross-border transactions or creating other barriers? Secondly, is the existing piecemeal approach to European legislation in contract law sufficient to remove such obstacles, or does it rather create further difficulties, such as an inconsistent application of European law in the various Member States? Thirdly, are there any options for legislative activities by the Community which are more appropriate for eliminating any existing trade obstacles?

In the following subsection we summarise some attempts to give an answer to these questions that have been made in the past, mainly on behalf of the Commission. In the next subsection we describe the set-up and methodology

---

[27] If a European contract law were to be enacted as an 'optional instrument' alongside the national contract law systems it could be argued that this would not be a measure for the 'approximation' of the laws of the Member States and that, consequently, Art 308 EC, and not Art 95 EC, would be the correct legal base. See, eg H-H Herrnfeld, in J Schwarze (ed), *EU-Kommentar* (Baden-Baden, Nomos, 2000), Art 95 EGV, notes 23, 37 (referring to the practice of the Council and to the ECJ in Opinion 1/94 [1994] ECR I-5267, para 59); for a different view, see S Leible, in R Streinz (ed), *EUV/EGV* (Munich, CH Beck, 2003), Art 95 EGV, notes 28–29. However, it is submitted that if the two requirements mentioned in the text are met, the requirements of Art 308 EC would be met as well.

[28] Cf above n 12, and S Weatherill 'European Contract Law: Taking the Heat out of Questions of Competence' (2004) 15 *European Business Law Review* 23. See also the contribution of Weatherill to this volume.

[29] COM(2001) 398, above n 13, paras 10, 15, 23, 40, 72–73 and COM(2003) 68, above n 15, paras 5–6.

of a major business survey conducted in 2005. In the third and final subsection we report the results of this survey in the belief that they shed new light on the level of demand among commercial undertakings for an EC contract law (of some type).

1. Previous Attempts to Evaluate the Attitudes and Expectations of Market Participants towards a European Contract Law

In order to find out more about the need for a European contract law it is helpful to go beyond the purely legal framework and to gain inspiration from economics and from behavioural theory, a subdiscipline of psychology. This was done in a series of seminars at the Maastricht-based Ius Commune Research School, the results of which have just been published. They are very much in favour of a cautious, step-by-step approach to further harmonisation, slowly leading to a restatement or to an optional contract code which would allow but not force the parties to choose a neutral system.[30]

The problem with this approach is that it provides theory where hard empirical data are needed. If we want to know whether the diverging contract laws in Europe really form a barrier to cross-border trade and impede on the proper functioning of the internal market, and whether the introduction of a comprehensive Community contract law would be a suitable and necessary means in order to remove such impediments, we should ask the main users of contract law: businesses and consumers. Perhaps surprisingly, this has hardly been done on a large scale. There are important older sociological studies on the general importance of contract law on business relationships in a national context.[31] As far as cross-border transactions are concerned, data have so far only been collected in the wake of the Commission's Green Paper on European Union Consumer Protection,[32] and thus in the context of business-to-consumer ('B2C') transactions.

Thus a survey conducted on behalf of the Commission amongst 15,043 European consumers from the then 15 Member States in January 2002 revealed that, on average, consumers perceive the level of protection to be higher in their country than abroad: only 32% of consumers consider their rights to be well protected in a potential dispute with a seller or manufacturer in another Member State, whereas 56% are confident of this with regard to their own country.[33] A comparable survey on cross-border shopping,

---

[30] J Smits (ed), *The Need for a European Contract Law: Empirical and Legal Perspectives* (Groningen, Europa Law Publishing, 2005) v–vii, 178–79.

[31] S Macaulay, 'Non-contractual Relations in Business: a Preliminary Study' (1963) 28 *American Sociological Review* 55, for Wisconsin; H Beale and T Dugdale, 'Contracts between Businessmen' (1975) 2 *British Journal of Law & Society* 45, for England.

[32] COM(2001) 531.

[33] Flash Eurobarometer 117, 'Consumers Survey' (January 2002) 33–39, available at http://www.europa.eu.int/comm/dgs/health_consumer/events/event42/eu_report_en.pdf.

conducted a couple of months later, found that only 13% of European consumers had bought or ordered products or services for private use from shops or sellers located in another Member State during the preceding 12 months. A quarter of all respondents stated that they felt less confident buying abroad than in their country of residence. The main reasons they gave for this were difficulties with the resolution of after-sales problems, such as complaints, returns, refunds and guarantees (88%), and the difficulty in taking legal action through the courts (83%).[34] These findings are supported by a survey amongst 12 of the then 14 European Consumer Centres on consumer advice conducted in May 2002. When asked what, in their experience, the main obstacles to cross-border trade were from the consumer's point of view, the consumer advisers ranked the same two reasons—after-sales problems and difficulty in taking legal action—top.[35] Both reasons are certainly related to problems of language and non-familiarity with business practices elsewhere, but they also depend on different legislative frameworks. It is therefore not surprising that, when asked about what measures could be taken to increase confidence in cross-border purchases, nearly eight out of ten consumers lacking such confidence mentioned (1) full harmonisation of consumer rights and protection or (2) being able to sue foreign sellers in the courts of the consumer's Member State under his or her national laws.[36]

In order to find out how businesses perceive obstacles to cross-border sales to consumers another survey was conducted on behalf of the Commission in August and September 2002. The results were based on responses from 2,899 companies, based in all 15 Member States and employing at least 10 persons. The survey revealed that only 13% of consumer sales in the preceding 12 months had been to final consumers who resided in EU countries other than the one in which the company operated. When asked about the most important factors causing difficulty in the development of sales and advertising throughout the EU, the first ranking obstacle mentioned was the need for compliance with different national regulations on commercial practices, advertising and other consumer protection regulations ('very important' or 'fairly important' for 47% of respondents). Almost equal importance (46%)

---

[34] Standard Eurobarometer 57.2, reported in 'Public Opinion in Europe: Views on Business-to-Consumer Cross-Border Trade' (14 November 2002) 3, 20, 39–40, available at http://europa.eu.int/comm/consumers/cons_int/safe_shop/fair_bus_pract/green_pap_comm/stu dies/eb57-fb128_final_report_en.pdf.

[35] GFA Management GmbH, *Ex-ante-Impact Assessment of the Options Outlined in the Green Paper on EU Consumer Protection: Final Report* (November 2002) 5, 18–19, 54, 69–71, available at http://europa.eu.int/comm/consumers/cons_int/safe_shop/fair_bus_pract/green_pap_comm/studies/gfa_report_en.pdf. European Consumer Centres (ECCs) are run by independent national consumer organisations, but financed by the European Commission.

[36] Standard Eurobarometer 57.2, above n 34, 45 (seen by 79% and 76% as 'very' or 'fairly important', respectively).

was attributed to difficulties caused by different fiscal regulations and to problems arising from resolving cross-border complaints and conflicts. Consequently, harmonisation of diverging national regulations in this area and the establishment of independent arbitration and conciliation services dealing with cross-border complaints and disputes were seen as efficient measures to make the development of sales and/or advertising throughout the Union easier. Such measures were considered to be 'very' or 'fairly' efficient for this purpose by 68% and 59% of respondents respectively. If national regulations were completely harmonised, 38% of the businesses surveyed estimated that the proportion of their marketing and advertising budget devoted to cross-border sales would increase, and 46% of the respondents would expect their cross-border sales to grow.[37]

The process initiated by the Commission in 2001 goes far beyond B2C contracts. Its scope potentially includes cross-border transactions between businesses ('B2B transactions') or between consumers ('C2C transactions'). Both businesses and consumers were amongst the interested parties who were invited in the 2001 Communication to give their views on the three major issues outlined at the beginning of this section. Four consumer associations responded, surely primarily with B2C transactions in mind. They declared that the current state of affairs deterred consumers from cross-border transactions, that the existing piecemeal harmonisation results in further problems, and that they favoured improvement of the existing Community legislation as a suitable remedy.[38] The results of the 47 responses collected under the heading 'business', almost all of them given by interest groups and business associations, were much more mixed and somewhat inconclusive. Neither was there a clear view on whether divergences in national contract law created obstacles to cross-border trade, nor were there strong complaints about inconsistencies created by piecemeal harmonisation. However, a clearer picture emerged as to future improvements: the most favoured option was to improve the quality of legislation already in place.[39]

Reacting to the 2003 Action Plan, the four consumer associations and most of the 29 businesses and business associations responding agreed on the need to improve existing legislation, and there was cautious support for the elaboration of a CFR. As to the optional instrument suggested by the Commission, a much more sceptical attitude prevailed.[40] Of course, by their very nature, the reactions received during the consultation exercise could not

---

[37] Flash Eurobarometer 128, reported in 'Public Opinion in Europe', above n 34, 33, 41–42, 52, 55, 57.

[38] COM(2003) 68, above n 15, annex, paras 3.1.3, 3.2.3, 4.1.3, 4.2.3, 4.3.3, 4.4.3.

[39] COM(2003) 68, above n 15, annex, paras 3.1.2, 3.2.2, 4.1.2, 4.2.2, 4.3.2, 4.4.2.

[40] Reaction to the Action Plan—A More Coherent Contract Law, paras 3.1.2, 3.1.3, 3.3.2, 3.3.3, available at http://europa.eu.int/comm/consumers/cons_int/safe_shop/fair_bus_pract/cont_law/analyticaldoc_en.pdf.

be representative and would not give a complete picture. The Commission itself acknowledged that much.[41]

2. The Business Survey Conducted in Early 2005: Respondents and Methodology

In our view, in early 2005, three and a half years after the Commission started its consultation exercise, it could hardly be said that the three questions raised at the outset of this section had received a conclusive answer. The case for further European intervention in the area of contract law had simply not been made. This is why, in the run-up to the conference, the contributions to which are collected in this volume, we embarked on a fresh start. In doing so, we acted as academic advisors to Clifford Chance, the world's biggest law firm and the co-organisers of the conference.[42] Clifford Chance had written a fairly critical response to the Commission's 2003 Action Plan,[43] and this was followed by an equally disapproving article by one of their partners, who reached the conclusion that

> before too many moves are made, serious research needs to be undertaken to estab-lish whether or not [users of contract law] really do find different legal systems an obstacle to trade and do want a uniform law to solve this.[44]

Since the bulk of previous research had been directed at consumers' affairs, it seemed appropriate to focus on the experiences, perceptions and expecta-tions of businesses. Thus a survey was conducted amongst 175 firms, based in eight Member States. The countries chosen seemed to offer a fairly represen-tative mix of larger and smaller economies, old and new Member States, and more 'Europhile' and more 'Eurosceptic' traditions. Two of them, Germany and the Netherlands, had recently undergone major revisions of their

---

[41] COM(2003) 68, above n 15, para 15. With respect to the responses to the 2001 Communication, this is also acknowledged by C Ott and H-B Schäfer, 'Die Vereinheitlichung des europäischen Vertragsrechts—Ökonomische Notwendigkeit oder akademisches Interesse' in C Ott and H-B Schäfer (eds), *Vereinheitlichung und Diversität des Zivilrechts in transnationalen Wirtschaftsräumen* (Tübingen, Mohr Siebeck, 2002) 203, 223–30, who nevertheless regard these statements as important for a 'first assessment', evaluate them systematically, establish that there is a 'uniform tendency against a common European law of contract' amongst business associations (224) and reach the conclusion that 'there are no clearly discernible economic reasons for the creation of a European contract law' (230). In the same collection of essays H Eidenmüller, 'Kommentar: Obligatorisches versus optionales Vertragsrecht' 237 casts doubt on the statistical basis and on the conclusions drawn by Ott and Schäfer.

[42] We are grateful to Clifford Chance LLP for giving us permission to use the data of the survey and to publish the results on which they hold the copyright.

[43] Available at http://europa.eu.int/comm/consumers/cons_int/safe_shop/fair_bus_pract/cont_law/stakeholders/4–5.pdf. Cf R Sherwood, 'Law Firm Hits Out at EU Plan on Contracts', *Financial Times*, 26 May 2003.

[44] S James, 'EU Plans to Harmonise Contract Law' (2003) 18 *Butterworths Journal of International Banking and Financial Law* 413, 416.

domestic contract laws (see Figure 1). The companies surveyed belonged to a wide range of industries, comprising consumer and retail, energy and resources, healthcare and life sciences, manufacturing and construction, professional and other services, technology, and transport (see Table 1). Most of them were major businesses (at least 250 employees), some of them national, European or even global players. However, care was taken that almost a fifth (19.4%) were small (10–49 employees) or medium sized (50–249 employees) enterprises (SMEs), conventional wisdom being that SMEs suffer most under the existing divergences between national contract laws.[45] Two-thirds of the individuals responding worked in the legal

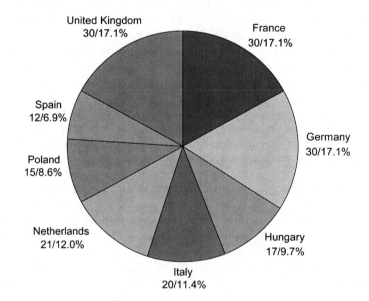

Figure 1: Participants in the survey—by country

Table 1: Participants in the survey—by industry

Total	Consumer and retail	Energy and resources	Healthcare and life sciences	Manufac- turing and construc- tion	Professional and other services	Technol- ogy	Transport	Other
175	38	11	16	42	21	27	16	4
100%	21.7%	6.3%	9.1%	24.0%	12.0%	15.4%	9.1%	2.3%

[45] Cf, eg COM(2001) 398, above n 13, para 30.

departments of their firms; the others were directors, vice presidents, company secretaries or similar.

The survey was commissioned by Clifford Chance and conducted by an independent firm, Gracechurch Consulting. It had two stages. The first stage consisted of a small number of 'qualitative' interviews in which the respondents were asked discursive, open questions about the subject. These were designed to find out the extent of their knowledge, their concerns, their interests, etc. The results of these interviews were used in order to compose the final questionnaire for the second, 'quantitative' phase, which comprised more box-ticking-style questions from which the real results of the survey were drawn.[46] For this stage prospective respondents were emailed to establish if they were prepared to participate. Those who agreed were sent a two-and-a-half-page background note.[47] This summarised the debate so as to give participants who were not entirely familiar with all the issues an opportunity to reflect on them before they were interviewed. The interviews were then conducted over the telephone and in the native language of the respective country. With very few exceptions, they took place in late January and early February 2005. All the questions for both stages of the survey and the background notes were approved, and in some cases formulated, by the academic advisors: we endeavoured to ensure not only that they were factually and legally correct but also that the issues were presented in a balanced and unbiased manner.

3. Results of the Survey

The survey comprised four groups of questions. One aimed at establishing some aspects of the respondents' current practice towards cross-border trade. The other three were designed to give answers to the three leading questions referred to above, ie whether differences in national contract laws presented obstacles to cross-border trade; whether the existing European legislation in the area had improved matters or created new problems; and, finally, whether further legislative intervention was desirable and, if so, what form it should take. The answers given by the respondents are summarised here.

Three preliminary remarks have to be made in this context. First, in the majority of cases there were no marked national variances; the results for different Member States usually did not diverge strongly. Secondly, it was a recurring observation that figures for SMEs were not significantly different from those for major enterprises. Thirdly, the figures did not differ strongly between different industries. In all these categories some variations existed, but they were usually not profound and did not aggregate in obvious

---

[46] The final questionnaire is reprinted in Appendix B.
[47] See Appendix A.

patterns. Thus, in what follows, we will not break down all the results according to the location, size and core business activity of the respondent companies, but only highlight these factors in cases where notable differences existed.

With regard to current practices of trans-border trade, participants were asked about their attitudes when choosing the law to govern a contract. The ability to choose from different contract laws across Europe was seen as an advantage by almost two-thirds of the businesses, with strong national variations and major enterprises expressing a much stronger preference for the possibility of choice of law than SMEs.[48] When asked about the ability to choose the governing law without limiting this to the European context, 83% of the respondents thought this was 'important' to them when conducting cross-border transactions (see Table 2). As would be expected, most of the

Table 2: Importance of ability to choose the governing law when conducting cross-border transactions

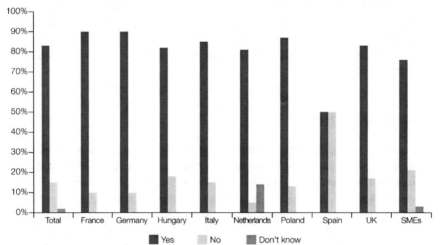

	Total	France	Ger-many	Hun-gary	Italy	Nether-lands	Poland	Spain	UK	SMEs
Yes	146 (83%)	27 (90%)	27 (90%)	14 (82%)	17 (85%)	17 (81%)	13 (87%)	6 (50%)	25 (83%)	26 (76%)
No	26 (15%)	3 (10%)	3 (10%)	3 (18%)	3 (15%)	1 (5%)	2 (13%)	6 (50%)	5 (17%)	7 (21%)
Don't know	3 (2%)	–	–	–	–	3 (14%)	–	–	–	1 (3%)

---

[48] 61% considered it to be an advantage (47% SMEs, 65% majors; only 38% in the Netherlands, 50% in the UK, 88% in Hungary), 33% (41% SMEs, 30% majors) did not.

respondents, namely two-thirds, preferred to choose their home law. However, that proportion varied considerably between different countries, ranging from 42% in Spain to 73% in France and up to 97% in the United Kingdom. It may be noted that both countries which had recently experienced a thorough reform of their contract laws, Germany and the Netherlands, scored below average, in the latter case particularly significantly (see Table 3).

More than four out of ten companies at least occasionally chose a foreign contract law because their local law was not suitable to achieve their aims (see Table 4).[49] When asked what law was used the most when conducting cross-border transactions, 'UK law' (for these purposes taken to mean English law) was mentioned by roughly a quarter of the respondents. It was chosen approximately two and a half times more frequently than any other law, no other country scoring more than 11% (France). Perhaps remarkably New York law was only said to be used in 1% of cross-border transactions; 2% referred to 'American law' (see Tables 5 and 6).[50] However, 41% of the respondents declared a willingness to choose a non-European law if no European law was suitable for their purpose (see Table 7). When asked which characteristics of contract law influenced their choice, most answered that a suitable contract law had to enable trade, and be predictable and fair. A

Table 3: Preferred choice of governing law when conducting cross-border transactions

	Total	France	Germany	Hungary	Italy	Netherlands	Poland	Spain	UK
Home law	115 (66%)	22 (73%)	19 (63%)	12 (71%)	11 (55%)	9 (43%)	8 (53%)	5 (42%)	29 (97%)
Other law	37 (21%)	4 (13%)	9 (30%)	3 (18%)	6 (30%)	8 (38%)	3 (29%)	3 (17%)	1 (3%)
Don't know/refused	23 (13%)	4 (13%)	2 (7%)	2 (12%)	3 (15%)	4 (19%)	4 (27%)	4 (33%)	–

[49] 17% (15% SMEs and 17% majors) do so 'often', 26% 'occasionally' (15% SMEs and 29% majors), 29% 'almost never', 21% 'never' (see Table 4).

[50] The most used laws were: UK 26%, France 11%, Germany 10%, Hungary 7%, Italy 6%, Poland 5%, the Netherlands 3% (see Table 5). There are two particularities to this result. First, an unusually high proportion of respondents to this question either did not know an answer (18%) or refused to give it (2%). Secondly, the result is obviously coloured by restricting the survey to companies from only eight Member States: if home choices are excluded only the figure for the UK remains constant; the others drop significantly (Germany 6%, France 1%), in most cases even to zero (see Table 6).

Table 4: Frequency of choosing foreign contract law because local law is not suitable to achieve aims

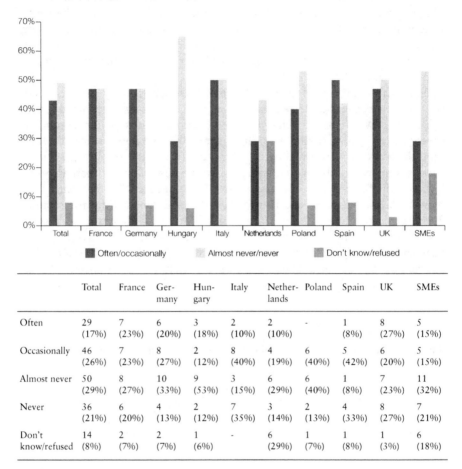

	Total	France	Germany	Hungary	Italy	Netherlands	Poland	Spain	UK	SMEs
Often	29 (17%)	7 (23%)	6 (20%)	3 (18%)	2 (10%)	2 (10%)	-	1 (8%)	8 (27%)	5 (15%)
Occasionally	46 (26%)	7 (23%)	8 (27%)	2 (12%)	8 (40%)	4 (19%)	6 (40%)	5 (42%)	6 (20%)	5 (15%)
Almost never	50 (29%)	8 (27%)	10 (33%)	9 (53%)	3 (15%)	6 (29%)	6 (40%)	1 (8%)	7 (23%)	11 (32%)
Never	36 (21%)	6 (20%)	4 (13%)	2 (12%)	7 (35%)	3 (14%)	2 (13%)	4 (33%)	8 (27%)	7 (21%)
Don't know/refused	14 (8%)	2 (7%)	2 (7%)	1 (6%)	-	6 (29%)	1 (7%)	1 (8%)	1 (3%)	6 (18%)

smaller number thought that it was important that the governing contract law be flexible, short and concise, or prescriptive.[51]

On the other hand, 42% of European businesses tended to avoid certain European jurisdictions because of their legal system. The countries named most frequently by those who occasionally avoid other contract laws were Italy (32%), France (23%), the UK (23%), Germany (16%), Spain (16%) and Greece (15%). The reasons given for this varied hugely. Some were very specific, such as 'the way in which liberation is handled in Germany,' but most

---

[51] Enable trade: 87%, predictable: 79%, fair: 78%, flexible: 66%, short and concise: 61%, prescriptive: 39%, other: 12% (based on all respondents who feel that choice of law is important when conducting cross-border transactions).

Table 5: Law most used when conducting cross-border transactions

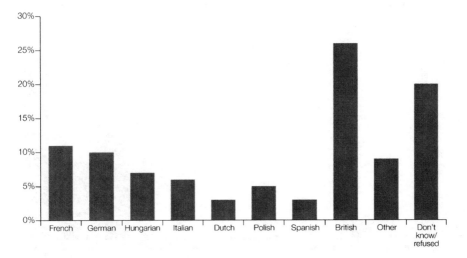

	Total	France	Ger-many	Hungary	Italy	Nether-lands	Poland	Spain	UK
French	19 (11%)	18 (60%)	–	–	1 (5%)	–	–	–	–
German	18 (10%)	–	13 (43%)	1 (6%)	–	1 (5%)	3 (20%)	–	–
Hungarian	12 (7%)	–	–	12 (71%)	–	–	–	–	–
Italian	11 (6%)	–	–	1 (6%)	10 (50%)	–	–	–	–
Dutch	6 (3%)	–	1 (3%)	–	–	5 (24%)	–	–	–
Polish	9 (5%)	–	–	–	–	–	9 (60%)	–	–
Spanish	5 (3%)	–	–	–	–	–	–	5 (42%)	–
British	45 (26%)	5 (17%)	6 (20%)	–	1 (5%)	8 (38%)	–	–	25 (83%)
Other	15 (9%)	2 (7%)	4 (13%)	1 (6%)	2 (10%)	2 (10%)	–	1 (8%)	3 (10%)
Don't know/refused	35 (20%)	5 (17%)	6 (20%)	2 (12%)	6 (30%)	5 (24%)	3 (20%)	6 (50%)	2 (7%)

were extremely vague, for instance the propositions that Belgian judges were 'too arbitrary,' that transactions and proceedings in Italy and Spain were 'too lengthy,' or that French law was 'too protectionist' and 'too focused on the

Table 6: Law most used when conducting cross-border transactions, excluding home choices

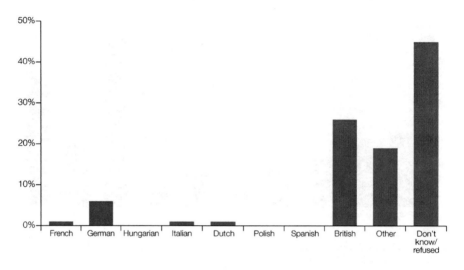

	Total (76)	France	Germany	Hungary	Italy	Nether-lands	Poland	Spain	UK
French	1 (1%)	n/a	–	–	1	–	–	–	–
German	5 (6%)	–	n/a	1	–	1	3	–	–
Hungarian	0	–	–	n/a	–	–	–	–	–
Italian	1	–	–	1	n/a	–	–	–	–
Dutch	1	–	1	–	–	n/a	–	–	–
Polish	0	–	–	–	–	–	n/a	–	–
Spanish	0	–	–	–	–	–	–	n/a	–
British	20 (26%)	5	6	–	1	8	–	–	n/a
Other	15 (20%)	2	4	1	2	2	–	1	3
Don't know/refused	35 (46%)	5	6	2	6	5	3	6	2

interest of their citizens.' Often the reasons given were coloured with a certain lack of knowledge, for example when a UK company declared that it avoided French and Italian law because 'they don't have a developed commercial law.' Quite revealingly, the reasons most frequently given for the avoidance of another jurisdiction's law were the extent to which it was

Table 7: Willingness to choose a law outside Europe if no European law was suitable for the specific purposes

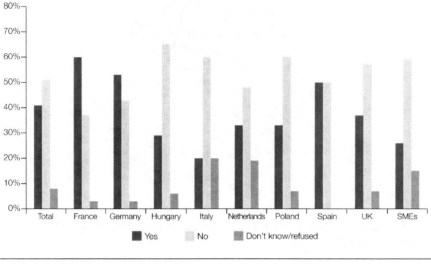

	Total	France	Ger-many	Hun-gary	Italy	Nether-lands	Poland	Spain	UK	SMEs
Yes	72 (41%)	18 (60%)	16 (53%)	5 (29%)	4 (20%)	7 (33%)	5 (33%)	6 (50%)	11 (37%)	9 (26%)
No	89 (51%)	11 (37%)	13 (43%)	11 (65%)	12 (60%)	10 (48%)	9 (60%)	6 (50%)	17 (57%)	20 (59%)
Don't know/refused	14 (8%)	1 (3%)	1 (3%)	1 (6%)	4 (20%)	4 (19%)	1 (7%)	–	2 (7%)	5 (15%)

'different' from their own jurisdiction's contract law and the unfamiliarity with the respective jurisdiction.

Given that businesses enjoy rather broad freedom to choose or to avoid particular domestic contract laws and that they frequently do so, does the existing divergence in national legal systems present an obstacle to cross-border trade at all? Almost two-thirds of European businesses experience 'some' (51%) or even 'large' (14%) obstacles to cross-border trade between Member States (see Figure 2 and Table 8).[52] But are these due to legal issues? We asked our respondents to rank seven factors which might impede their ability to conduct cross-border transactions. The list comprised both

[52] This experience was more widespread in Poland (80% having experienced 'large' or at least 'some' obstacles), Germany (77%) and the UK (74%) than in the Netherlands (62%), Hungary (59%), Spain (59%), France (57%) and Italy (50%) (see Table 8).

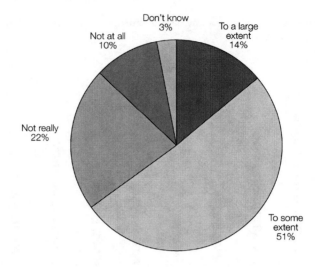

Figure 2: Extent to which obstacles to cross-border trade exist between EU Member States (1)

policy- and non-policy-induced obstacles, ie factors that can or cannot, in principle, be addressed by legislation. Five factors belonged to the first group: tax, variations between legal systems, the cost of obtaining foreign legal advice, the differences in implementation of European directives and bureau-cracy/corruption. They were seen as slightly more significant than the non-policy-induced obstacles listed, namely cultural differences and language (see Table 9). Thus it is clear that legal divergences have a comparably strong adverse impact on cross-border trade. However, these obstacles are generally not perceived to be insurmountable. As one respondent observed, in 'fringe areas, it might make a difference between whether a deal is viable or not, but it wouldn't get into the way of a lucrative deal.' Still, 10% of those who felt there were obstacles considered them to have a 'large' financial impact, 52% thought they had 'some' and 27% believed they had a 'minimal' financial impact on their organisation (see Table 10).[53] And more than a quarter of the companies perceiving such obstacles were 'often' (7%) or 'sometimes' (21%) deterred from conducting cross-border transactions (see Table 11).[54] More than four out of ten (43%) were 'not very often' deterred.

Given that variations between legal systems and the cost of obtaining foreign legal advice constitute obstacles to cross-border trade that are at least

---

[53] Taking into account those who thought that there were no obstacles, the overall number of those for whom these obstacles have 'large' or 'some' financial impact drops from 62% to 57%.

[54] Taking into account those who thought that there were no obstacles, the overall number of those who are 'often' or 'sometimes' deterred from cross-border trade drops from 28% to 25%.

Table 8: Extent to which obstacles to cross-border trade exist between EU Member States (2)

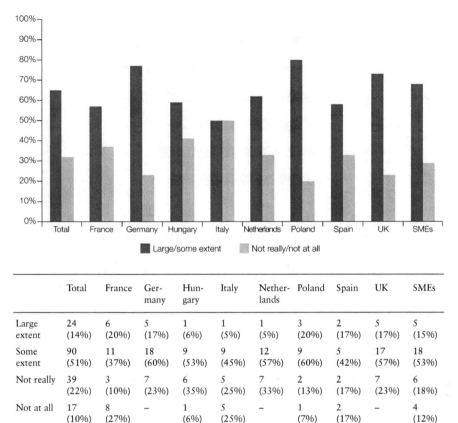

	Total	France	Ger-many	Hun-gary	Italy	Nether-lands	Poland	Spain	UK	SMEs
Large extent	24 (14%)	6 (20%)	5 (17%)	1 (6%)	1 (5%)	1 (5%)	3 (20%)	2 (17%)	5 (17%)	5 (15%)
Some extent	90 (51%)	11 (37%)	18 (60%)	9 (53%)	9 (45%)	12 (57%)	9 (60%)	5 (42%)	17 (57%)	18 (53%)
Not really	39 (22%)	3 (10%)	7 (23%)	6 (35%)	5 (25%)	7 (33%)	2 (13%)	2 (17%)	7 (23%)	6 (18%)
Not at all	17 (10%)	8 (27%)	–	1 (6%)	5 (25%)	–	1 (7%)	2 (17%)	–	4 (12%)
Don't know	5 (3%)	2 (7%)	–	–	–	1 (5%)	–	1 (8%)	1 (3%)	1 (3%)

not entirely insignificant, have the legislative measures enacted by the EC so far proved to be appropriate means to remove these obstacles? A huge majority of the businesses surveyed (59%) said that EU directives and regulations had indeed reduced obstacles to cross-border trade in Europe, whereas 8% considered that they had actually increased them. Over a quarter (29%) thought the legislative activities of the EU had made no difference (see Table 12).[55] But clearly, there is a feeling that the national bodies responsible for

[55] There were huge national variations in the answer to this question. In the UK and Poland, for instance, only 34% and 36% respectively said that the EU had reduced obstacles, whereas in Hungary and Italy the figures were 88% and 80%. This feeling was also not shared widely amongst SMEs (41%) (see Table 12).

Table 9: Factors impeding the ability to conduct cross-border transactions

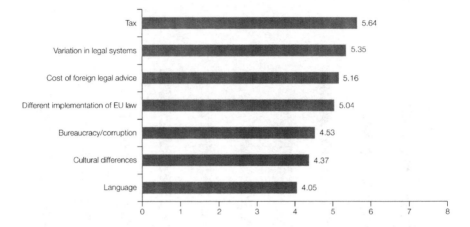

	Total (153)	France	Ger-many	Hun-gary	Italy	Nether-lands	Poland	Spain	UK	SMEs
Language	4.05 (2.62)	4.05 (2.54)	3.67 (2.34)	3.31 (3.16)	4.53 (2.77)	4.00 (2.49)	3.07 (2.46)	5.22 (2.44)	4.76 (2.68)	4.00 (2.58)
Variations between legal systems	5.35 (2.40)	5.55 (2.46)	6.20 (2.51)	4.88 (2.09)	5.67 (2.50)	4.79 (2.02)	5.08 (2.25)	4.89 (3.30)	5.07 (2.36)	5.48 (2.52)
Cultural dif-ferences	4.37 (2.19)	4.90 (2.00)	4.07 (2.07)	3.56 (2.42)	4.67 (2.26)	4.70 (2.13)	3.50 (1.65)	4.11 (2.47)	4.86 (2.40)	4.28 (2.83)
Differences in implementa-tion of EU directives	5.04 (2.29)	5.72 (2.89)	4.76 (2.42)	5.21 (2.05)	6.13 (1.36)	4.70 (2.32)	4.23 (2.24)	4.56 (2.56)	5.00 (2.07)	5.46 (2.50)
Bureaucracy/corruption	4.53 (2.55)	3.78 (2.82)	4.57 (2.37)	4.75 (2.46)	5.36 (2.50)	5.45 (2.69)	5.85 (2.76)	3.78 (2.59)	3.43 (1.95)	5.59 (2.95)
Cost of obtaining for-eign legal advice	5.16 (2.54)	5.35 (2.30)	6.13 (2.27)	3.47 (2.48)	6.47 (1.60)	4.56 (2.43)	5.82 (3.34)	5.00 (3.12)	4.41 (2.37)	5.48 (2.82)
Tax	5.64 (2.38)	6.18 (2.13)	6.70 (2.12)	4.81 (2.97)	5.33 (1.68)	6.06 (1.96)	5.00 (2.83)	4.67 (1.87)	5.18 (2.63)	4.89 (2.73)

implementing and applying directives could do better. Six out of ten respondents had experienced significant differences in the implementation and interpretation of directives across the Member States.[56] Almost two-thirds of

---

[56] Implementation: 15% 'very significant', 50% 'significant'; interpretation: 13% 'very significant', 45% 'significant'.

Table 10: Financial impact of obstacles to cross-border trade in the EU

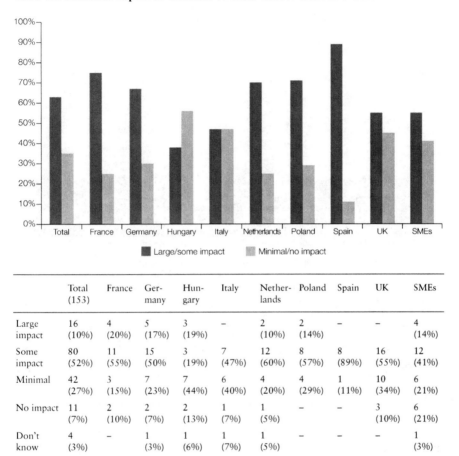

Large/some impact   Minimal/no impact

	Total (153)	France	Ger-many	Hun-gary	Italy	Nether-lands	Poland	Spain	UK	SMEs
Large impact	16 (10%)	4 (20%)	5 (17%)	3 (19%)	–	2 (10%)	2 (14%)	–	–	4 (14%)
Some impact	80 (52%)	11 (55%)	15 (50%	3 (19%)	7 (47%)	12 (60%)	8 (57%)	8 (89%)	16 (55%)	12 (41%)
Minimal	42 (27%)	3 (15%)	7 (23%)	7 (44%)	6 (40%)	4 (20%)	4 (29%)	1 (11%)	10 (34%)	6 (21%)
No impact	11 (7%)	2 (10%)	2 (7%)	2 (13%)	1 (7%)	1 (5%)	–	–	3 (10%)	6 (21%)
Don't know	4 (3%)	–	1 (3%)	1 (6%)	1 (7%)	1 (5%)	–	–	–	1 (3%)

those who had experienced such differences did not think that they impinged on their ability or desire to conduct cross-border trade. That still leaves approximately a third who are concerned by the issue, and even more so in Germany and in the UK.[57] One British respondent, for instance, maintained that 'basically, in some countries we have to change our trading patterns because of their interpretation/understanding of directives.' Another respondent claimed that such differences had caused his firm 'to restructure otherwise standard business models, principally in relation to the acquired

---

[57] Does not impinge: 64% (Germany 43%, UK 52%); does impinge: 31% (Germany 53%, UK 45%).

Table 11: Deterrence from conducting cross-border trade in the EU because of obstacles

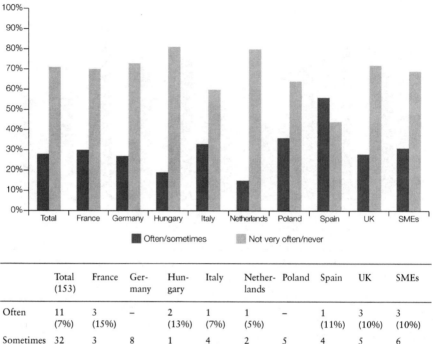

	Total (153)	France	Ger-many	Hun-gary	Italy	Nether-lands	Poland	Spain	UK	SMEs
Often	11 (7%)	3 (15%)	–	2 (13%)	1 (7%)	1 (5%)	–	1 (11%)	3 (10%)	3 (10%)
Sometimes	32 (21%)	3 (15%)	8 (27%)	1 (6%)	4 (27%)	2 (10%)	5 (36%)	4 (44%)	5 (17%)	6 (21%)
Not very often	66 (43%)	7 (35%)	9 (30%)	5 (31%)	6 (40%)	12 (60%)	9 (64%)	3 (33%)	15 (52%)	14 (48%)
Never	42 (27%)	7 (35%)	13 (43%)	8 (50%)	3 (20%)	4 (20%)	–	1 (11%)	6 (21%)	6 (21%)
Don't know	2 (1%)	–	–	–	1 (7%)	1 (5%)	–	–	–	–

rights directive and its different interpretation in France to the rest of Europe.'

Given that the existing state of European contract law does not seem to provide an adequate solution, are there any options for legislative activities by the Community which are more appropriate for eliminating any existing trade obstacles? The answer was an unequivocal 'Yes'. Some 83% of all businesses—and 88% of all SMEs—surveyed approved of the concept of a harmonised European contract law (see Table 13).[58] In some countries the

---

[58] To the question 'How favourably do you view the concept of a harmonised contract law?' 38% (SMEs: 41%) responded 'very favourably' and 45% (SMEs: 47%) responded 'favourably'.

Table 12: Impact of EU directives and regulations on cross-border transactions

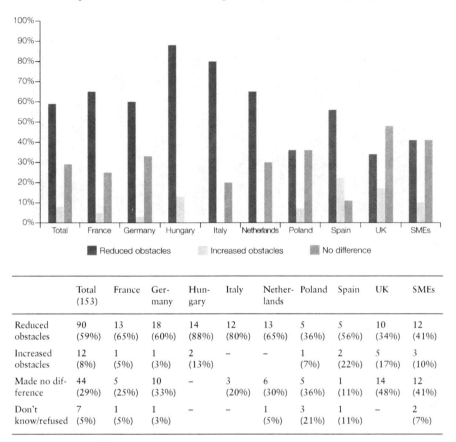

	Total (153)	France	Ger-many	Hun-gary	Italy	Nether-lands	Poland	Spain	UK	SMEs
Reduced obstacles	90 (59%)	13 (65%)	18 (60%)	14 (88%)	12 (80%)	13 (65%)	5 (36%)	5 (56%)	10 (34%)	12 (41%)
Increased obstacles	12 (8%)	1 (5%)	1 (3%)	2 (13%)	–	–	1 (7%)	2 (22%)	5 (17%)	3 (10%)
Made no dif-ference	44 (29%)	5 (25%)	10 (33%)	–	3 (20%)	6 (30%)	5 (36%)	1 (11%)	14 (48%)	12 (41%)
Don't know/refused	7 (5%)	1 (5%)	1 (3%)	–	–	1 (5%)	3 (21%)	1 (11%)	–	2 (7%)

figures were significantly higher, reaching 95% in Italy and 100% in Hungary. By far the least enthusiastic responses came from the UK, where 20% viewed the concept 'not at all favourably', but even there 64% of the businesses were positively predisposed towards the idea. Amongst industries, the services sector was markedly more sceptical than other areas, with only 67% being favourably disposed.

The question then arises as to how best to achieve a harmonised European contract law. When offered three choices, 38% opted for improvements on the basis of the status quo, namely for a more uniform implementation and interpretation of directives. This somewhat more conservative route was especially popular amongst French (50%) and UK (43%) businesses. Of all respondents, 28% favoured the option of having a European contract law in addition to the existing national contract laws. Finally, 30% advocated the bold step of introducing a European contract law that would replace national

Table 13: Disposition to the concept of a harmonised European contract law

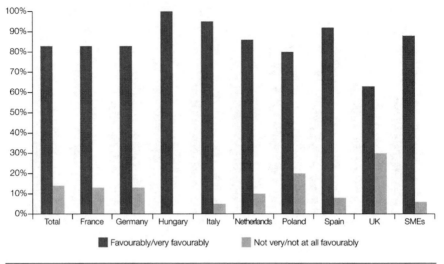

	Total	France	Ger-many	Hun-gary	Italy	Nether-lands	Poland	Spain	UK	SMEs
Very favour-ably	67 (38%)	11 (37%)	10 (33%)	8 (47%)	12 (60%)	5 (24%)	4 (27%)	9 (75%)	8 (27%)	14 (41%)
Favourably	79 (45%)	14 (47%)	15 (50%)	9 (53%)	7 (35%)	13 (62%)	8 (53%)	2 (17%)	11 (37%)	16 (47%)
Not very favourably	16 (9%)	3 (10%)	4 (13%)	–	1 (5%)	2 (10%)	2 (13%)	1 (8%)	3 (10%)	–
Not at all favourably	8 (5%)	1 (3%)	–	–	–	–	1 (7%)	–	6 (20%)	2 (6%)
Don't know	5 (3%)	1 (3%)	1 (3%)	–	–	1 (5%)	–	–	2 (7%)	2 (6%)

laws. This was, overall, the most favoured option amongst SMEs (38%, as opposed to 28% amongst majors), but it was the most unpopular route in the UK, where it was favoured by only 13% (see Table 14).

Clearly, as has been shown above, the introduction of a European contract law that replaces national contract laws is presently not on the Commission's agenda. However, in view of the Commission's thoughts on an 'optional instrument', the establishment of a European contract law in addition to existing national contract laws does not seem to be entirely unrealistic. If such a contract law were to be established, we asked, should it be mandatory or optional? Only a fifth of the respondents thought that it should be mandatory for all cross-border transactions. As opposed to this, 74% wanted some form of optionality. They were fairly evenly spread amongst those who favoured

Table 14: Preferred approach as to further harmonisation

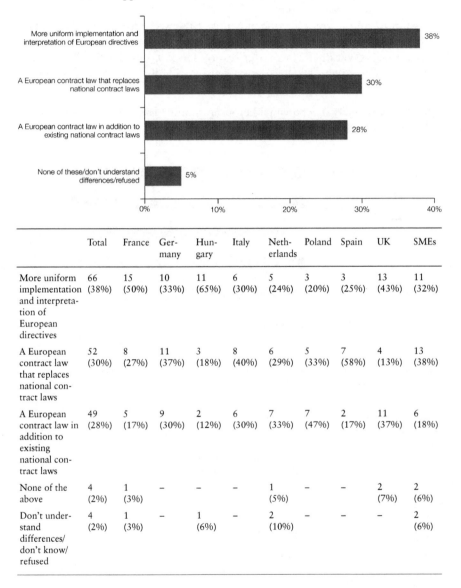

	Total	France	Ger-many	Hun-gary	Italy	Neth-erlands	Poland	Spain	UK	SMEs
More uniform implementation and interpretation of European directives	66 (38%)	15 (50%)	10 (33%)	11 (65%)	6 (30%)	5 (24%)	3 (20%)	3 (25%)	13 (43%)	11 (32%)
A European contract law that replaces national contract laws	52 (30%)	8 (27%)	11 (37%)	3 (18%)	8 (40%)	6 (29%)	5 (33%)	7 (58%)	4 (13%)	13 (38%)
A European contract law in addition to existing national contract laws	49 (28%)	5 (17%)	9 (30%)	2 (12%)	6 (30%)	7 (33%)	7 (47%)	2 (17%)	11 (37%)	6 (18%)
None of the above	4 (2%)	1 (3%)	–	–	–	1 (5%)	–	–	2 (7%)	2 (6%)
Don't under-stand differences/ don't know/ refused	4 (2%)	1 (3%)	–	1 (6%)	–	2 (10%)	–	–	–	2 (6%)

an additional regime for all cross-border transactions, be it with a possibility to opt in (21%) or to opt out (21%), and those who supported an additional regime for all contracts, cross-border and national, be it with a possibility to opt in (19%) or to opt out (13%) (see Table 15). These findings correspond with the general importance attached to the ability to choose the governing law of contract reported above.

Assuming an optional European contract law were to be established, how likely would European businesses be to use it in connection with cross-border transactions? Overall, 82% of the respondents would be 'likely' or 'very likely' to use it. Again, UK businesses were decidedly less enthusiastic (54%)

Table 15: Optionality of a potential European contract law to be established in addition to existing national contract laws

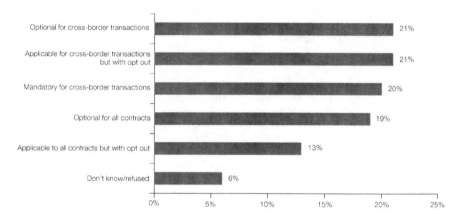

	Total	France	Ger-many	Hun-gary	Italy	Neth-erlands	Poland	Spain	UK	SMEs
Optional for all cross-border transactions	37 (21%)	6 (20%)	7 (23%)	3 (18%)	2 (10%)	5 (24%)	3 (20%)	3 (25%)	8 (27%)	8 (24%)
Applicable, in principle, for all cross-border transactions but with the option to opt out	37 (21%)	7 (23%)	6 (20%)	1 (6%)	5 (25%)	8 (38%)	2 (13%)	–	8 (27%)	9 (26%)
Mandatory for all cross-border transactions	35 (20%)	1 (3%)	10 (33%)	3 (18%)	3 (15%)	2 (10%)	5 (33%)	6 (50%)	5 (17%)	5 (15%)
Optional for all contracts	33 (19%)	8 (27%)	4 (13%)	7 (41%)	1 (5%)	–	3 (20%)	2 (17%)	8 (27%)	6 (18%)
Applicable, in principle, for all contracts with the option to opt out	23 (13%)	6 (20%)	1 (3%)	2 (12%)	8 (40%)	2 (10%)	2 (13%)	1 (8%)	1 (3%)	3 (9%)
Don't know/refused	10 (6%)	2 (7%)	2 (7%)	1 (6%)	1 (5%)	4 (19%)	–	–	–	3 (9%)

than their counterparts on the continent, notably in Poland (100%), Hungary (95%) and Italy (95%) (see Table 16). Incidentally, despite the widespread approval of an optional contract law in principle, there is strong scepticism as to whether it can be achieved in practice. Only 54% of the respondents thought that further harmonisation of contract law is achievable (see Table 17).

Obviously, the willingness to use an optional European contract law would very much depend on its scope and its quality. Final judgment on these matters can only be passed once a draft is on the table. It is, however, possible to gauge the expectations of the business community. If there were to be a European contract law it should, according to 57% of the respondents, be confined to general issues concerning all contracts. Eighteen per cent would

Table 16: Likelihood of making use of an optional European contract law for cross-border transactions

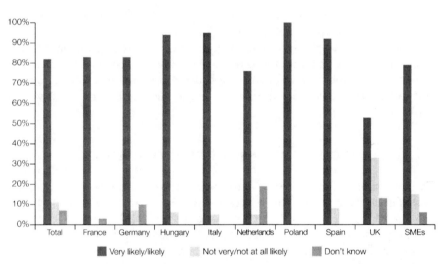

	Total	France	Ger-many	Hun-gary	Italy	Nether-lands	Poland	Spain	UK	SMEs
Very likely	59 (34%)	9 (30%)	9 (30%)	4 (24%)	12 (60%)	5 (24%)	7 (47%)	8 (67%)	5 (17%)	9 (26%)
Likely	84 (48%)	16 (53%)	16 (53%)	12 (71%)	7 (35%)	11 (52%)	8 (53%)	3 (25%)	11 (37%)	18 (53%)
Not very likely	16 (9%)	3 (10%)	2 (7%)	1 (6%)	1 (5%)	1 (5%)	–	1 (8%)	7 (23%)	4 (12%)
Not at all likely	4 (2%)	1 (3%)	–	–	–	–	–	–	3 (10%)	1 (3%)
Don't know	12 (7%)	1 (3%)	3 (10%)	–	–	4 (19%)	–	–	4 (13%)	2 (6%)

Table 17: Perspectives for achieving a harmonisation of European contract law

	Total	France	Germany	Hungary	Italy	Netherlands	Poland	Spain	UK	SMEs
Very achievable	16 (9%)	–	8 (27%)	2 (12%)	–	3 (14%)	–	2 (17%)	1 (3%)	2 (6%)
Achievable	78 (45%)	16 (53%)	10 (33%)	11 (65%)	14 (70%)	8 (38%)	10 (67%)	1 (8%)	8 (27%)	18 (53%)
Not very achievable	58 (33%)	11 (37%)	11 (37%)	4 (24%)	4 (20%)	6 (29%)	5 (33%)	3 (25%)	14 (47%)	9 (26%)
Not at all achievable	15 (9%)	1 (3%)	–	–	1 (5%)	–	–	6 (50%)	7 (23%)	2 (6%)
Don't know	8 (5%)	2 (7%)	1 (3%)	–	1 (5%)	4 (19%)	–	–	–	3 (9%)

like it to contain rules on specific contracts as well, and another 18% wished it also comprised rules in other areas of law which are closely related to contract law. As to the substance of individual provisions, European businesses have a mix of expectations that are not always easy to reconcile. They want their contract law, in decreasing order of importance, to enable trade and to be fair, predictable, short and concise, flexible and prescriptive (see Table 18).[59]

V. CONCLUSIONS: WHERE TO GO NEXT

To summarise our findings: European businesses enjoy far-reaching possibilities of choosing the contract law most applicable to a particular cross-border transaction, and they make ample opportunity of this. It is certainly not impossible or even unduly burdensome to engage in cross-border trade in the internal market. However, two-thirds of companies face costly obstacles to trading with others in a different jurisdiction. A major reason for this is the existence of different legal systems. As a result, roughly a quarter of all businesses are effectively deterred from cross-border trade. The piecemeal approach hitherto adopted towards harmonisation in the area of contract law is not perceived to be an effective remedy: almost two-thirds of European businesses have experienced divergences amongst various Member States in the implementation and interpretation of directives, and a third of that group felt that these impinged on their ability or desire to conduct cross-border trade. Thus, we would submit, a case can be made for further Community action in the field of European contract law on the basis of Article 95 EC.

[59] The results thus widely mirror those reported in n 51.

Table 18: Factors making for a good law of contract

	Total	France	Germany	Hungary	Italy	Netherlands	Poland	Spain	UK	SMEs
Fair	8.50	8.00	9.03	7.47	8.75	8.05	9.60	7.73	8.93	8.75
	(2.09)	(2.52)	(1.35)	(2.40)	(1.62)	(2.14)	(1.30)	(2.65)	(2.03)	(1.72)
Predictable	8.21	8.07	8.87	7.76	7.28	7.89	9.60	6.08	8.83	8.12
	(2.00)	(1.44)	(1.91)	(2.46)	(1.97)	(1.49)	(1.30)	(3.32)	(1.05)	(2.50)
Short and concise	7.59	8.40	7.60	8.12	7.95	7.25	8.13	6.75	6.53	8.48
	(2.18)	(1.55)	(2.01)	(1.65)	(1.64)	(2.22)	(2.48)	(2.80)	(2.61)	(1.81)
Flexible	6.62	6.59	6.87	7.53	6.40	6.30	6.47	6.00	6.59	6.82
	(2.32)	(2.50)	(2.40)	(2.18)	(2.42)	(2.08)	(2.56)	(2.22)	(2.21)	(2.46)
Prescriptive	5.94	6.05	5.33	5.65	7.74	6.30	4.60	6.25	5.80	6.22
	(2.37)	(1.99)	(2.62)	(2.29)	(1.73)	(2.20)	(2.38)	(1.60)	(2.59)	(2.28)
Enable trade	8.60	8.87	8.93	9.06	8.60	7.35	9.53	6.75	8.83	8.64
	(1.76)	(1.28)	(1.80)	(1.14)	(1.47)	(2.06)	(0.92)	(2.67)	(1.49)	(1.85)

As to the way ahead, a surprising 83% of businesses view the concept of a harmonised contract law favourably.[60] In order to achieve this, the solution favoured by a small margin is an improvement in the implementation and interpretation of existing directives. However, taken together, almost six out of ten respondents would like to see a more comprehensive European contract law, either substituting existing national contract laws or in addition to them. But businesses would like to retain the freedom to choose another, more suitable law. So if a European contract law were to be established alongside national contract regimes, only 20% would like it to be mandatory for all cross-border transactions. If they were offered the choice of an optional European contract law, 82% of European companies believe they would be likely to use it at some stage. Thus it seems inevitable to conclude that the 'way forward' proposed by the Commission in 2004 is, in principle, met with approval by the business community: European business wants an improvement in the implementation and interpretation of the existing directives, and the suggested qualitative improvement of the *acquis* would certainly help to

---

[60] This result was reaffirmed by a straw poll of 200 UK companies conducted by the British In-House Lawyers' Association (IHLA), a newly formed breakaway group from the established Commerce & Industry Group (C&I), in March 2005. The organisation favours a single contract law for the European market, arguing that businesses do not want to obtain 25 different legal opinions when one will do. It emailed a background note outlining its views to its members and asked for their reactions. An overwhelming majority of the respondents backed greater contract law harmonisation. Only one of the 200 in-house counsel objected, assuming that a European contract law which, he assumed, would probably be based on continental principles would provide less legal certainty than English contract law. However, the result has to be treated with care: the straw poll was relatively informal, the background note was extremely short and it only presented arguments in favour of harmonisation. We are grateful to Anthony Armitage, IHLA Chairman, for providing us with information on the poll.

this effect. Furthermore, European business has a strong interest in having an optional instrument at its disposal and it would be highly likely to use it; the elaboration of a CFR is certainly a useful step into this direction (albeit not the only option; other possibilities might well be imagined).

So far, the Commission has justified the elaboration of the CFR as a necessary condition for the improvement of the *acquis*. To many observers, especially in Britain, this seemed implausible, far-fetched and, ultimately, slightly disingenuous. In the future, on the basis of our survey's findings, it will be possible to justify the project as a useful step towards a possible optional instrument which in turn can be presented as *one* possibility to overcome obstacles to cross-border trade. Thus the Commission, moving on its 'way forward' announced in 2004, seems to be on the right track.[61]

Accordingly our survey lends a degree of support to the Commission's initiatives. We believe that the survey advances the quality of the debate, and we present it in that spirit. However, we admit openly that it does not conclude it. Our sample of 175 companies from eight Member States clearly is not one from which one could deduce with complete confidence the opinion of 'European business'. Results for Spain, for example, have to be treated with caution as they are based on only 12 respondents. As opposed to this, the 2002 survey of European companies referred to above[62] was based on nearly 200 interviews per Member State. Furthermore, our sample is not in line with the distribution of enterprises by size in Europe: there are 85% small, 12% medium and under 3% large businesses in the EU. However, according to the experts working for the consultancy which conducted the survey, the overall conclusions are unusually consistent and thus relatively robust. The results of our survey, despite its relatively modest sample size, gain further credibility as it is the first such survey to be conducted without any involvement of the Commission. Moreover, Clifford Chance had voiced strong scepticisms about the Commission's initiatives in 2003,[63] and the academic advisors would not consider themselves to be uncritical enthusiasts of the Commission's proposals either. In short, we cannot but be persuaded that the accumulated objective evidence is more supportive of the Commission's activities than we had expected.

It is also pertinent to note the questions we did *not* ask. We did not, for instance, include a question on the respondents' attitudes towards the CFR. And we constantly referred to 'cross-border transactions' without distinguishing B2B and B2C transactions. Furthermore, we did not touch upon business attitudes to the inclusion and the status of mandatory, rather than

---

[61] However, it clearly has to step up its efforts at informing businesses: prior to being contacted for the purposes of the survey, only 61% of the respondents had been aware that the Commission is currently looking into various levels of harmonisation of European contract law, ranging from only 8% in Spain to 73% in the UK.

[62] Flash Eurobarometer 128, above n 37.

[63] Cf n 43.

non-mandatory, rules in an optional instrument. More broadly, in drafting a manageable questionnaire, we chose not to ask questions about the potential negative consequences of introducing a European contract law, such as adjustment or transition costs, although ample reference was made to these in the background note sent out before the telephone interviews were conducted; incidentally, in this vein, we were intrigued to note that, although this issue must have been on the mind of the German respondents who had just undergone a similarly painful process with the introduction of a new law of obligations in 2002, German companies remained as favourably disposed towards an EU contract law as the average of all countries surveyed (83% 'favourable' or 'very favourable'). No survey can be fully comprehensive, and suffice it to say that the questions of our survey were much more comprehensive and much more attuned to the current debate than those asked in the aforementioned 2002 survey of European companies.[64]

Let us finally acknowledge that, even if businesses unanimously wished to have a uniform contract law, this does not mean that it has to be given to them. If asked, they would probably also want to have zero taxes and the lowest possible standards of consumer protection. There may be valid reasons, in the interests of consumers and society as a whole (or, in this case, societies as a whole), not to go ahead with further harmonisation. These will have to be assessed and balanced as the political process towards a European contract law unfolds. This will be a complex exercise, embracing appreciation of the potentially competing values of diversity, local autonomy, coherence and uniformity in Europe and in European law, all of which is way beyond the scope of this chapter. However, it should have now become clear that it is impossible to deny this process any constitutional legitimacy from the outset.

[64] Flash Eurobarometer 128, above n 37.

APPENDIX A: BACKGROUND INFORMATION

The following background note was sent to those who had indicated their willingness to participate in the survey. It was meant to give them an opportunity to reflect on the key issues before being interviewed over the telephone.

A European Contract Law?

The EU is taking tentative steps that could eventually lead to a European contract law. Is this the direction in which the users of contract law, such as financial institutions and other companies, both big and small, want to move?

Introduction

The EU's traditional approach to law reform has been sectoral, ie it has identified particular problems and legislated to cure them (eg commercial agents, late payments and doorstep selling). However, since 1989 the European Parliament has passed a series of resolutions arguing that the single internal market required the harmonisation of all civil law across the EU. In 2001, the Commission responded with a consultation paper on the possible harmonisation of contract law rather than civil law as a whole.

The Commission asked whether different national contract laws really did obstruct the functioning of the internal market by, for example, increasing costs, giving a competitive advantage to suppliers in the home state or discouraging consumers or small businesses from undertaking cross-border transactions through ignorance of foreign legal systems. The Commission also asked whether existing EU legislation in the area of contract law was satisfactory.

If problems were identified in these areas, the Commission suggested four possible remedies. First, do nothing. Second, promote the development of common European contract law principles in the hope that they would be useful to those drafting contracts and, perhaps, lead to the creation of a customary law. Third, improve the quality of existing EU legislation. Fourth, adopt new comprehensive legislation, ultimately a set of rules which would replace national laws.

The Commission's Action Plan

In February 2003, the Commission published a paper, entitled *A More Coherent European Contract Law—An Action Plan*. This recorded the problems caused by differences in national contract law identified by its respondents. These included, for example, differing approaches to the transfer of property in moveable goods and securities, to reservation of title, to assignments of receivables, and to insurance contracts. The Commission also set out the reaction to its four possible remedies. The first, do nothing, met with little support. The overwhelming majority supported the Commission's third proposal, to improve EU legislation. There was also 'considerable support' for the Commission's second proposal, to develop common principles of European contract law, but a majority was against the fourth, a comprehensive European contract law.

The Commission's solution was to accept the need to improve the EU's existing legislation but also to say that this improvement required the creation of a 'common frame of reference [CFR], establishing common principles and terminology in the area of European contract law'.

In a further paper, published in October 2004, the Commission said that the CFR will provide definitions of legal terms, fundamental principles, and coherent model rules of contract law, drawing on the EU's existing legislation in this area and on the best solutions from the member states. This paper said that the CFR could cover the requirement of good faith, pre-contractual obligations, the definition of a contract, how a contract is concluded, the interpretation of contracts, terms, performance, remedies, assignment and prescription, as well as specific contracts like sale of goods and insurance.

The Commission also commented that there may be problems arising from the different interactions between contract and property law in the Member States, and those preparing the CFR would need to consider how to resolve these problems.

The Commission is in the process of appointing academic research groups to prepare the CFR. These groups will include the Study Group on a European Civil Code and another group which will consider insurance law. The groups are proposing to hold some 32 workshops over the next three years with the Commission's 'stakeholder experts'—representatives of business and consumer groups, practising lawyers, and others who have expressed an interest—on topics such as service contracts, insurance law, pre-contractual obligations, notion/functions of contract, unfair terms, good faith, assignment, loan agreements and other financial services, security rights in movables, and e-commerce. Shortly before each workshop the researchers will distribute drafts on the topics, which will then be discussed.

The researchers' work is expected to be completed by the end of 2007, at which point the Commission will consider whether the product meets its needs. These needs include helping to improve the EU's existing legislation on contract law, but also extend to assisting arbitrators in finding unbiased and balanced solutions to resolve conflicts between contracting parties, the development of a possible optional instrument of EU contract law, incorporation into Commission contracts, and inspiring the European Court of Justice when faced with contractual issues.

Parallel with the preparation of the CFR, the Commission intends to continue its reflections on whether an optional instrument of EU contract law is needed. The Commission was keen to stress in its most recent paper that 'it is [not] the Commission's intention to propose a "European civil code" which would harmonise contract laws of the Member States.' It reports that most of those who have responded to its papers favour an opt-in instrument, rather than one requiring the parties to opt out.

Is a European Contract Law Necessary?

Contract law does not exist in an ivory tower. It is a practical tool regulating the circumstances in which one party can enforce a bargain made with another. These bargains are fundamental to commercial activity. Ultimately it is for consumers of the law—the businesses big and small, as well as individuals, who make bargains—to determine whether a European contract law would serve their purposes better than individual national laws or would provide a valuable additional tool. The only way to find out what the consumers of law want or need is to ask them. That is the purpose of the survey Clifford Chance has commissioned.

It may be that a single contract law for Europe would, for example, reduce transaction costs and avoid differences in the implementation of existing EU legislation. The rules for choosing what law governs a contract are set out in a EU treaty (the Rome Convention), and it might be a logical step to bring substantive contract law within a European framework. Even if national laws remain, an additional, neutral, contract law might in itself be valuable.

On the other hand, a single contract law, whether in addition to or as a substitution for national laws, might be a disproportionate reaction. For example, England and Scotland have distinct contract laws, as do individual states in the USA, but there is no evidence that this obstructs trade within the UK or the USA. The process of change may also impose costs out of proportion to any gain. If a European law is in addition to existing national laws, any unpredictability in the results it offers law might mean that parties never choose it.

Finally, the content of any European contract law cannot be ignored. France codified its contract law in 1804, Germany did so in 1900 (and has recently completed a significant review) and the Netherlands has just finished a major revision of its code. There are significant differences in style and approach between these codes and other codes, and still further differences between these and the common law systems of England and Ireland. Harmonisation of European contract law might in principle remove obstructions within the single market, but will a sufficient majority of users consider the new law to be better than the old law they were used to? Is competition between legal systems the best way to ensure that the needs of users are met?

The Survey

The purpose of our survey is to find out what the users of contract law think of the direction in which the European Commission is proposing to go. If the different contract laws within the EU do obstruct business, it is a powerful reason for change; but if it is not so, then the European Commission should direct its energies into other areas.

The European Commission's publications on this matter, and many of the responses it has received, can be found at: http://europa.eu.int/comm/ consumers/cons_int/ safe_shop/fair_bus_pract/cont_law/index_en.htm

APPENDIX B: QUESTIONNAIRE

The following questionnaire was used for the telephone interviews conducted mostly in late January and early February 2005. Unless otherwise indicated questions were put to all respondents.

Harmonisation of European Contract Law

This survey aims to gain your reaction to the European Commission's thoughts on the potential harmonisation of European contract law and other options for an EU contribution to the development of contract law.

General Awareness

1. Prior to receiving the introduction e-mail, were you aware that the European Commission is looking into various levels of harmonisation of European contract law?

Obstacles to Cross-Border Trade

2. To what extent do obstacles to cross-border trade exist between the European Union member states?

   a. To a large extent

   b. To some extent

   c. Not really

   d. Not at all

3. How much do the following factors impact on your ability to conduct cross-border transactions?[65] *(Please rate on a scale of 1–10, where 1 is no impact and 10 is a high impact)*
   — Language
   — Variations between legal systems
   — Cultural differences
   — Differences in implementation of EU directives
   — Bureaucracy/corruption
   — Cost of obtaining foreign legal advice
   — Tax
   — Other_____

4. How much of a financial impact do these obstacles have on your organisation?
   a. Large impact
   b. Some impact
   c. Minimal impact
   d. No impact

5. How often do the obstacles and their financial impact deter you from conducting cross-border transactions?
   a. Often
   b. Sometimes
   c. Not very often
   d. Never

6. In your opinion, how have EU directives and regulation affected cross-border transactions in Europe? *(Would you say that EU directives have . . .)*
   a. Reduced obstacles to cross-border trade
   b. Increased obstacles to cross-border trade
   c. Made no difference

Implementation of EU Directives

I want to ask you about the way EU directives are implemented and interpreted across member states.

---

[65] Base for questions 3–12: all who think that there are obstacles to cross-border trade.

7. First, in your experience, how significant are differences in *implementation* of EU directives across member states?

   a. Very significant

   b. Significant

   c. Not very significant

   d. Not at all significant

8. Secondly, how significant are differences in *interpretation* of EU directives across member states?

   a. Very significant

   b. Significant

   c. Not very significant

   d. Not at all significant

9. How, if at all, do these differences in the implementation and interpretation impinge on your ability or desire to conduct cross-border trade?

   _____
   _____
   _____
   _____

10. In which countries does this present the most significant problems?

    _____
    _____
    _____

What Makes for Good Contract Law

11. How important do you feel the following factors are in developing good contract law? *(Please rate how important these factors are in developing good contract law, where 1 is not important and 10 is very important).* The law should be...

    — Fair

    — Predictable

    — Short and concise

    — Flexible

    — Prescriptive

    — Enable trade

    — Other_____

Choice of Governing Law

12. When conducting cross-border transactions, what is your preferred choice of governing law?

13. Overall, which law is the most used when conducting cross-border transactions?

14. Is the ability to choose from different contract laws across Europe an advantage?

15. How often do you choose a foreign contract law as the governing law because the local law is not suitable to achieve your aims?[66]

    a. Often

    b. Occasionally

    c. Almost never

    d. Never

16. Are there any jurisdictions in Europe that you tend to avoid because of their legal system?

17. Which countries are they?[67]

18. Why do you tend to avoid those jurisdictions?

    _____
    _____
    _____
    _____

19. If no European law was suitable for your purposes, would you choose a law outside Europe that was?

20. When conducting cross-border transactions, is it important to you to be able to choose the governing law?

21. If yes, what factors influence your choice? The governing law has to be...[68]

    — Fair

    — Predictable

    — Short and concise

---

[66] Base for questions 15 and 16: all who feel that differences in implementation and/or interpretation are at least to some extent significant.

[67] Base for questions 17 and 18: all who tend to avoid jurisdictions in Europe because of their legal system.

[68] Base for question 21: all who feel that it is important to be able to choose the governing law when conducting cross-boder transactions.

— Flexible
— Prescriptive
— Enable trade
— Other_____

Would Harmonisation be a Good Thing?

22. How favourably do you view the concept of a harmonised European contract law?

a. Very favourably

b. Favourably

c. Not very favourably

d. Not at all favourably

(If not very/not at all, why not?)

_____
_____
_____
_____

23. Would you prefer:

a. A European contract law that replaces national contract laws

b. A European contract law in addition to existing national contract laws

c. More uniform implementation and interpretation of European directives

d. None of the above

e. Don't understand the difference/can't answer

(If none of the above, why not?)

_____
_____
_____
_____

24. If a European contract law was to be established in addition to existing
national contract laws, would you prefer it to be:

a. Optional for all contracts

b. Optional for all cross-border transactions

c. Mandatory for all cross-border transactions

d. Applicable, in principle, for all contracts with the option to opt out

e. Applicable, in principle, for all cross-border transactions with the option to opt out

25. If there was to be a European contract law, should it contain rules:

a. On general issues concerning all contracts *(formation, interpretation, third party rights, etc)*

b. On specific contracts *(sale, lease, insurance, etc)*

c. On areas of law closely related to contract *(transfer of title, securities, unjust enrichment, etc)*

26. In your perception, how achievable is a harmonisation of European contract law?

a. Very achievable

b. Achievable

c. Not very achievable

d. Not at all achievable

27. If an optional European contract law were to be established, how likely would you be to use it in connection with cross-border transactions?

a. Very likely

b. Likely

c. Not very likely

d. Not at all likely

8

Harmonisation of and Codification in European Contract Law

GUIDO ALPA

I. CONTRACT LAW BETWEEN GENERAL AND SPECIAL RULES

The process of convergence left up to the 'natural' evolution of legal systems in European countries is very slow and its results are only empirically perceptible. As for classifications, the situation seems replete with difficulties, given the differences among national cultures.

Comparison teaches us many things, above all to assume that terminology and categories are marked by a high degree of relativity—relativity of meaning and relativity of aspects relating to both time and function. If we just briefly consider, by way of example, the French experience and the British experience, which may be taken as sufficiently significant models, we will find categories similar, analogous or functionally comparable to our own. In those countries as well, jurists either proceed as if nothing had happened, and thus think about 'adapting' existing categories to new needs, or else they, too, wonder about their destiny; or perhaps they do not even concern themselves with the systematic problem, but rather concentrate on adhering to the reality as it evolves, which leads them to put aside questions of a more dogmatic nature, following the flow of economic relations.

In delineating the characteristics of *Droit privé européen* during a conference organised a few years ago by the Centre de recherche en droit des affaires of the Université de Reims-Champagne-Ardenne,[1] Christophe Jamin assumed 'European' contract law to be a phenomenon regarding only general rules on the contract per se, though his study was aimed at ascertaining the existence of a European law relating to contracts. In any event, his conclusion was negative, in the sense that, notwithstanding the transplantations, circulation of models and shared solutions for some problems, the national character of systems is so strong that just raising the issue of European

---

[1] Under the direction of Pascal de Vareilles-Sommières (Paris, Economica, 1998).

contract law seems to reflect wishful thinking rather than confidence in a realisable project.[2] What is more, he argued that derived EC law, ie the complex of rules imposed by the European Community through its directives, not only leaves ample margins and many gaps, but also ends up playing a much more limited, less ambitious role, which consists simply in circulating ideas and bringing national experiences closer together. Even the planning of a 'restatement' of common principles of contract law appeared to him to be a merely cosmetic operation, which, given the flexibility of the terms and concepts used, would not be able to lend the certainty that specialists needed. In the same context, Richard Crone, for his own part, focused on international private law, the only body of rules that needed to be taken as a basis in order to achieve a more substantial, reliable harmonisation.[3]

Those who describe the regulation of civil and commercial contracts (corresponding to the bipolarity of codes) venture into a more complex subject. Here it is noted that the different stages marking French history as regards the general and specific rules on contracts have caused interpreters to reject the initial classifications and adopt new ones. In this regard, François Collart Dutilleul and Philippe Delebecque observe that the common rules to be observed in all agreements, as established by the Napoleonic Code—which also reflected the influence of canonical doctrine—are no longer judged valid by contemporary jurists because in France a transition had been made from the general law of contract to the law of 'très speciaux' contracts; in addition, two opposite trends have manifested themselves: the general law has become more specialised, whereas special law has become more generalised. This is due to the existence of new sources, the creative power of jurisprudence and the intervention of independent administrative authorities, so that today 'la catégorie des contrats commerciaux n'existe pas en tant que telle.'[4]

French jurists who have directly addressed the problem of a European codification of contracts appear less hasty to rule out the possibility of a solution. But here as well a priority is placed on analysing problems relating to contracts in general rather than those involving special contracts. This choice is not, however, shared by everyone. Now not only is the classification of contracts coming under challenge, but also the very foundation of a general contract theory.[5]

British jurists offer a more concrete analysis of the impact of EC law on commercial law.[6] Here, with reference to the regulation of 'commercial'

---

[2] C Jamin, 'Un droit européen des contrats?' in P de Vareilles-Sommières (ed), *Le droit privé européen* (Paris, Economica, 1998) 47.

[3] R Crone, 'Problèmes pratiques des contrats européens' in de Vareilles-Sommières, *ibid*, 61.

[4] F Collart Dutilleul and Ph Delebecque, *Contrats civils et commerciaux* (Paris, Dalloz, 1996) 20.

[5] E Savaux, *La théorie générale du contrat, mythe ou réalité?* (Paris, LGDJ, 1997).

[6] C Quigley (ed), *Droit communautaire des contrats* (The Hague, Kluwer Law International, 1998).

contracts, a description is given of all the problems related to payments, the rules of competition and the rules for individual economic transactions, with particular emphasis on distribution agreements. On the other hand, we all know that in the common law the distinction between contracts in general and special contracts, between civil law and commercial law, is based upon criteria very different from our own: it is empirical and concrete, shuns classifications, and above all rebuffs every attempt at systematisation.

There are still those who hold the opinion, which in some eyes appears old-fashioned, that it is possible to formulate a general description of contract rules.[7] This view has, however, come under criticism, since the status of the contracting parties is by no means irrelevant to the issue of uniform regulation.[8]

But we also find something new on the opposite front, with respect to consumer contracts. The social ambitions that had driven the first initiatives for directives designed to protect the economic interests of consumers have been abandoned within the European Community framework. Consumer law now seems oriented toward protecting citizens as such, and many rules derived from fragments of law pertaining to individual contract types have ended up being extended to all contract relationships. This has led many jurists to envisage the development of a single European civil code governing all relationships, irrespective of the status of the parties.[9] On the other hand, the push to harmonise national rules in the consumer sector has been taken by some as a negative sign of where EC law is headed, since harmonisation at the highest level stifles national identities, the adoption of general principles and clauses undermines the certainty of law, and reliance on self-regulation ends up accentuating rather than reducing differences in status.[10]

In short, again invoking the theory of relativity as regards legal categories and contract classification, it would seem that distinguishing between contracts between professionals, on the one hand, and contracts between professionals and consumers, on the other hand, does not provide a solution. The distinction may be justified only as long as the regulation of contracts belonging to the two categories pursues different purposes, but it is destined to disappear once the rules converge.

In the meantime, however, another distinction has been added regarding the sources. That is, a distinction is made between contracts regulated by provisions that influence the freedom of negotiation and contracts that allow

---

[7] See, eg E McKendrick, *Contract Law* (6th edn, Basingstoke, Palgrave Macmillan, 2005).

[8] R Brownsword, *Contract Law. Themes for the Twenty-first Century* (London, Butterworths, 2000).

[9] H Micklitz, 'De la nécessité d'une nouvelle conception pour le développement du droit de la consommation dans la Communauté européenne' in *Mélanges en l'honneur de Jean Calais-Auloy* (Paris, Dalloz, 2004) 725.

[10] G Howells and T Wilhelmsson, 'EC Consumer Law: Has it Come of Age?' (2003) 28 *EL Rev* 370.

ample space for private autonomy. In the latter case, the parties are free to decide the contents, methods, times, formation etc of their agreements; in the former case they must follow the models devised by third parties, who may be legislators (national and European), administrative authorities (national and European) or trade associations with their codes of conduct, collective bargaining agreements or ethic codes.

II. FREEDOM OF CONTRACT AND MARKET REGULATION

We now come to the central issue: the relationship between negotiating autonomy and market regulation. This is a subject that Hugh Collins dealt with in a brilliant and acute manner a few years ago. The chosen perspective considers precisely the new techniques for regulating contracts. The conclusion of his investigation may be summed up in a few phrases. Collins reports that 'private' law—construed, according to its traditional meaning, as the reign of free will, not subject to outside intervention—is progressively losing ground to 'public' law; he also draws attention to the normative construction of markets and the increasingly broad role of the authorities involved in this process.[11] His argument is based upon the premise that no market, even if it is free or may become so, can do without rules—a subject that Natalino Irti has repeatedly invited us to reflect upon—or ignore personal values. This subject is also highly familiar to Italian jurists, so familiar that it requires no further examination or remarks, though we should at least mention the contributions of Giorgio Oppo and Pietro Rescigno, Massimo Bianca, Adolfo di Majo, Giovanni B Ferri, Nicolò Lipari, Pietro Perlingieri and Stefano Rodotà, as well as the contributions of all those colleagues who, as authors of recent essays on contracts, defenders of civil rights, proponents of the values of equity and solidarity or theorists of so-called contract justice, have addressed this problem and suggested solutions.

From this perspective as well, however, many things have changed. Just 10 years ago, when presenting some publications on commercial contracts, bearing the more analytic title of *I contratti del commercio, dell'industria e del mercato finanziario*,[12] Franco Galgano ventured to observe that

> the principal tool of juridical innovation today is the contract. Classic conceptions of law do not include the contract among normative sources; but if we were to continue conceiving the contract as a mere application of law, and not as a source of new law, we would deny ourselves the possibility of understanding how law changes in our own times.[13]

---

[11] H Collins, *Regulating Contract* (Oxford University Press, 1999).
[12] (Turin, Utet, 1995).
[13] F Galgano, above n 12, xxvii.

The emergence of non-typical contracts, international practices and the new *lex mercatoria*—added Galgano—have endowed the business community with the power to set itself up as the 'sovereign ruler', of which national states 'become the secular arm': in other words, the rules of contracts—and of commercial contracts above all—are transmitted and implemented through contractual models.

Today, however, we seem to be witnessing a reversal in the trend: not only has the protection of consumer and investor interests required *ab externo* intervention, but even some of the contracts typically left up to free negotiation between entrepreneurs have fallen subject to the imposition, *ab externo*, of models, contents and rules limiting negotiating autonomy, as they express a different conception of the contract relationship. Contract relationships, though innovative, no longer depend on the free determination of the parties, but are rather subordinated to rules from different legislative, administrative and ethical sources, in a context characterised by an increasingly extensive regulatory framework. The interests underlying a contract, regardless of the parties' status, are no longer only 'private', but must rather conform to the needs of the community, even if it is made up exclusively of businessmen.

This state of affairs generates complexity and uncertainty, and will continue to do so at least as long as the two trends, the one described by Galgano and the one I shall attempt to describe in these pages, develop at the same rate without cancelling each other out. The complexity may be governed by drawing up one or more sets of general principles;[14] and the uncertainty—which depends on the changing relationship between imperative rules and dispositive rules, the judicial interpretation of contracts or judicial remedies for their incompleteness[15]—may be governed by the hermeneutic community, that is, by consolidating interpretative models designed to reduce the arbitrary discretion of judges and arbiters.

But there is more. Beyond the processes of national codification or recodification that are spreading throughout Europe,[16] beyond the expansive force of EC law and beyond the different interpretations that may be given to the formula of 'private European law',[17] the need for coordination, clarification and simplification is felt everywhere and has had the effect of kindling new codification aspirations, of arousing interest in new standardisation techniques, new normative unification projects regarding individual sectors of legal systems, individual sectors of economic relations and individuals segments of the market.

---

[14] G Oppo, 'Impresa e mercato' [2001] I *Rivista di Diritto Civile* 430.
[15] A Gambaro, 'Contratto e regole dispositive' [2004] I *Rivista di Diritto Civile* 1.
[16] Most recently S Patti, *Diritto privato e codificazione europea* (Milan, Giuffrè, 2004).
[17] Recently discussed by V Roppo, 'Sul diritto europeo dei contratti. Per un approccio costruttivamente critico' [2004] *Europa e diritto privato* 439.

Contract relationships, including those, like 'commercial contracts', ascribed to the area enjoying the greatest freedom of negotiation up to a decade ago, are thus not immune to these phenomena, which, though still fragmentary and localised, are not isolated. As it is impossible to draw a complete and organic outline of the situation, it may be useful to cite a few examples of what, as I previously suggested, shows all the signs of being an authentic reversal in the trend. It not only transcends the dualism between statute law and case law, or the dualism between authoritative rules and persuasive rules or hard law and soft law, but also relies on other means whose significance is much more difficult to decipher. Among those means, the most evident are:

1. intervention of regulatory subjects who represent a 'third' player alongside legislators and judges;
2. intervention of rules governing activity and conduct, rather than the substantial relationship established between the parties;
3. intervention of rules designed to resolve disputes between the parties.

These do not form a homogeneous set of expedients or techniques. Contract models, once adopted by richer and more solid traditions, no longer suffice to regulate contractual relationships, since the basic rules are *imposed* by law. Little does it matter whether we are talking about a simple 'connotation', partial provisions or a complete regulatory model: mandatory rules prevail over and are more numerous than dispositive ones. In all of these cases legislators do not limit themselves to regulating the essential minimum content of contracts but, rather, go so far as to specify how a contract should be concluded and drawn up and even how the parties should behave.

It is this aspect which most strikes the interpreter: the legislator, who once relied on vague and generic definitions of general concepts such as good faith, fairness, public law and order or standards such as diligence, now introduces new categories (abuse of a dominant position, abuse of economic dependence, prevention of unfair surprise, limitation of conflicts of interest) and detailed rules for controlling the parties' behaviour. Furthermore, non-compliance with normative requirements is punishable by both administrative and civil sanctions, which have repercussions on private acts resulting from the violation of the prescribed rules of behaviour. Conduct prior to the conclusion of a contract is more relevant than when the simple requirement of good faith was enforced. Legislators have imposed obligations related to the disclosure of information and delivery in advance of the contract document, obligations to ascertain that the contents of the contract rules are thoroughly understood and obligations to report conflicts of interest.

The most recent initiative regarding consumer protection refers precisely to conduct—also with respect to contractual negotiation. It involves rules of fair practice, presently the subject of a proposal for a directive[18] which dictates guidelines on how a company should behave in relation to techniques of communication with potential customers or, more specifically, 'aggressive' or deceptive practices. On attaining final approval, the directive will need to be adapted, which will also entail the compilation of codes of conduct.[19]

Conduct—this time of third parties, vis-à-vis the contract parties—is likewise a concern of the directives on the prevention and repression of money laundering.[20] On behalf of the public interest, the new anti-money laundering regulations make it obligatory for third parties participating in a contract's formation—eg lawyers, notaries, accountants—to report any suspicious transactions to the competent authorities, after having ascertained their client's identity, the identity of the economic beneficiary of the transaction and the source of the client's economic resources, and to refrain from performing any acts or even providing advice when the transaction shows evidence of criminal reprehensibility.

With respect to financial relationships, the legislator's control over conduct is even more invasive. Intermediaries are obliged to behave according to principles of diligence, fairness and transparency, act in the interest of customers (irrespective of their status) and protect the integrity of markets, assuring fair treatment of customers, and engage in sound and prudent management practices.[21]

This expanding legislative process is also manifested, as I mentioned earlier, through initiatives aimed at codifying entire sectors of economic relations, as the European Commission is trying to do with consumer law, and the Italian Government did in many fields of the Italian legal system. In the last case we are no longer talking about laws assembled into consolidated acts, but rather about a systematic arrangement of regulations incorporating the corrective adjustments necessary to bring domestic regulatory provisions into

---

[18] COM(2003) 356 final (18 June 2003). See now, subsequent to the completion of this paper, Directive 2005/29 [2005] OJ L149/22.

[19] Regarding this point, see in particular H Micklitz and J Kessler (eds), *Marketing Practices Regulation and Consumer Protection in the EC Member States and the US* (Baden-Baden, Nomos, 2002); H Collins (ed), *The Forthcoming EC Directive on Unfair Commercial Practices: Contract, Consumer and Competition Law Implications* (The Hague, Kluwer Law International, 2004).

[20] There is a second directive, Directive 2001/97/EC of the European Parliament and of the Council of 4 December 2001 amending Council Directive 91/308/EEC on prevention of the use of the financial system for the purpose of money laundering [2001] OJ L344/76, implemented in Italy with Legislative Decree No 56 of 20 February 2004. There is a proposal for a third directive, dated 9 August 2005 (OR.en. PE-CONS 3631/05), on the prevention of the use of the financial system for the purpose of money laundering and terrorist financing.

[21] See Art 21 of Consolidation Act No 58 of 1998, as well as Directive 2004/39/EC of the European Parliament and of the Council of 21 April 2004 on markets in financial instruments of 21 April 2004 and Commission Directive 2004/72/EC of 29 April 2004 implementing Directive 2003/6/EC of the European Parliament and of the Council as regards accepted market practices, the definition of inside information in relation to derivatives on commodities, the drawing up of lists of insiders, the notification of manager's transactions and the notification of suspicious transactions OJ L162/70.

line with EC law. Such initiatives are based on delegated laws that are broad in content and allow greater freedom and more complex operations than in the past.[22] Italian examples include the 'intellectual property code', the 'code of consumer rights' and the 'private insurance code' recently drafted by the government and enacted in autumn 2005.

A lack of confidence in private autonomous decision making, or a need to protect 'weak interests' or to streamline the normative complex regulating markets? If we subscribe to the teaching of Roy Goode[23] we will see this as a trend postulated by the market itself—by the international market as well—to lend greater certainty, greater efficiency and greater fairness to the relationships among entrepreneurs. And the trend is all the more significant given its acceptance (not without some reluctance and even a bit of regret) in a context such as English law, which had always upheld the 'sanctity' of the contract and the free determination of economic operators in the conducting of their private business affairs.

However, what strikes us most about the English experience is the fact that the theory of the sanctity of the contract was conceived to 'armour' the will of the parties and keep their business safe from any meddlesome intervention by a judge. No thought had been given to applying it to prevent interventions by legislators: such occurrences were not frequent, and in the majority of cases they were dictated by contingent exigencies.

Now, however, even the UK is witnessing a sizeable expansion in contract-related statute law, as will be evident to anyone who leafs through the annual volumes of Acts, or visits the Houses of Parliament website. This expansion is justified not only by factors tied to the implementation of EC directives, but also by the need to adapt the system to continental models, as has occurred in the case of third-party contracts with the adoption of a law that facilitates insurance company contracts. In short, even in the English experience, where freedom of contract seemed to reign, the system is becoming increasingly rigid. It is interesting to note that this legislation-based regulatory approach is in harmony with projects for European civil codes.

III. NEW SCENARIOS OF CONTRACT LAW

Usages and codes of conducts, that is to say 'soft law', are characteristic concerns of 'professionals'. But, apart from a few aspects already alluded to in this paper, usages and codes of conduct do not represent the most relevant new development in this sector in the new millennium.

In other words, the idea that the market of the third millennium should or inevitably would be relegated entirely to the sphere of private autonomy, while the only task left to the authorities—or institutions—would be 'soft'

---

[22] l. 23.8.1988, no 400; l. 29.7.2003, no 229.
[23] R Goode, *Commercial Law in the Next Millennium* (London, Sweet & Maxwell, 1998).

regulation and ex post monitoring of economic transactions, seems to be contradicted by this expansion of legislation, which means expansion of 'hard law' instead of 'soft law'.

Rather than being merely a relic of old law, of the old way of conceiving the contract and commercial contracts, these phenomena tend to support the opinion that neither model, considered on its own, appears to be satisfactory in a context such as the European Community or Europe in a broader sense, where personal values of the individual, ethical values and representation in a democratic society that is not merely mercantilist represent the fundamental features of the new European society, as reflected in the Nice Charter, the European Constitution and the rules that must be applied in Europe, whatever their source.

Some conceptual revisions are thus necessary in order to adapt national cultures to this new trend. As regards the general rules of contracts, the trend as reflected by EC directives regarding certain types of services and the relationships between professionals in general appears to place an emphasis on principles of fairness in pre-contractual information, principles of fairness in the formulation of contract texts and deterrents to the abuse of power. At the same time, it is also possible to perceive a slow, gradual, but constant extension of the rules already established for consumer contracts to relationships between professionals.

The margin left to private autonomy is thus narrower. Of course a distinction should be made between types, as it is not possible to generalise. Nonetheless the freedom of the parties appears to be limited:

1. in the choice of the contracting party;
2. in the choice of contents (extra-minimal);
3. in the choice of remedies;
4. in the choice of the formulation of clauses;
5. in the choice of the types of individual clauses adopted; and
6. in the choice of applicable law and applicable procedure.

Regulation is thus based upon normative models of a legislative type, sometimes detailed, sometimes expressed through broad formulas. In this case we may speak of a sort of rebirth, or 'revival', of general principles, by now widely disseminated also at the EC level.[24]

Regulations of a 'legislative' and administrative type are joined by codes of conduct, which tend to replace usages. In this case as well, however, it must be pointed out that, although codes of conduct are an expression of the professional categories concerned, their adoption is imposed by numerous directives.

---

[24] F Toriello, *I principi generali del diritto comunitario. Il ruolo della comparazione* (Milan, Giuffrè, 2000).

But, as I suggested at the beginning, private autonomy is also being challenged in the sphere of conflict resolution. By now, numerous directives require the Member States to set up special bodies for settling disputes out of court. This obviously does not mean that judges are denied access; however, preference is shown for an approach to conflict resolution based on principles of independence, impartiality, competence, procedural simplicity and efficiency, which can guarantee users of the 'service' an opportunity to verify the legitimacy of the rights claimed through proceedings that are simpler and faster than those employed by ordinary courts.[25]

At this point an investigation should be conducted into the costs and benefits, also from an economic perspective, of a 'system' in which contracts are increasingly removed from the sphere of private autonomy. And we should try to answer the basic question of whether it is better to 'maintain the status quo', so to speak, or support the trend I have attempted to describe.

To my knowledge, the issue has not been raised at the EC level, since in most cases commissioners and offices are concerned with assuring not only a maximum degree of competition but also maximum simplification of relations to facilitate market integration. However, it is significant that, based on a broad analysis of the effects of Directive No 13 of 1993 on unfair terms, the Commission has let it be understood that it is preferable to work with uniform contract models purged of unfair terms rather than relying on the free choice of professionals as regards their inclusion in the contracts drawn up by them and submitted to judicial control.[26]

IV. RECODIFICATION INITIATIVE: FROM 'DECODIFICATION' TO 'RECODIFICATION'

Twenty-five years ago, a famous lawyer, Natalino Irti, investigated the phenomenon of the gradual removal of entire sections of rules from the Italian civil code to special laws.[27] The 1942 codification, apart from unifying the 1865 *Codice civile* (civil code) and the 1882 *Codice di Commercio*, had intended to incorporate the main principles of all the regulations regarding the law on trade into the single code, as well as the basic rules concerning property law. The Italian civil code appeared to be an 'adhesive', a kind of connective tissue which set out the benchmarks for the private legal system. However, since its introduction, the civil code had begun to suffer from a kind of haemorrhage. The special nature of the rules concerning categories of interest affected by law, the technicality of the rules and their minute details

---

[25] On this latter point, see G Alpa and R Danovi (eds), *La risoluzione stragiudiziale delle controversie e il ruolo dell'avvocatura* (Milan, Giuffrè, 2004).

[26] European Commission, *The 'Unfair Terms' Directive. Five Years On* (Brussels, 2000).

[27] N Irti, 'Leggi speciali (dal mono-sistema al polisistema)' [1979] I *Rivista di Diritto Civile* 141.

had led the law-maker to betray his codifying purpose, and to entrust to single laws, even with a general scope, the task of regulating entire sections of law. This phenomenon ended up by weakening the meaning of the civil code and creating many microsystems, where the relations of private individuals were regulated (although sometimes in an incomplete manner).

However, in practice, the civil code resisted, continued to carry out its main function and formed the connective tissue to fill the holes, settle conflicts and provide behavioural models for private individuals through the judges' adaptative (ie interpretation rule according to which a judge is supposed to opt for that rule meaning which comes closer to the relevant higher level provisions), creative interpretations.

Since the 1960s, the Italian civil code has begun to feel the impact of the new Constitution: the direct application of constitutional rules to relations between individuals, the declaration of the illegitimacy of the code's provisions in contrast with the constitutional rules and the interpretation of its provisions in the light of constitutional values. Case law, supported by a powerful control of legal literature and scientific elaboration, managed to correct the obsolete texts. Taking advantage of the elastic rules contained in the code, it also managed to adapt legal forms to the new economic and social demands.

During the same period, with the entry of EC law into the domestic system, entire sections of the Italian code were subject to principles deriving from that law, at least for the subjects governed by the EC. EC law was one of the engines behind change and adaptation. Many of the directives were implemented by special laws, but two in particular originally were included in the body of the civil code: Directive No 13 of 1993, on unfair terms in consumer contracts, which is now reflected in articles 1469 bis ff, and Directive No 44 of 1999, on certain aspects of the sale of consumer goods and associated guarantees, now reflected in articles 1519 bis ff. Due to the Legislative Decree 6.9.2005 no 206, these provisions have been included in the 'code of consumer rights'.

The plans for a new code that had arisen initially following the fall of the corporate system and then at the beginning of the 1960s came to nothing. At the end of the twentieth century, however, a pressing need to renew the text of the code was felt once again, as the judges' corrective, adaptative and creative interpretations could no longer be considered sufficient.

Hence a process of recodification also began in Italy. This process is based on certain ideas:

1. that the idea of a 'code' does not need to be universal, but rather put into relative terms, historically and ideologically speaking;
2. that a 'code' can still be useful in the society of the third millennium, if it does not claim to be universal and if it contains mechanisms to adapt to a rapidly changing world; and

3. that the 'code' cannot even claim to regulate all relations in detail, but rather it can expect to dictate the general principles on which individual sectors can be referred to.

In Italian history, in which the country's unity has been hard won but is still, from a certain angle, incomplete, the 'code' can only derive from the national law-maker. Regionalist claims cannot play a part (indeed, it is true that the reform of Articles 117 and 118 of the Constitution has maintained the state's exclusive competence to make laws as regards the civil system). In the words of a famous legal historian, Paolo Grossi:

> it is clear that the State cannot escape from establishing fundamental guidelines, but it is also clear that a form of delegification is establishing itself, abandoning the enlightened mistrust of social aspects and establishing an authentic form of legal pluralism with private individuals active in both legal organisation and social change.[28]

In Italy, work on recodification began in 1975, with the reform of family law, and continued in 2001 with the reform of corporate law, which renewed much of Book V of the Code. Book I is currently being revised, to adapt its regulations to the various forms of non-profit organisations.

Alongside these measures are new techniques of law making, which involve the drafting of organically structured consolidation acts for each industry, and the adaptation of domestic law to EC law (eg the consolidation acts on insurance, consumer law, cultural heritage).

The recodification process has also involved other countries, which have considered the results achieved in Italy, especially in the field of obligations, along with the drafting of general principles, such as the UNIDROIT Principles of International Contract Law and the Principles laid down by the Commission coordinated by Lando and Beale on European contract law.[29] The German system is one of the most significant in Europe. In Germany, recodification took place with Book II of the BGB (German Civil Code), relating to obligations. In France a study group has been set up for the reform of the civil code, and a debate has begun on whether to abandon the Code civil or to substantially modernise it. Brief mention must also be made of measures emerging from other types of legal system. For example, there is the codification of the Catalan and Scottish civil codes. These are phenomena that are taking place in countries very different from Italy, in which the need for identification of nations within multinational states emerges through having a code that becomes a symbol for large linguistic or cultural minorities.

---

[28] In P Cappellini and B Sordi, *Codici* (Milan, Giuffrè, 2002) 599.
[29] S Patti, 'Tradizione civilistica e codificazioni europee' [2004] I *Rivista di Diritto Civile* 521.

(a) Recodification in Germany

Precisely at the time of the first centenary of the German code,[30] the German law-maker, after having extended the code to East Germany, which had become an integral part of the Federal Republic after unification and the abolition of the civil code of the German Democratic Republic introduced in the 1970s, hastened to continue the work on recodification that had begun in the early 1980s. In 2002, the new version of the German Civil Code came into force. This reformed Book II and a section of Book I.[31] The change had been preceded by the inclusion in Book I of the general definitions of the 'consumer' and the 'professional'. The reform re-established the regulations for the binding relationship, introduced the rules on general contract conditions, on immovable properties on a timeshare basis, 'door to door' contracts and e-commerce contracts, consumers' loan and financing agreements, but it also introduced elements that had emerged from creativity in judicial practice, such as assumption, pre-contractual liability and obligations towards third parties. It does not represent a code with merely general principles, but a code that continues to represent a complete, detailed regulation of sectors of social life.[32] Moreover, the whole of consumer law—derived partly from the existing special laws and partly from the implementation of EC directives—supplemented the civil law. The regulations are redrafted with regard to impossibility of performance, compensation for damages and dissolution of the contract (in the sense of there being no alternative between rescission and withdrawal). The general, abstract figure of the obligation was maintained; according to Cian,

> the oldest of the legal systems derived from Roman law, whose enduring validity and effectiveness are difficult to do without for a modern law-maker with our legal tradition.[33]

The law of 25 July 2002 continued the recodification work, introducing rules into the German Civil Code concerning compensation for non-financial damage and capacity referred to extra-contractual liability. Further, a new concept of liability was introduced, concerning the fraudulent or seriously negligent preparation of expert testimony.[34]

In Germany the debate has begun on the European codification of the law of obligations and the question has been raised as to whether the German

---

[30] G Cian, *I cento anni del codice civile tedesco in Germania e nella cultura giuridica italiana* (Padoa, Cedam, 2002).

[31] Gesetz zur Modernisierung des Schuldrechts of 26 November 2001.

[32] G Cian, 'Significato e lineamenti della riforma dello Schuldrecht tedesco' [2003] I *Rivista di Diritto Civile* 5.

[33] *Ibid*, 18; see also G Cian, 'La figura generale dell'obbligazione nell'evoluzione giuridica contemporanea fra unitarietà e pluralità di statuti' [2002] I *Rivista di Diritto Civile* 491.

[34] See G Cian, 'La riforma del B.G.B. in materia di danno immateriale e di imputabilità dell'atto illecito' [2003] II *Rivista di Diritto Civile* 125.

recodification could be an example to follow. Apart from the many calls for measures to draft a European civil code,[35] fears have been raised concerning the knowledge and thus the certainty of law, on the possibly negative impact on commercial relations and on the fact that it may threaten the principle of contractual autonomy. These are all issues that have also been the subject of criticism of the German reform.[36]

(b) The Debate on Recodification in France

It has emerged from France that a movement is being formed proposing the modernisation of the Code civil. This is taking place at the same time as the celebrations for the second centenary of its introduction. This is not a strange coincidence, nor is it making bold parallels with the German system, but rather a natural consideration that is made in the mind of anyone attempting to evaluate a code: whether the text needs to be preserved or whether it should be shelved or substantially amended.

This celebration was preceded by the celebration for the bicentenary of the 1789 Declaration of Rights. Even at that time, lawyers had considered the innovative scope of the French Revolution in the field of law, including private law. The Napoleonic Code's two centuries of existence were marked primarily by the reprinting of the original text.[37] Indeed, since the original, over time, the text had undergone significant changes and adaptations: wide reforms of family law had also been introduced in France, a few years earlier than in Italy. The law on 'private life' had been codified, and many 'consolidation acts' had been linked to the code, ie complex systems of rules which set out the provisions for implementing the EC directives. However, in France, constitutional regulations were never directly applied to private law, nor was there even a discussion on general principles. Neither of these aspects, although present in legal culture, were successful: the former, due to the persistent, clear-cut separation between (constitutional) public law and private law; the latter because of the French legal system's natural aversion to abstract, structured categories.

The meditations on the Code civil's past and present thus imposed a consideration on the future, and even here a debate emerged about whether or not to introduce a code at the European level. In the extensive literature that has grown on the subject, with reviews, specific writings and historical reconstructions of the protagonists of codification, two publications stand out due to their importance: *Le Code civil, 1804–2004. Livre du Bicentenaire*,[38] by the Cour de Cassation (French Supreme Court), the Board of

---

[35] See H Schulte-Nölke, 'Ein Vertragsgesetzbuch für Europa?' [2001] *Juristenzeitung* 917.
[36] B Dauner-Lieb, 'Vers un droit européen des obligations? Enseignements tirés de la réforme allemande du droit des obligations' (2004) 56 *Revue internationale de droit comparé* 559.
[37] JD Bredin, *Code civil des Français 1804* (Paris, Dalloz, 2004).
[38] (Paris, Dalloz, 2004).

Lawyers at the Conseil d'Etat and the Henri Capitant Association, and *1804–2004. Le Code civil. Un passé, un présent, un avenir,*[39] edited by the University Panthéon-Assas (Paris II). Both books offer a reinterpretation of the Code from a historical point of view, but they are most concerned with outlining its future.

The first book, in particular, looks towards the years to come, as it includes recodification among 'general problems', then studies the individual Books and fundamental institutions of the Code separately (people, family, general theory of contract, special contracts, civil liability, succession and gratuities, assets, personal security), the relations between these materials and international private law and administrative law, in view of the difficulties of recodification, and closes the overview with an analysis of certain national systems that have adopted the French code as a model for civil codification. Considered in these pages are phenomena such as the explosion of special rules outside of the Code, the reformulation of domestic sources, the proliferation of international sources. Mention is then made of the serious omissions in the Code, for example, in the rules regarding persons, now obsolete, the somewhat contrived inclusions such as the 'family solidarity clauses' and the de facto relations, while one tends to think that the Code should not be abrogated completely, but only substantially redrafted. In short, a general review appeared to many to be absolutely necessary, without the expectation that the Code could incorporate all matters concerning civil law. Not even a brief mention was made of the idea of unifying the Code civil and the Code de Commerce, while there is appreciation of the creative work of judicial practice, which has also been considerable in this system. The programme for modernisation of the Code thus involves the elimination of outdated provisions, such as many rules concerning property, for a re-writing of provisions that were of doubtful interpretation at the outset, the integration with provisions that reflect the needs of modern society. The law on property and the law on obligations should be the first sections to be redrafted.

The second work also offers a historical analysis of the Code and its reformulation during its two centuries of existence. It highlights its 'constitutional' function,[40] retraces the story woven between the creative interpretation of the Code and the evolution of civil law, analyses the relationship between the Code and commercial law and public law, describes the influence of the Code in the countries of the world where its structural model has been adopted, and then devotes a large section to its future. This is the most intriguing sector, since one can observe the tension between the justified pride of those who bear their history[41]—because the Code civil, as stated by Carbonnier, is a

---

[39] (Paris, Dalloz, 2004).

[40] J Gaudemet, 'Le Code Civile; "Constitution civile de la France"' in *1804–2004, ibid,* 297.

[41] See the following contributions in *1804–2004, ibid:* F Malaurie, 'Le Code Civil: "Constitution civile de la France"' at 1; F Terré, 'Inestimable Code civil' at 899; J Carbonnier, 'Le lieux de mémoir' at 1045.

historical monument, the vessel containing the memory of historical divisions, the result of a historic compromise[42]—and the awareness that this text cannot be preserved as it is, since it is forced to submit to the challenges of globalisation, EC law and the European Convention on Human Rights.

In particular, there are three influences that appear to be most pervasive: EC law, the possible constitutionalisation of private law and plans for European codification.

1. EC law has a dual impact: not only does it amend the existing regulations or introduce new rules, following the loss of sovereignty by the national government in favour of the EC Parliament, but, when laws implementing the directives are included in the Code, it ends up by altering their structure and balance.[43] This is a problem shared by all the codifications in Europe, a clear feature of both German and Italian literature; to this we could add the indirect, even 'expansive' influence of EC law on civil law, even beyond the subjects that are now reserved to it.

2. The 'constitutionalisation of private law', although hoped for by certain authors,[44] and with the exception of the work of the Conseil d'Etat, cannot have much success as long as the Code is considered, as per Carbonnier, to be 'the country's true constitution.' However, the surprising thing is not so much the fact that the direct application of constitutional regulations to relations between private individuals is not common ground between French lawyers, as it is between Italian lawyers and German lawyers (and even, with regard to fundamental laws, English lawyers), but that in France the situation is reversed, and it is considered that the fundamental concepts of private law can be elevated to constitutional values. This is a 'dream' that is still cherished by a few lawyers, but it has been the target of fundamental criticisms by those who are familiar with the *Drittwirkung* theory.[45]

3. Plans for European codification are appearing on the horizon, which is also the subject of a vast amount of literature and great debate in France. Authoritative lawyers doubt that the Code, which has become a shadow of its former self, without losing its image as a 'monument to global legal thought,' could be subjected to a simple modernisation.[46] On the contrary, they suggest that it is appropriate to consider what happens in other systems, where recodification has taken stock of the plans to standardize legislation at international level or even the plans for a European code that are currently being drafted. In short, there is a question as to whether what is at stake (the reformulation of an old text such as the Code) is in fact worth it, and whether it is

---

[42] Carbonnier, *ibid*, 1046.
[43] Leveneur, in *1804–2004*, above n 39, 925.
[44] L Favoreu, 'La constitutionnalisation du droit' in J-B Auby et al (eds), *L'Unité du Droit. Mélanges en Honneur à Roland Drago* (Paris, Economica, 1996) 25.
[45] E Zoller, 'L'Unité du droit communautaire' in *ibid*, 988.
[46] D Tallon, 'Conclusions' in *ibid*, 1002.

not more appropriate to wait for a European code, rather than commencing an extremely complex project destined to have a short life.[47]

La Revue des Contrats[48] has published the work of prestigious lawyers on the expediency and/or feasibility of the reform of Book III, chapter III, of the Code civil, concerning 'Des contrats ou des obligations conventionelles en général.' A lawyer's first impression when studying this charter is that, during the two centuries of the Code's existence, almost nothing has changed with regard to contracts and obligations, as only 31 articles of the total 238 have been amended. This longevity is due, according to Catala,[49] to two concurrent reasons: the first is that the new contract law developed outside of the Code, the second is that the Code contains few mandatory regulations, mainly referring to family relationships, while the rest is made up of non-mandatory provisions that protect the autonomy of the contracting parties. Rémy adds a third reason:

> the historic structure of contracts and contractual obligations is so abstract that it was well able to survive the broadest of time spans.[50]

The policy of contract law has also gradually changed: from the dirigism that included contract law in what is known as the 'ordre public économique' we have returned to liberalism. The drafting of legislative texts outside of the body of the Code was justified by the unequal position of the parties and the requirement to protect the weaker party. This led to the birth of consumer law. However, these events cannot, in Catala's opinion, leave the Code unaffected. According to Ghestin,[51] the effects of EC law and international law have ended up by changing the systematic structure of the code, creating duplicated systems, as happens in the area of sales.

The most significant amendments to chapter III have involved the review of the penal clauses, the law on default interest, the cooling-off period and the admission of evidence via new technologies.

The text has thus been renewed through the creative work of judicial practice, that has affected the form of the contract, the flexible concepts of loyalty, good faith, proportionality, the pre-contract stage, *l'avant-contrat*, and unjust enrichment. Following Demogue's theories, judges have approved the distinction between obligations of performance and obligations of diligence, and have invented the 'obligation de sécurité' and gross negligence. They have also discovered, starting from the agency agreement, the concept of 'common interest' that governs open-ended obligations; even before

---

[47] *Ibid*, 1008.

[48] [2004] issue 4, 1145.

[49] P Catala, 'Au-delà du bicentenaire' [2004] *Revue des Contrats* 1145, 1148.

[50] Ph Rémy, 'Réviser le titre III du livre troisième du Code civil ?' [2004] *Revue des Contrats* 1169, 1170.

[51] J Ghestin, 'Le futur: exemples étrangers. Le Code civil en France aujourd'hui' [2004] *Revue des Contrats* 1152, 1158.

Directive No 44 of 1999 was introduced, the judges had distinguished between contracts for professionals and consumer contracts, included within the guarantee for defects.

Unlike the opinion that now prevails in Italy, whereby the decisions of the courts are assigned the role of a source of law, Catala considers that this admirable work by judges cannot be elevated to the status of law, and therefore is not only changeable but does not give effective judicial certainty in contractual relations. Ghestin also shares this opinion, believing that many of the judgments of the *Corte di Cassazione* (Italian Supreme Court) are equivocal and give rise to uncertainties when applying the Code.[52]

A number of areas are not covered by the Code. Nothing is mentioned about formation of the contract, nor about negotiations and the 'avant-contrat'. The regulation of vices only deals with consent, and does not consider the obligation for cooperation between the parties when exchanging information prior to the conclusion of the contract. The law on consideration also requires amendments, since it should control the usefulness of the economic transaction and the balance of performance. As far as execution of the contract is concerned, Catala suggests relying on the contract in the interests of the third party to introduce the direct action. Other problems to be resolved are the issue of 'negotial link' (ie *interdependence* between two *contracts*), the issue of one side failing to perform during the contract and the creditor's right to early termination.

In this regard, Ghestin considers that it is precisely the part of the Code dedicated to the conditions and effects of termination of the contract that represents a symptomatic example of the problems that led the French system to rely on the sole intervention by courts in this area. This is because, unlike the provisions of the German Civil Code, the Code civil does not provide for unilateral termination of the contract, as termination must be obtained through the courts. The isolated cases in which the *Cour de Cassation* (French Supreme Court) has admitted unilateral termination in the case of non-performance during the contract by only one of the parties are founded on reasons of 'urgency'.[53] According to Ghestin, urgency is not sufficient, and it is necessary to add a further requirement, involving the 'relevance of the non-performance'.[54]

The regulations on retroactive effects of termination, although created by case law, also require clarification, since these effects are only admitted in the case of a unitary contract. In any case, there are conflicts concerning the date from which the effects of termination should run. There continues to be much confusion concerning the division between 'résiliation judiciaire' and 'résolution judiciaire', as only the first term has retroactive effects, not the

---

[52] *Ibid*, 1153.
[53] Cass com, 4.2.2004, quoted by J Ghestin, above n 11, 1155.
[54] J Ghestin, above n 51, 1155.

second. For this reason, Ghestin[55] suggests unifying the regulations of the two institutions.

In the same way, the general regulations of obligations are also in need of systematic reformulation. There are many problems to resolve. Ghestin[56] only highlights one, which is certainly one of the most significant: the issue of *cause*. This issue has been resolved rather drastically in the Principles of European Contract Law (PECL) by Lando and Beale, by abolishing the institution. Ghestin does not agree with this solution, since *cause* enables a control on the lawfulness of the transaction, and moreover its non-existence would affect the certainty of relations. The question is then transferred to the definition of '*cause*', which should comply with the principles of fairness of exchange and the certainty of the obligation. The fact that the concept of *cause* has survived over the past two centuries is proof—in Ghestin's opinion[57]—of its longevity and that it is essential. Having thus rejected the idea of abolishing it, three different concepts remain that are still being discussed in French legal literature today.

The first concept gives a flexible meaning, designed to regulate contractual justice, the equivalence and proportionality of performance. The second one suggests an articulated notion that differs according to the individual sectors in which it intervenes. The third makes it an instrument 'hidden' amid the depths of the provisions regulating the formation of the agreement, being the provisions that justify its existence, sanction its immorality or unlawfulness and therefore govern its function, invalidate the agreement's conflict with public order or acceptable customs and thus impede its effects.

Ghestin suggests writing a text that is similar to the PECL, but making use of the term '*but*' (aim) instead of '*cause*'; the control of the existence of the *cause* could be replaced by a control on the *objet*. Likewise for the inclusion of third-party interests in a contract on behalf of a third party, which could also replace *cause* in that context, also due to the negligible extent (imaginary or derisory nature) of the counter performance.[58] The recurring question contains a worrying dilemma: do we correct the code or wait for European codification? Ghestin supports recodification of the law of obligations,[59] but considers that the drafting of a European code is to be hoped for, although not in the immediate future. In any case, the two options are, in his words, incompatible. This led to the initiative to set up a study group, initially formed of 'five scholars' (Carbonnier, Foyer, Cornu, Malaurie and Ghestin; then reduced to four after the death of Carbonnier), to draw up an 'avant-propos' to be submitted to the Ministry of Justice.

---

[55] *Ibid*, 1157.
[56] *Ibid*, 1163.
[57] *Ibid*, 1164.
[58] *Ibid*, 1166. See also J Ghestin, 'Faut-il conserver la cause en droit européen des contrats?' (2005) 1 *European Review of Contract Law* 396.
[59] *Ibid*, 1159.

For his part, Rémy wonders whether recodification could not be, so to speak, 'light' or 'trouble-free', as in the past. However, this opens up another worrying issue: should the review of the Code maintain the original elements or should it be more similar to the PECL or the plan for standardised obligation law put forward by von Bar, thus including the sources of obligations other than the contract? Considering the structure of the Code civil, Rémy wonders whether the *summa divisio* between contracts and contractual obligations on the one hand and obligations that are formed without an agreement (non contractual obligations) on the other should be preserved, or whether the German route, which distinguishes legal acts from legal facts, should be followed. Instead of choosing to construct the new chapter on the unilateral manifestation of will, Rémy prefers to maintain the old distinction that puts the greatest emphasis on the 'deal', ie the agreement of one or more parties, which can then be followed by rules concerning the other situations. Again, Rémy rejects the idea of regulating obligations in general, considering that the general regulations of contracts should be maintained instead. This is the decision that has been taken by the Lando–Beale Commission, since the PECL do not include a section devoted to the obligation relation, or to obligations in general.[60] However, he certainly agrees with abolishing the category of 'quasi contracts' in the Code, along with the distinction between 'delicts' and 'quasi delicts' (which are already removed by judicial practice). An ordered structure would emerge that has been adopted by the Italian code, which governs civil liability, unjust enrichment and undue enrichment separately, but Rémy does not acknowledge this.[61] He therefore excludes that the definition of the contract should be included in the Code, while he agrees with the inclusion of the general principles on contractual liability that introduce the PECL.

Those who have more openly declared their support for recodification on a par with the PECL, or for recodification that gives an indication of a European code in which French culture plays an active part, suggest that this is not simply a technical work; it is essential—for such an important reform—that the political reasons of the initiative be expressed clearly.[62] In this context, Tallon[63] relies on the consideration of foreign models, so that French recodification does not retain the uncertainties that have arisen from codes in force in other European countries. In this sense, while he states his approval of the amendment to the rules on judicial termination, enabling the debtor to perform or pay compensation, or enabling the judge to redefine the contract as a result of supervening events (and therefore criticises the *Cour de*

---

[60] Ph Rémy, above n 50, 1176.

[61] *Ibid*, 1178.

[62] A Sériaux, 'Vanitas vanitatum. De l'inanité d'une refonte du livre III du titre III du Code civil' [2004] *Revue des Contrats* 1187, 1189.

[63] D Tallon, 'La rénovation du titre III, livre III du Code civil: une approche comparative' [2004] *Revue des Contrats* 1190, 1192.

Cassation, which refrains from amending the clauses negotiated by the parties), he is more concerned about other decisions of the PECL, such as the rules on damage limitation.

The way is therefore open towards recodification even in a system that, in the words of Rémy,[64] seemed to be more reluctant to abandon that 'merveilleux conservatoire de fragments de Pothier, de Domat, du Digeste ou des Institutes.'

V. CONCLUSION

Competition applies for all purposes other than making agreements: it is better to have uniform conditions more acceptable for consumers than mutually competing contract models. The same line of reasoning applies for contracts between professionals. This will also hurt competition among legal systems as we move toward increasing harmonisation of normative rules and contract conditions. But uniformity helps increase the certainty of the parties' legal positions, the intelligibility of their acts and the fairness of their conduct. In other words, the sacrifice of private autonomy is counterbalanced by the positive effects produced by regulation, to the advantage of the parties, the operators concerned and markets.

[64] Ph Rémy, above n 50, 1179.

9

Contracts and European Consumer Law: an OFT Perspective

SIR JOHN VICKERS[1]

I. INTRODUCTION

Competition law and consumer law are basic elements of the legal framework in which contracts are made. Each is being harmonised, at least to some degree, across Europe. The Office of Fair Trading (OFT), like the US Federal Trade Commission but rather unusually in Europe, has enforcement responsibilities in relation to both competition law and consumer law. My aim in these remarks is not to enter the depths of contract law, but to discuss, based on OFT experience, some possible implications for contract law and questions about its European harmonisation arising from harmonising developments in EC competition and consumer law.

I will focus mainly on issues in consumer law, where a series of EC directives has provided steps towards harmonisation. A particularly important directive—on unfair commercial practices[2]—is now in train. But I will start with some comments on competition law, where, perhaps naturally, European harmonisation has occurred differently, and gone further, than has happened so far with consumer law.

Let me say at the outset that I do not see harmonisation as an end in itself: it has costs as well as practical benefits. One question for the debate on the harmonisation of contract law is how far the benefits can be achieved, without undue cost, by appropriate degrees of harmonisation in relevant associated areas of law, such as competition and consumer law. How deeply

---

[1] The views expressed in this paper, which was delivered when I was Chairman of the OFT, are personal and not necessarily those of the OFT. For help in preparing the paper I am most grateful to my OFT colleagues Tabitha Bonney, Simon Brindley, Agatha Coker, Jessica Farry, Paul Gurowich, Karen Johnston, Sarah Kaye, Jennifer Thompson, Ray Woolley, and especially Colin Brown.
[2] Directive 2005/29/EC of the European Parliament and of the Council of 11 May 2005 concerning unfair business-to-consumer commercial practices in the internal market [2005] OJ L149/22 ('Unfair Commercial Practices Directive').

into the private law arena need harmonisation go to achieve its practical benefits? Another issue for the debate concerns the effectiveness and coordination of law enforcement, as distinct from harmonisation per se, across Europe—for example, against scams and other kinds of manifestly unfair trading. Without that, harmonisation might be more theoretical than real in important respects.

II. CONTRACTS AND THE HARMONISATION OF COMPETITION LAW

Competition law impinges on contracts mainly, but not only, through its prohibition of anti-competitive agreements. Thus Article 81 of the EC Treaty and its equivalents in domestic law apply to agreements between undertakings and concerted practices that have as their object or effect the prevention, restriction or distortion of competition. The scope of those provisions goes well beyond contracts, for the 'concurrence of wills' that is the hallmark of an agreement or concerted practice need not take contractual form. Collusive agreements and practices, for example, are usually not contractual, and moreover they can be passively accepted.[3]

Harmonisation of European competition law has occurred in three reinforcing ways. The first is the enforcement over more than 40 years of Articles 81 and 82 (formerly Articles 85 and 86) by the European Commission and Community Courts. Second is the more recent introduction of national laws that mirror EC competition law. Thus the UK Competition Act 1998, which came into force in March 2000, contains prohibitions of anti-competitive agreements and abuse of dominance that echo Articles 81 and 82. Moreover, section 60 of the Act requires that they be applied consistently with EC jurisprudence. Thirdly, the Modernisation Regulation,[4] which came into effect on 1 May 2004, makes Articles 81 and 82 directly applicable by national competition authorities and courts. It also prevents national competition law going beyond Article 81 in respect of agreements that may affect trade between Member States.

Together with increasingly harmonised public enforcement, there is growing scope for private competition law actions. In principle these have long been possible under Articles 81 and 82, but in practice they have been rare. However the *Crehan* litigation concerning beer supply agreements has established that, as well as third parties, a party to an agreement in breach of

---

[3] A recent discussion of this point is in the judgment of the Competition Appeal Tribunal in the replica football kit price-fixing cases. See, eg: 'it is . . . plain that an undertaking may be passively party to an infringement', *Allsports v OFT* [2004] CAT 17 at [1043].

[4] Council Regulation (EC) 1/2003 of 16 December 2002 on the implementation of the rules on competition laid down in Arts 81 and 82 of the Treaty [2003] OJ L1/1 ('Modernisation Regulation').

Article 81 may bring a claim for damages arising from it.[5] The litigation now continues before the House of Lords, inter alia, on the question of the scope of the obligation of a national court to adopt findings of fact in a decision of the European Commission.[6] Scope for private competition law actions has also been enhanced by some national legislation (the UK again being a prime example) and by the Modernisation Regulation ending the notification system for agreements.

All this amounts to quite extensive European harmonisation of substantive competition law, and hence of an important element of the law relating to contracts.

Several background factors may have been favourable to the European harmonisation of competition law. It is only recently that systematic competition law was introduced in most Member States. Only Germany had such competition law, and only just, ahead of its introduction in the EEC in 1962.[7] Other Member States have come later, and have followed suit inasmuch as they have adopted laws reflecting EC law and jurisprudence. This in turn has facilitated the devolution of the Modernisation Regulation. Thus competition law has not grown out of contract law but been grafted onto it.

III. CONTRACTS AND THE HARMONISATION OF CONSUMER LAW

The historical situation is very different with respect to consumer law, which often has grown from various origins in contract law by providing for some public action at national and local level to seek results that the ordinary consumer may be ill-placed to achieve individually through private action. Accordingly, whereas EC competition law has for decades been applied centrally by the Commission, subject to the Community Courts, there is no enforcement of consumer law by the Commission.

EC consumer law has nevertheless come into being through a number of directives that have been variously implemented and applied in Member States alongside their respective bodies of contract law relating to consumers. For example, there are directives on:

— misleading advertisements
— doorstep selling
— consumer credit
— package travel

---

[5] Case C–453/99 *Courage Ltd v Crehan* [2001] ECR I–6297 at [36].

[6] On appeal from the judgment of the Court of Appeal in *Courage Ltd v Crehan (No.1)* [1999] EWCA Civ 1501, [1999] UKCLR 110.

[7] The Treaty of Rome was signed in 1957. The competition provisions (then Arts 85 and 86, now Arts 81 and 82) became directly effective in the original six Member States on 13 March 1962.

— unfair contract terms
— timeshare
— distance selling
— sale of goods and guarantees
— electronic commerce
— injunctions

The underlying problems for consumers that such measures seek to address are of three broad kinds—information problems pre-purchase; duress and undue pressure at the time of purchase; and undue surprises post-purchase.[8]

From the list above, the following discussion focuses on unfair contract terms. Then the impending directive on unfair commercial practices, which deals with a wide range of pre-contractual issues, are considered. Finally, the paper turns to the practical arrangements for public enforcement of consumer law across borders.

1. Unfair Terms in Consumer Contracts

The challenges and opportunities for national implementation of directive-based consumer law are well illustrated by the regulations on unfair terms in consumer contracts, which provide the closest approach to date to harmonisation of general contract law principles. The Directive on Unfair Terms in Consumer Contracts[9] owed much more to continental contract law jurisprudence than to English common law of contract. Nevertheless, the UK has been energetic in its practical application.

The directive was implemented in the UK by the Unfair Terms in Consumer Contracts Regulations of 1994 and 1999 (UTCCRs).[10] The regulations say that unfair standard terms in consumer contracts are not binding on consumers. Their scope excludes the terms—sometimes called the 'core' terms—that define the main subject matter of the contract and the price of the goods or services supplied. A term is unfair if, contrary to the requirement of good faith, it causes a significant imbalance in the parties' rights and obligations under the contract to the detriment of the consumer. In the words of Lord Bingham:

---

[8] An economic discussion of these issues is in my 2003 Keynes Lecture, 'Economics for Consumer Policy' (2005) 125 *Proceedings of the British Academy* 287.

[9] Council Directive 93/13/EEC of 5 April 1993 on unfair terms in consumer contracts [1993] OJ L95/29 ('Unfair Terms in Consumer Contracts Directive').

[10] The Unfair Terms in Consumer Contracts Regulations 1994, SI 1994/3159 and 1999, SI 1999/2083. The 1999 Regulations replaced those of 1994, without major substantive change but so as to reflect more closely the wording of the Directive and, in particular, to allow other 'qualifying bodies' to enforce the Regulations alongside the OFT.

The requirement of good faith in this context is one of fair and open dealing. Openness requires that the terms should be expressed fully, clearly and legibly, containing no concealed pitfalls or traps. Appropriate prominence should be given to terms which might operate disadvantageously to the customer. Fair dealing requires that a supplier should not, whether deliberately or unconsciously, take advantage of the consumer's necessity, indigence, lack of experience, unfamiliarity with the subject matter of the contract, weak bargaining position or any other factor listed in or analogous to those listed in schedule 2 to the Regulations.[11] Good faith in this context is not an artificial or technical concept; nor, since Lord Mansfield was its champion, is it a concept wholly unfamiliar to British lawyers. It looks to good standards of commercial morality and practice.[12]

The OFT is the lead UK enforcer of the UTCCRs. As in other areas of consumer law, our strategy has had three main strands:

— publishing written guidance, with emphasis on illustrative examples, aimed at particular economic sectors;[13]
— working with businesses to improve trading practice (eg by assisting the revision of standard form contracts);[14]
— law enforcement, including the pursuit of cases to clarify the law.

Two early cases in which unfair contract terms were removed without litigation illustrate the application of the regulations. One concerned the length of the notice period for consumers wanting to terminate mobile phone contracts. The seven companies approached agreed with the OFT in 1997 to introduce major improvements to their contracts, which included reductions in notice periods to not more than one month. The second example is a case involving City Mortgage Corporation, which concerned the permanent near-doubling of interest rates against borrowers who had committed even one act of default and unfairly high charges on borrowers redeeming loans early. Following OFT action, the company agreed in 1998 to limit the circumstances in which rates could be increased, sharply reduce the increase that would occur and cut its early redemption charges. The OFT's guidelines on non-status lending also address these issues and industry practice appears generally to be in keeping with them.

---

[11] This is a reference to schedule 2 of the 1994 Regulations, which disappeared on reissue of the Regulations in 1999 as being an unnecessary statement of factors which the Unfair Terms in Consumer Contracts Directive (above n 9) anyway required to be taken into account via its recitals.

[12] *Director General of Fair Trading v First National Bank plc* [2001] UKHL 52, [2002] 1 AC 481 at [17].

[13] See, eg the OFT published guidance on unfair contract terms relating to package holidays, entertainments, care homes, health and fitness clubs, and tenancy agreements. As well as general guidance aimed to help compliance by suppliers, the OFT has issued consumer leaflets on all of these.

[14] In nearly 1,000 cases, over 6,000 contract terms have been deleted or amended following OFT action.

Lending practices were also at issue in the *First National Bank* case,[15] which was appealed to the Court of Appeal, where the OFT won, and then to the House of Lords, where the OFT lost. The challenged contract term stipulated that contractual interest would be charged *after*, as well as before, any court judgment against the borrower. So even though a borrower was meeting repayment instalments ordered by the court, contractual interest would nevertheless build up.

The Lords accepted that the sort of situation at hand was unacceptable but judged, on balance, that the problem arose not from the unfairness of the term but from the lack of procedural safeguards for the consumer at the stage of default—in particular, concerning awareness of provisions of the Consumer Credit Act 1974 that empower courts to amend underlying contract terms when making orders relating to borrowers in default.

Though naturally disappointed to have lost the case, the OFT found the Lords' judgment very helpful in other respects, particularly in clarifying the scope and substance of the Regulations in a way that confirmed the main lines of interpretation developed by the OFT.

As to the lack of harmonisation of European contract law, there is an interesting statement in the *First National Bank* judgment by Lord Hope:

> It has been pointed out that there are considerable differences between the legal systems of the member states as to how extensive and how powerful the penetration has been of the principle of good faith and fair dealing . . . But in the present context there is no need to explore this topic in any depth. The Directive provides all the guidance that it needed as to its application.[16]

On this and more generally the Lords saw no need to refer any issue to the European Court of Justice in Luxembourg.

Stepping back from the particular context of UK consumer credit law, the *First National Bank* case is therefore a strong example of a national court—indeed the highest court, the House of Lords—finding itself able to apply the provisions of a European consumer contract regulation, and to do so with considerable clarity, notwithstanding the diverse nature of European contract laws.

A quite different point about the scope of the UTCCRs arose in the recent *Newham* case.[17] Important issues of law, which could potentially affect millions in rented accommodation, arose in this case, which primarily concerned the Council's responsibility to certain homeless persons. Do the Directive on Unfair Terms in Consumer Contracts and UTCCRs apply to contracts relating to land (eg tenancy agreements) and to public authorities such as the Borough Council? The OFT intervened as an interested party to

---

[15] *First National Bank*, above n 12.
[16] *Ibid* at [45].
[17] *London Borough of Newham v Khatun et al* [2004] EWCA Civ 55, [2005] QB 37.

establish that the UTCCRs did so apply, and the High Court and Court of Appeal both agreed.

In the process the courts had to deal, inter alia, with the lack of harmonisation of European language. The word equivalent to 'goods' in the French text—'biens'—includes immovables, and likewise in Italian, Spanish and Portuguese. Under the principle that European law is to be read as a single whole, this helped trump the argument that in English 'goods and services' does not generally embrace land.[18] Whether or not clearer drafting in legislation or transposition would have avoided ambiguity in the first place, one advantage of a common frame of reference might be to resolve such issues efficiently.

The *Newham* case is therefore another illustration of European-derived consumer contract law being both enforced by a national public authority and applied with clarity by a national court, despite the diversity of contract (and, indeed, property) law across the EU. More generally, the regulations on unfair terms in consumer contracts show the scope for harmonisation notwithstanding underlying diversity, and practical improvements in the marketplace for consumers in the UK and elsewhere.

The harmonisation of substantive consumer law as between Member States through measures such as the Directive on Unfair Contract Terms just discussed only goes so far. For example, this legislation covers what is in contracts but not the process of contracting. There are moreover other important dimensions of the harmonisation of consumer law and policy, including consistency across market sectors, and of law enforcement as between Member States.

2. The Unfair Commercial Practices Directive

Harmonisation of consumer law relating to a wide range of largely pre-contractual conduct is precisely the aim of the Unfair Commercial Practices Directive. At the time of writing, the Directive has been adopted by the European Parliament and the Council but awaits transposition by Member States.[19] The directive also brings an important element of cross-sectoral consistency by adopting a principles-based approach.

Because sectoral regulation is drawn up with existing products and services in mind, disreputable traders can circumvent its purpose by adapting their activities to go just beyond the regulation, but still within the law. A good example is the emergence of the 'holiday club' market from the timeshare market.

---

[18] *Ibid* at [68], [70].
[19] Unfair Commercial Practices Directive, above n 2.

The 1994 Timeshare Directive[20] had a substantial impact on the timeshare sector. It requires traders to provide consumers with a 10-day cooling off period, and not to take a deposit during that time, for contracts with a duration of 36 months or more. This, together with consumer demand for more flexible products, led to the development of holiday club programmes, which were in some cases specifically designed to avoid the operation of the Timeshare Directive—for example, by offering 35-month contracts where the directive applies to contracts for 36+ months. Many such programmes have been sold using all the dubious pressure-selling techniques perfected in the heyday of timeshare mis-selling, against which the cooling-off period was intended to guard.[21]

There have been calls for amendments to the Timeshare Directive to close the loopholes that allow holiday clubs to trade unfairly and deceptively. Although such amendments would be welcome, they would only catch up with the most recent market developments. It is all too likely that a number of companies would adjust the detail of their market offering to put their sales operations once again beyond the reach of public law enforcers, meaning that many consumers would continue to lose out. Specific sectoral legislation can mean that the law and the enforcement agencies are perpetually running to arrive at where bad but imaginative and resourceful traders were the day before yesterday.

The Unfair Commercial Practices Directive[22] takes a very different approach and, provided it is well implemented, the result should be better regulation. The directive sets a benchmark for fairness for all business-to-consumer transactions. It marks the culmination of a move away from the tradition of prescriptive sector-specific legislation which is then amended over time to react to recent developments. It also goes beyond the more recent approach of dealing with single aspects of transactions, such as advertising, doorstep selling and distance selling. It is based on the general principle 'not to trade unfairly'. This principles-based approach follows closely that of the longer tradition of competition law, where bans on anti-competitive agreements and on the abuse of a dominant position have safeguarded competition across markets generally.

The directive contains a general clause, underpinned by two tests—professional diligence and material distortion—which can be used to assess whether

---

[20] Directive 94/47/EC of the European Parliament and the Council of 26 October 1994 on the protection of purchasers in respect of certain aspects of contracts relating to the purchase of the right to use immovable properties on a timeshare basis [1994] OJ L280/83 ('Timeshare Directive').

[21] After protracted negotiations the OFT has recently obtained undertakings from two businesses operating in Spain which have agreed to give cooling-off periods and improved contracts. Negotiating such voluntary undertakings across borders requires painstaking work and is often slowed down by differences between the two countries' implementations of directives.

[22] Unfair Commercial Practices Directive, above n 2.

a commercial practice is unfair and therefore actionable. Furthermore, as one of the key determinants of unfairness the directive points to the omission or obscuring of pre-contractual information that the average consumer needs to take an informed transactional decision.

The directive contains a clear list of practices in annex I which, according to the heading of the annex, 'are in all circumstances considered unfair,' thus providing certainty for business and enforcers that these particularly egregious practices will be regarded as a breach. The list can be amended only by revision of the directive and must be implemented in the same form in all Member States.

Examples from this list of 'always unfair' practices are: [23]

— Making a materially inaccurate claim concerning the nature and extent of the risk to the personal security of the consumer or his family if the consumer does not purchase the product.
— Creating the false impression that a consumer has already won, will win, or will on doing a particular act win, a prize or other equivalent benefit, when in fact . . . there is no prize or other equivalent benefit . . .
— [Running] a pyramid promotional scheme where a consumer [pays] for the opportunity to [get money from bringing] other consumers into the scheme rather than from the sale or consumption of products.
— Claiming that the trader is about to cease trading or move premises when he is not.

The consumer problems caused by holiday clubs mostly relate to how they are sold, and they would be caught by the directive under one or more of the general or annexed provisions. Companies that re-engineered the product or service on offer, or changed only one aspect of their marketing, would not escape the provisions of the directive except by trading fairly.

The Unfair Commercial Practices Directive therefore aims to provide a broader base for the harmonisation of contracts and the conditions under which those contracts are established. More importantly, it should improve those conditions and should create a better legal environment for all fair-trading businesses, as well as for consumers. The directive will be accompanied by a rationalisation of the existing consumer protection directives listed earlier. We should expect a parallel process within national jurisdictions.

In some Member States consumer law is already based on a general duty to trade fairly. For example, in Finland the Consumer Protection Act has a general clause that simply states:

---

[23] Unfair Commercial Practices Directive, above n 2, annex I [12], [31], [14], [15].

No method that is contrary to good practice or that is otherwise unfair from the point of view of consumers shall be used in marketing. Marketing that does not convey the necessary information in respect of the health or economic security of consumers shall always be deemed unfair.

Belgium and Germany also have general principles legislation. Other countries, such as the UK, have no single general duty but instead have a mixture of legislation and common law rules pertaining to sectors and specific practices. In this country the Department of Trade and Industry (DTI) has already begun consulting publicly on the style of transposition, particularly on how radical the redesign of consumer law should be. The directive should bring with it a substantial deregulatory dividend in respect of accumulated specific regulations. This simpler, clearer consumer law regime should bring substantial gains to business, consumers themselves and to those entrusted with enforcing consumer law.

3. Consistency of Law Enforcement

For practical purposes, the harmonisation of consumer law cannot be viewed in isolation from the consistency—or otherwise—of consumer law enforcement. Across Europe there is a surprising variety of enforcement systems. In the UK public bodies such as the OFT and the trading standards service have long pursued cases where poor trading practices harm consumers, but in some Member States there are no such public bodies and all cases are dealt with by private organisations—either consumer associations or self-regulatory bodies sponsored by business—or by individuals.

Especially for cross-border activity, these differences can cause problems for business by creating a set of awkward barriers to buying and selling across borders and thereby raising the costs of expanding into other countries. Consumers are left confused and often disappointed at the lack of action when things go wrong. This in turn diminishes consumer confidence in purchases made across national boundaries. So, despite a growing level of formal harmonisation of consumer protection law, practical unevenness in application slows down the development of the internal market for consumer goods and services. The same lack of consistency can also create problems for public agencies trying to enforce the law across Europe, though far greater problems face individual consumers trying to take private actions across borders.

Cross-border actions by public agencies are in their infancy, but are growing. In part this is because the agencies are now better placed to take them, but it is also because traders increasingly use borders as a shield for rogue practices.

The EC Injunctions Directive,[24] first implemented in the UK in the Stop Now Orders Regulations 2001[25] and then in Part 8 of the Enterprise Act in 2002, provides standing for nominated Community Qualified Entities (CQE) to take action before the courts of other Member States to seek a cessation of infringements of obligations under the listed consumer directives in the foreign jurisdiction.

When seeking to enforce consumer directives, the OFT has discovered significant divergence in the way those directives have been implemented and interpreted. In some Member States the provisions of directives have been implemented in different civil codes and actions would be heard in a variety of courts—for example, misleading advertising cases may be actionable in tort or come before criminal courts, while unfair contract terms cases come before contract courts. This can make it logistically difficult for a foreign qualified entity to initiate a single Injunctions Directive action against a trader.

The most significant hurdle to effective cross-border public enforcement of consumer law has been the lack of a fully effective network of enforcers with powers under the Injunctions Directive. The OFT in 2004–5 held the presidency of the International Consumer Protection Network (ICPEN) and its European offshoot, ICPEN Europe. Members of this body are primarily public or publicly funded enforcers, and some are ministerial representatives. This network of primarily public bodies is excellent in many respects, but when it comes to action under the Injunctions Directive our counterparts often tend to be private consumer bodies. Indeed. many Member States provided Community Qualified Entity status only to private consumer bodies. These generally do not have the resources or expertise to assist a foreign public body, nor do they have equivalent powers of investigation or duties of administrative law.

We therefore welcome the European Consumer Protection Cooperation Regulation,[26] which now requires each Member State to have a single public liaison office and provides for certain investigative powers which can be exercised on behalf of other Member State enforcers. Bodies like the OFT will be able to rely on the cooperation of an agency in each other Member State when pursuing cross-border breaches of consumer law. The Commission will monitor the implementation arrangements to ensure consistency and will set up a regulatory committee to share experience and communicate plans between equivalent regulators.

---

[24] Directive 98/27/EC of the European Parliament and of the Council of 19 May 1998 on injunctions for the protection of consumers' interests [1998] OJ L166/51 ('Injunctions Directive').

[25] Stop Now Orders (EC Directive) Regulations, SI 2001/1422 ('Stop Now Orders Regulations 2001').

[26] Regulation (EC) 2006/2004 of the European Parliament and of the Council of 27 October 2004 on cooperation between national authorities responsible for the enforcement of consumer protection laws [2004] OJ L364/1 ('European Consumer Protection Cooperation Regulation').

The OFT has pursued cross-border cases with some success, but the following two examples of cases illustrate some of the complexities faced by public bodies that the Consumer Protection Cooperation Regulation should greatly reduce. Both involve distance selling and buying from home, one via the post and the other via the web.

Cross-Border Cases

The first is a case in which the OFT used the Injunctions Directive to pursue a trader in a foreign court—the first ever such cross-border action of its kind. In December 2004 the Brussels Commercial Court ruled in favour of the OFT's injunctive action against Duchesne SA, trading as TV Direct Distribution and Just 4 You. Complaints about the company concerned unsolicited mailings received by large numbers of UK consumers with the strong implication that the recipient is the winner of a big cash prize. The mailings appeared to require consumers to place an order from a catalogue of general household goods in order to receive their 'prize'.

When the OFT takes a case abroad it always approaches the authorities and Community Qualified Entities in the Member State in which the infringement originated in the first instance. Originally we anticipated that in most cases the authorities locally would be best placed to act. However, contact with our counterparts in Belgium highlighted the practical difficulties in collaborative working across borders. The CQE there is a private consumers' association, Test Achats. As the mailings were not disseminated in Belgium and therefore did not affect Belgian consumers, they could not justify the costs of taking the case and did not have the remit to protect overseas consumers. The ICPEN member, and public body, the Ministry of Economic Affairs could not take action as it was not a CQE and could not bring an Injunctions Directive action.

Domestic authorities have a level of local expertise that a foreign authority cannot expect to possess. Unilateral investigations from afar, which are not supported by powers to demand information, are time-consuming and complex. Though we were very pleased with the outcome in this case, the OFT will only take unilateral action as a last resort. Especially in view of the difficulties that we experienced as a public authority, it is imperative to have systems in place to protect consumers rather than expecting them to conduct time-consuming, complex, cross-border litigation themselves.

The second case is that of Jestel KG (gobuyeurope.com), a German trader selling clothing and footwear on the internet. The case demonstrates the sort of collaborative working between organisations that we hope the Consumer Protection Cooperation Regulation will make routine. It is also a good illustration of the differences between modes of enforcement of European consumer law in different countries.

The OFT became aware of numerous complaints about the trader in respect of late goods and non-delivery. The trader's contract terms sought to allow for delay and non-delivery, contrary to the regulations on unfair contract terms. The OFT provided a dossier of concerns and an analysis of breaches to a private German body, ZBUW,[27] which is funded by business primarily to enforce compliance with the law on unfair contract terms and misleading advertisements. ZBUW approached the trader and obtained undertakings that they would amend their terms and conditions to comply with the German implementation of the Unfair Terms in Consumer Contracts Directive.[28] These undertakings took the form of a contract between the company and ZBUW, with a financial penalty clause for any future breach. The case took two months from the first report of the problem to receipt of undertakings.

These two recent examples show that while unilateral cross-border action is better than nothing, practical cross-border cooperation is by far the best approach. Indeed, it would seem essential for effectively harmonised consumer law.

IV. CONCLUSIONS

Competition law and consumer law have been and are being harmonised across Europe to a considerable extent. Since those areas of regulatory law are fundamental parts of the framework for contracting, a degree of contract law harmonisation has occurred in the process. This has gone much further with respect to consumer contracts than with business-to-business contracts, which is probably appropriate.

Harmonisation has happened notwithstanding the underlying diversity of contract laws across Europe. Harmonisation of competition law is perhaps the easier process since national competition laws were mostly grafted onto contract law in the first place, rather than having grown out of it, and many reflect EC law and jurisprudence anyway.

Consumer law, by contrast, has generally grown from private contract law to make public action possible on behalf of consumers in general, compensating for the difficulty that individual consumers face in taking private action. It regulates the conditions under which contracts are formed and the non-core terms of those contracts. Its European harmonisation has in the past taken the form of a lengthy list of directives, some aimed at specific selling practices and some at specific sectors.

For the average citizen in Europe those directives have helped to create a reasonably consistent level of consumer protection, although laws and enforcement mechanisms vary a great deal. This situation is not itself

---

[27] Zentrale zur Bekämpfung unlauteren Wettbewerbs eV.
[28] Unfair Terms in Consumer Contracts Directive, above n 9.

problematic when people buy and sell within their borders. However, these variations make both trade and consumer protection difficult in what is supposed to be a single market. Goods and services can be difficult to buy and sell across borders and consumer rights are hard to enforce.

The OFT has tried as hard as any other national authority to make the existing laws work for cross-border trade, but this takes time and resources. We therefore particularly welcome the further steps of European consumer law and policy harmonisation that are now under way. The Unfair Commercial Practices Directive should bring improvement—as well as convergence—of substantive consumer law, and the Consumer Protection Cooperation Regulation will create an effective network of consumer enforcement bodies which will enable cross-border cases to be handled more efficiently. Those reforms should be good for consumers and fair-dealing businesses across Europe.

I am quite unable to judge the prospective benefits and costs of more radical harmonisation of European contract law. It would, however, seem important to assess them in the light of, among other things, the practical experience of steps towards the European harmonisation of competition and consumer law.

10

The Commission's Communications and Standard Contract Terms

ULF BERNITZ

I. EUROPEAN PRIVATE LAW AND STANDARD TERMS AND CONDITIONS

The ongoing development of European private law is affecting the use and content of standard terms and conditions used when concluding contracts. The primary example is the 1993 Directive on Unfair Terms in Consumer Contracts, which is the fundamental European legislative act on the use of standard contract terms in business-to-consumer (B2C) contracts; one of the most comprehensive and far-reaching pieces of European private law legislation so far.[1] Several of the specific consumer law directives are aimed at regulating unfair standard contract terms in more detail within the particular types of contract covered by the Directive. Well-known examples are the Directives on Consumer Credit,[2] Package Tours[3] and Guarantees Used in the Sale of Consumer Goods.[4]

However, existing European legislation also has an effect, although to a lesser extent, on the use of standard terms and conditions in business-to-business (B2B) contracts. First of all, the mandatory provisions in the consumer law directives have a spillover effect on the drafting of the underlying contracts between firms dealing with the consumers and their providers. But European legislation also includes to some extent mandatory provisions which are explicitly aimed at onerous standard terms in B2B contracts. A

---

[1] Council Directive 93/13/EEC of 5 April 1993 on unfair terms in consumer contracts [1993] OJ L95/29. Unfortunately, the Directive has been implemented in the Member States in a number of different ways, something that reduces the harmonisation effect considerably.

[2] Council Directive 87/102/EEC of 22 December 1986 for the approximation of the laws, regulations and administrative provisions of the Member States concerning consumer credit [1987] OJ L42/48.

[3] Council Directive 90/314/EEC of 13 June 1990 on package travel, package holidays and package tours [1990] OJ L158/59.

[4] Directive 1999/44/EC of the European Parliament and of the Council of 25 May 1999 on certain aspects of the sale of consumer goods and associated guarantees [1999] OJ L171/12.

well-known example is Article 4 in the Directive on Consumer Guarantees which gives the seller a right of redress in relation to his providers further back in the contractual chain. Another example is one of the first private law directives, the 1986 Directive on Self-employed Commercial Agents,[5] which regulates commercial agency contracts, an area where the use of standard terms is commonplace. Of particular importance is Article 17 of this directive, which gives the commercial agent a right to indemnity or compensation after termination of the agency contract. The European Court of Justice upheld this provision as mandatory law in the *Ingmar* case, where the contract referred to Californian law, which lacks similar legal protection of agents, as the law of the contract.[6] There are other examples. The 2000 Directive on Combating Late Payment in Commercial Transactions, for instance, is specifically aimed at addressing certain types of unfair payment clauses in standard term contracts.[7] According to the preamble, this directive is aimed particularly at easing the administrative and financial burdens placed on small and medium-sized businesses as a result of excessive payment periods and late payment.[8]

Standard terms are also affected by other parts of European law, eg the Brussels Regulation on International Private Law.[9] Cooperation within a trade association on the drafting or use of common standard terms can be contrary to Article 81 EC Treaty on the prohibition of anticompetitive agreements, in particular if the terms agreed directly affect prices charged, such as index clauses. However, most terms common in standard form contracts probably do not have an appreciable effect on competition and would fall outside the scope of Article 81.[10]

Thus, standard contract terms in B2B contracts is not at all an area that can be considered to be outside the reach of the emerging European private law. However, the effect of European law on standard terms used outside the B2C sector has so far been fairly limited, except in certain specific sectors. Nor has there been any coherent European approach towards standard terms and conditions in the B2B sector.

To what extent can we foresee a change of this situation as a result of the Commission's Communications on contract law and harmonisation ambitions? This is the issue discussed here. I start by looking at the Commission's Communications from the viewpoint of their treatment of standard terms

---

[5] Council Directive 86/653/EEC of 18 December 1986 on the coordination of the laws of the Member States relating to self-employed commercial agents [1986] OJ L382/17.

[6] Case C–381/98 *Ingmar GB Ltd v Eaton Leonard Technologies Inc* [2000] ECR I–9305. The principal was established in California, the agent in the EU.

[7] Directive 2000/35/EC of the European Parliament and of the Council of 29 June 2000 on combating late payment in commercial transactions [2000] OJ L200/35.

[8] *Ibid*, recital 7.

[9] Council Regulation (EC) No 44/2001 of 22 December 2000 on jurisdiction and the recognition and enforcement of judgements in civil and commercial matters [2001] OJ L12/1.

[10] Case C–215/96 *Bagnasco v Banco Popolare di Novara et al* [1999] ECR I–135, on standard terms used by banks, supports this conclusion.

and conditions, particularly in the B2B sector (section II). I then discuss critically the positions and priorities taken by the Commission. In section III, I reflect on the relation to the *lex mercatoria* and the work in the area by non-governmental organisations (NGOs). In section IV the importance of the elimination of legal obstacles to the development of EU wide standard terms and conditions is observed. In section V two final points are made.

II. THE COMMISSION'S COMMUNICATIONS FROM THE VIEWPOINT OF STANDARD TERMS AND CONDITIONS IN B2B CONTRACTS

There was no specific discussion of standard terms and conditions in the initial 2001 Commission Communication on European Contract Law,[11] although the presentation in the Annex to the Communication of the state of the Community *acquis* is a valuable source of information which includes B2B contracts. The starting point is rather the Commission's Action Plan for a More Coherent European Contract Law of 2003[12] ('Action Plan'), which contains a specific discussion on how to promote the elaboration of EU-wide standard contract terms.

In the Action Plan, the Commission takes a favourable general attitude towards the use of standard terms and conditions in B2B contracts and declares its intention to promote the establishment of such terms, in particular in cross-border transactions.[13] The Commission recognises the principle of contractual freedom as the centrepiece of contract law in all Member States. In the B2B sector, the Commission finds the contractual freedom to be limited only to a minor extent by mandatory contract law provisions or by other compulsory legal requirements. The Commission observes that parties are often interested in using standard terms and conditions, in particular for fairly straightforward and often repeated transactions, but notes that the terms are frequently drafted by the party possessing sufficient bargaining power to impose its contract terms. The Commission finds standard terms and conditions developed by contracting parties on both sides, ie agreed documents, to be more rare. It notes further that most of the standard terms and conditions have been developed by parties from a single Member State; such terms may therefore be less adapted to the particular needs of cross-border transactions.

The Commission concludes that a wider use of standard terms and conditions developed to fit cross-border transactions could solve some of the

---

[11] Communication from the Commission to the Council and the European Parliament on European Contract Law, COM(2001) 398 final.

[12] Communication from the Commission to the European Parliament and the Council on A More Coherent European Contract Law: an Action Plan, COM(2003) 68 final.

[13] *Ibid*, paras 81ff.

problems and disincentives connected to contract law. On this point the Commission refers to its general conclusion in the Action Plan that there exist obstacles and disincentives to cross-border transactions, deriving directly or indirectly from divergent national contract laws or from the legal complexity of these divergences, which are liable to prohibit, impede or otherwise render less advantageous such transactions.[14] In short, the Commission finds the promotion of the development of EU-wide standard terms and conditions to be an important method to overcome obstacles to cross-border commerce related to divergences in the existing contract law of the Member States.

In the Action Plan, the Commission discusses different methods to promote development in this direction.[15] As a first step the Commission mentions the establishment of a list of existing initiatives, both at the European level and within the Member States. Such a list would make it possible for parties interested to obtain information about similar initiatives and to learn from the mistakes and experience of others in order to establish 'best practices'. The Commission also announces its intention to set up a website where companies, persons and organisations could, on their own responsibility, list information on existing or planned initiatives in this area. However, the Commission reminds the business community that its general support for the elaboration of standard terms and conditions on an EU-wide scale should not be interpreted as a blanket approval. The standard terms and conditions should not violate EU rules, eg the Unfair Contract Terms Directive or other mandatory EU law, nor run counter to EU policies, such as competition law. Moreover, the Commission finds it important to ensure standard terms and conditions are jointly elaborated by representatives from all relevant groups, including large, small and medium-sized industry, traders, consumers and legal professionals. The Commission declares its intention to publish guidelines, the purpose of which would be to remind interested circles of the applicable limits.

The Action Plan has been followed up in the Commission's Communication of 2004, 'The Way Forward'.[16] This focuses primarily on the development of a 'common frame of reference' (CFR), a topic not discussed here. However, in 'The Way Forward' the Commission has presented some more detail on its intentions to promote EU-wide standard terms and conditions in the B2B sector and also standard terms in relations between business and governments, primarily public procurement contracts—so-called 'B2G' contracts.[17] The Commission has found a number of examples of EU-wide standard terms and conditions being used successfully, but has also found a lack of awareness of such EU-wide solutions. The Commission assures that it

---

[14] *Ibid*, para 25.
[15] *Ibid*, paras 86ff.
[16] Communication from the Commission to the European Parliament and the Council on European Contract Law and the revision of the *acquis*: the way forward, COM(2004) 651 final.
[17] *Ibid*, para 2.2.

does not intend to draw up the contract terms but only act as a facilitator and an 'honest broker', ie bringing interested parties together without interfering with the substance. It reiterates its intention to host a website on which market participants can exchange information about the EU-wide standard terms and conditions they are currently using or plan to develop, but—contrary to what had been expressed the year before in the Action Plan—the Commission states that it does not intend at this stage to publish guidelines on the development and use of standard terms and conditions.

In 'The Way Forward' the Commission announces a new type of measure to promote EU wide standard terms and conditions, namely to identify and rectify legislative obstacles to the use of EU-wide standard terms and conditions.[18] The Commission declares its intention to examine such obstacles, together with interested parties, with a view to eliminating them where needed and appropriate. This could be done by voluntary action by the Member State concerned, infringement proceedings by the Commission where the obstacles violate EU law, or other EU action, such as legislative measures, where they do not. In the first instance the Commission will organise a survey of existing obstacles after having consulted with stakeholders on its content and structure.

However, the latest developments include a withdrawal of the Commission's proposal to host a website for the presentation of EU-wide standard terms and conditions used or proposed by private parties or trade associations. The ongoing work on drafting Common Frames of Reference seems to be focusing primarily on B2C contracts although B2B contracts have not been excluded from the agenda. To some extent, stakeholders have been invited to workshops and other meetings for discussion of the establishment of EU-wide standard terms and conditions and neighbouring matters.[19] However, so far, the Commission's proposals in relation to EU-wide standard terms and conditions and other measures affecting standard terms in business contracts do not seem to have been met with enthusiastic reactions among stakeholders. My impression is that private organisations and associations within different fields of trade and commerce, often having been active in the area of developing and revising standard form contracts for a long time, are not keen to accept the European Commission as a new principal actor in their

---

[18] *Ibid*, para 2.2.3.3.

[19] A workshop on standard terms and conditions was held in Brussels on 19 January 2004 where the ORGALIME contracts for the European mechanical, electrical, electronic and metalworking industries were subject of a case study. Of particular importance is the standard contract ORGALIME S 2000, General Conditions for the Supply of Mechanical, Electrical and Electronic Products. It is partially based on the Internordic standard contract in the area which has existed for a very long time. At the workshop, also other standard terms and conditions were presented, eg the model contracts developed by the International Chamber of Commerce (ICC) in Paris, available at http://europa.eu.int/comm/internal_market/contractlaw/ 2004workshop_summary_en. A network of stakeholder experts took part in the Moving Forward Together Conference, organised by the Commission later in 2004.

field. Time will show whether or not the Commission will overcome this resistance.

In its First Annual Progress Report on European Contract Law and the Acquis Review (First Progress Report), the Commission explains why it has dropped the proposed website for the exchange of standard terms and conditions.[20] In short, the reasons given are the following: if the standard terms and conditions are to be enforceable in all Member States they need to comply with the most restrictive national law, which would greatly reduce their attractiveness. Standard terms and conditions are typically drafted for a specific sector, and thus the contractual clauses would not be of use for other sectors. Standard terms and conditions are constantly updated, which makes their posting on a website less useful. Standard terms and conditions are reviewed at a great cost in terms of legal fees, and thus parties would not be eager to share the results with competitors for free. Finally, the establishment and upkeep of the website would be very costly for the Commission.

These reasons look like excuses. Neither standard terms and conditions nor national legislation in the field had a different character a few years ago than is the case today, and the cost of maintaining a website has not increased in the meantime—if anything, the opposite is true. In my view, the Commission's decision to drop the website seems to reflect the general lack of enthusiasm among the stakeholders for the Commission's EU-wide standard terms and conditions project.

The First Progress Report does not contain any other, positive information on the Commission's activities or plans in relation to standard terms and conditions in the B2B or B2G sectors. Nor does it indicate whether the Commission is planning to introduce any other instruments in lieu of the website project in order to realise its intentions, stated in the Action Plan, to act as an 'honest broker' to further the development of 'best practices' as benchmarks. It also does not give any new information on the Commission's intentions, announced in 'The Way Forward', to introduce new measures to identify and rectify legislative obstacles to the use of EU-wide standard terms and conditions.

To sum up, the Commission is at present concentrating on the realisation of the CFR (certainly in itself a very large and difficult project), and its ambitions in the standard terms and conditions sector, as announced primarily in the Action Plan, seem largely to have been put on hold. In my opinion, this is not very surprising. The way in which the Commission has presented its proposal and set its priorities can be criticised on several grounds, as I will discuss in the following.

---

[20] Report from the Commission, 'First Annual Progress Report on European Contract Law and the Acquis Review' COM(2005) 456 final, para 4.1.

III. THE RELATION TO LEX MERCATORIA AND THE WORK OF NON-GOVERNMENTAL ORGANISATIONS

The Commission's general description in the Action Plan of standard terms and conditions used in B2B contracts seems somewhat problematic and not quite balanced. According to the Commission, the standard terms and conditions are normally applied only within one Member State and not adapted to the needs of cross-border transactions. The Commission finds that the terms are usually drafted by the party possessing sufficient bargaining power to impose its contract terms on the other party and that agreed documents to be rare. The Commission's description is, in part, certainly correct. No doubt, there exists an abundance of standard terms drafted by individual firms or specific trade associations which are unbalanced and sometimes clearly unfair. In addition, standard contracts, in particular those emanating from individual firms, might at times be rather poorly drafted from a legal point of view.

However, the Commission's description in the Action Plan lacks the proper recognition and acknowledgement of all the important work that has been done by NGOs, international trade associations, etc in order to improve the situation. In particular, one finds no mention in the Commission's Communications of the rapid development of the international *lex mercatoria*. There is no agreement on the definition of what *lex mercatoria* is, but in general terms *lex mercatoria* is not national legislation but rather a non-national system of principles and rules generally accepted in international commerce.[21] The *lex mercatoria* is expressed in generally recognised international codes, established commercial usage and the like.

This immensely important area of law[22] includes, inter alia, principles on international contracts of sale, payment modalities, eg letters of credit, guarantees and warranties, trade terms, transport contracts, eg bills of lading and documents used for multimodal transports, transport insurance, international financing contracts and principles for the resolution of international commercial disputes. Principles intended for general international use have been laid down in important documents, eg the 2004 version of the UNIDROIT Principles of International Commercial Contracts with detailed comments.[23] The International Chamber of Commerce (ICC), an NGO, has been very active. As is well known, the ICC has elaborated the meaning of different trade terms by developing its system of Incoterms, abbreviation for *i*nternational *c*ommercial terms. They exist now in their version of

---

[21] J Ramberg, *International Commercial Transactions* (3rd edn, The Hague, Kluwer, 2004) 20.

[22] See, in particular, R Goode, *Commercial Law* (3rd edn, London, LexisNexis, 2004). A comprehensive work in the field is J Dalhuisen, *Dalhuisen on International Commercial, Financial and Trade Law* (2nd edn, Oxford, Hart, 2004). See also CM Schmitthoff, *The Export Trade* (10th edn, London, Sweet & Maxwell, 2000).

[23] See www.unidroit.org. The 2004 UNIDROIT Principles are reprinted in, eg Ramberg, above n 21, 227.

year 2000[24] and define terms as cif, fas, fob, ex works etc. ICC uniform rules and model contracts have been prepared in a number of important fields.[25] In the area of resolution of disputes one should recall the 1998 ICC Rules on Arbitration and the 1985 UNCITRAL Model Law on International Commercial Arbitration.[26]

This vast body of law has at least the status of soft law but is certainly an influential general source of law, inspiring legal writing, the drafting of standard contracts—which sometimes expressly integrate international codes or model contracts[27]—and the application and interpretation of national law on issues involving international commercial transactions. It might also express usage. Article 1.9 of the UNIDROIT Principles of 2004 states expressly that parties are bound by a usage that is widely known to and regularly observed in international trade by parties in the particular trade concerned except when the application of such usage would be unreasonable.[28] In this regard, the Incoterms of 2000 would be a good candidate.

It is difficult to understand why the Commission has not recognised in its Action Plan and in 'The Way Forward' the internationalisation of commercial law and the important work carried out in other fora. Standard terms and conditions used in transactions between the EU Member States cannot be separated from that work, and standard terms and conditions used in export and import transactions between EU countries and other parts of the world are no less important from the EU perspective than are intra-EU transactions. The EU is one of the world's two trade giants. There should be no reason to reinvent the wheel or for the Commission to set up a new competing organisational structure. An assessment of the importance of the Convention on Contracts for the International Sale of Goods for the formation of standard terms in B2B contracts would also have been welcome, the UK being the only major EU country not to have ratified it. In any case, the Commission Communication should have supported its proposals by including an analysis of what would be the shortcomings, in the view of the Commission, of what is going on and has been achieved by others. Possibly, the Commission might have found the work in other fora to have too little focus on small and middle sized firms and the relation to consumer law, but that is only a speculation on my part; the Commission has not said so. However, the Commission's

---

[24] ICC, *Incoterms 2000, ICC Publication No 560* (Paris, 2000).

[25] Goode characterises ICC as 'the prime mover in the codification of international trade usage'; above n 22, 14.

[26] *Ibid*, 1162ff.

[27] *Ibid*, 11ff; CM Schmitthoff, 'The Unification and Harmonisation of Law by Means of Standard Contracts and General Conditions' (1968) 17 *ICLQ* 551.

[28] A similar provision is found in Art 9(2) of the CISG, the UN Convention on Contracts for the International Sale of Goods (also known as the 'Vienna Convention'): 'The parties are considered, unless otherwise agreed, to have impliedly made applicable to their contract or its formation a usage of which the parties knew or ought to have known and which in international trade is widely known to, and regularly observed by, parties to contracts of the type involved in the particular trade concerned.'

initiative emanates primarily from the DG Sanco, ie the Directorate responsible for consumer law. The general lack of recognition of the work done by others is probably a primary explanation why the Commission's initiative has hardly been met with enthusiasm among the stakeholders. It is understandable they do not see how to place the Commission in the role of an 'honest broker' furthering the development of 'best practices'.

IV. ELIMINATION OF LEGAL OBSTACLES TO THE USE OF EU-WIDE STANDARD TERMS AND CONDITIONS

In my opinion, the Commission has announced a more fruitful approach, fitting the general role of the Commission better, in 'The Way Forward' when it points at the legislative obstacles to the use of EU-wide standard terms and conditions. As already mentioned, the Commission declares its intention in the Communication to examine such obstacles, together with interested parties, with a view to eliminating them where needed and appropriate. The Commission mentions different possible methods that could be used: voluntary action by Member states concerned, infringement proceedings to eliminate obstacles and harmonisation via specific legislation. According to the Communication, the Commission will start by organising a survey of existing obstacles.

Such a survey of existing obstacles should be welcomed and might bring to light a considerable number of legal obstacles related to contract law which function as hindrances to the free flow of cross-border trade and transactions or, at least, involve unnecessary costs and legal risks. In particular, one should look at specific provisions in national law which might function as 'traps' for uninformed parties in other Member States. It is well known that national law differs greatly between the Member States when it comes to the requirement of formalities, eg that contracts have to be set up, formulated or verified in a certain way. If the law is functioning very well in certain Member States without requiring such formalities as are deemed necessary in other Member States, it should be possible to draw conclusions based on these findings.

There are, in particular, two Member States that have specific legislation of a general character in relation to standard terms and contracts: Italy and Germany. According to Article 1341(2) of the Italian Civil Code, certain types of standard conditions, prepared in advance of one of the parties, have to be specifically approved in writing; if not, they are ineffective. Limitation of liability and arbitration clauses belong to the types of clauses mentioned in the statutory text.[29] This means that Italian standard contracts must be signed

---

[29] Art 1341 of the Italian Civil Code reads in English translation: '(1) Standard conditions prepared by one of the parties are effective as to the other, if at the time of the formation of the contract the latter knew of them or should have known of them by using ordinary diligence. (2) In any case, conditions are ineffective, unless specifically approved in writing, which establish, in

in a special way; the party must approve specifically in writing all such restrictive clauses covered by the provision in the Code. To take an example, a customer opening an account in an Italian bank has to sign the pre-prepared contract on more or less every page.

This provision was originally introduced as a measure aimed at protecting the weaker party. However, one might suggest that the measure has now developed into an empty formality, or at least ask if it is necessary to keep the measure in contracts having an EU dimension.

In Germany, the special Act on General Business Conditions (*Allgemeine Geschäftsbedingungen*, AGB) was made part of the *Bürgerliches Gesetzbuch* (BGB), the German Civil Code, in 2002; it is now contained in sections 305–310 BGB. The legislation includes an impressive list of black or grey standard terms which are only applicable in B2C contracts. However, the general clause in section 307 BGB is applicable also in B2B contracts and opens up for a court based control of the unfairness of standard terms used.[30] Based on both previous case law and new case law under that article, there has emerged an enormous body of law related to the assessment of particular terms used in standard contracts.[31] To an outside observer it seems as if practically every possible type of contract term has been the object of assessment in case law and legal doctrine. As a result, many types of contract terms are ineligible in German law and for many other terms it is necessary to know exactly how they should be phrased in order to avoid their censure by the courts.

The German AGB law forms an impressive body of law, largely unique in Europe. It offers protection, particularly for the weaker party, against standard terms which are too unbalanced in favour of the other party. However, in most other European countries businesses, including small businesses, seems to be able to function well without access to a similar protection. It is not for me to take a position whether or not the German protection of businesses against unbalanced standard terms has been carried too far in legal practice, but in relation to the issue of the establishment of EU wide standard terms and conditions one cannot avoid looking into the question. Obviously, a standard contract intended for EU-wide use cannot include terms which are unenforceable in the Union's largest Member State. It is worth remembering

---

favour of him who has prepared them in advance, limitation on liability, the power of withdrawing from the contract or of suspending its performance, or which impose time limits involving forfeitures of the other party, limitations on the power to raise defences, restrictions on contractual freedom in relation to third parties, tacit extension or renewal of the contract, arbitration clauses, or derogations from the competence of courts.' Text taken from M Beltramo, GE Longo and JH Merryman (eds), *The Italian Civil Code* (New York, Oceana Publishing, 1991ff) (looseleaf publication).

[30] '[E]ntgegen den Geboten von Treu und Glauben unangemessen benachteiligen.'
[31] A comprehensive presentation of this, mostly clause based, case law is found in the well-known handbook by O Palandt, *Bürgerliches Gesetzbuch* (Munich, CH Beck).

that, in the area of B2C contracts, the European Directive of 1993 on Unfair Terms in Consumer Contracts was drafted according to the German model, ie the harmonisation of European law was based on the German pattern. If we want EU-wide standard terms and conditions in the B2B sector, the same problem crops up again. One solution would be to accept the requirements of German law, characterised by a very well-developed control of the content of the terms, as the basis for the EU-wide standard terms and conditions; another would be to achieve a certain reduction of the German control ambitions.

What would be the opinion of the Commission on this very important point? We do not know; the Commission has chosen not to mention the problem in its Communications. However, this can hardly be the 'way forward' towards EU-wide standard terms and conditions in the B2B sector. The issue needs to be addressed further.

V. TWO FINAL POINTS

I will finish by mentioning two final points. First, the Commission should fully acknowledge the important work going on in other fora, eg NGOs, on the improvement of the law on international commercial transactions and standard contracts used in such transactions, and should avoid any duplication. Secondly, the Commission should give priority to its proposal to identify and rectify legislative obstacles in the law of Member States to the use of EU-wide standard terms and conditions in order to stimulate cross-border transactions and reduce unnecessary formalities and costs. As a first step, a survey of existing obstacles, including different kinds of formality requirements in the Member States, would be much welcomed.

11

Non-Legislative Harmonisation: Protection from Unfair Suretyships[*]

AURELIA COLOMBI CIACCHI

I. THE ADVANTAGES OF NON-LEGISLATIVE HARMONISATION

The debate on the creation of a common contract law for Europe has so far concentrated predominantly on legislative harmonisation. Here 'legislative harmonisation' means not only legislation in the strict sense, but also non-binding, optional instruments which are drafted in the form of model laws, no matter whether they are issued by public bodies or private entities. Non-legislative instruments of harmonisation have attracted some consideration in the Commission's communications on European contract law, but only with regard to voluntary, non-authoritative measures, such as the approximation of standard contract terms in the business practice.[1]

This paper will concentrate instead on the major authoritative system of non-legislative harmonisation: judicial governance. It starts from the assumption that harmonised written legal provisions are neither necessary nor sufficient to assure equally effective protection of the same basic interests in different legal systems. They are not necessary because the same degree of protection of a certain interest can be achieved by applying widely divergent legislative provisions or case-law doctrines. This is shown by comparative law studies based on a factual approach, such as the Trento project 'The Common Core of European Private Law'.[2] They are not sufficient because

---

[*] For a longer version of this paper see A Colombi Ciacchi, 'Non-Legislative Harmonisation of Private Law under the European Constitution: The Case of Unfair Suretyships' (2005) 13 *European Review of Private Law* 285.

[1] See the communications 'A More Coherent European Contract Law: An Action Plan' COM(2003) 68 final (12 February 2003) paras 52ff, 81ff; and 'European Contract Law and the revision of the *acquis*: the way forward' COM(2004) 651 final (11 October 2004) para 2.2.

[2] This project aims at discovering similar solutions in the case-law of the Member States behind the veil of the different provisions or doctrines applied. See M Bussani and U Mattei, 'The Common Core Approach to European Private Law' (1997) 3 *Columbia Journal of European Law* 339. For more information about the Common Core project, see http://www.jus.unitn.it/dsg/common-core.

the application of even totally uniform rules can lead to different degrees of protection from country to country, according to each different system of remedies and court practices.

A more effective and sensitive way of harmonising the standards of protection of certain basic interests of European citizens could be convergence in the case-law of the Member States. It could be more effective because the intensity of protection of a certain right depends primarily on the law in action, not the law in books.[3] It could be more sensitive because case-law convergence operates even in the context of the great diversity of legal cultures.[4] All that matters is that the courts of different European States achieve similar results in the same cases, regardless of which norms, doctrines or procedures they apply in order to reach this end.

To illustrate how the standards of protection in European contract law could be approximated via case-law convergence, this paper will refer to one specific example: the protection of non-professional guarantors from unfair suretyships.

II. UNFAIR SURETYSHIPS AND CASE-LAW CONVERGENCE

Non-professional guarantors, such as family members of the debtor, often sign suretyships without being aware of their potentially ruinous consequences. Neither the debtor nor the bank has any interest in advising the potential guarantor about the financial risk of the contract.

However, sometimes the surety's substantive freedom of contract is impaired even when the guarantor is perfectly aware of the contractual risk. For example, family members of the main debtor often have little choice, if any: either they agree to stand surety or they risk impairing their familial relationship by refusing to do so.[5]

For these reasons, since the 1970s—and with particular intensity in the 1990s—the Courts and legislatures of several Member States (such as the UK,[6] France,[7] Germany,[8] Austria[9] and the Netherlands[10]) have looked for

---

[3] Cf R Pound, 'Law in Books and Law in Action' (1910) 44 *American Law Review* 12.

[4] On the constitutional, cultural and economic objections to legislative harmonisation, see S Weatherill, 'Why Object to the Harmonisation of Private Law by the EC?' (2004) 12 *European Review of Private Law* 633. On the connection between private law and cultural identity, see H Collins, 'European Private Law and the Cultural Identity of States' (1995) 3 *European Review of Private Law* 353.

[5] Cf B Fehlberg, 'The Husband, the Bank, the Wife and her Signature' (1994) 57 *MLR* 467; 'The Husband, the Bank, the Wife and her Signature. The Sequel', (1996) 59 *MLR* 675; D Geary, 'Notes on Family Guarantees in English and Scottish Law—A Comment' (2000) 8 *European Review of Private Law* 25.

[6] A milestone in the 1970s was *Lloyds Bank v Bundy* [1975] QB 326, later overruled by *National Westminster Bank v Morgan* [1985] 1 All ER 821. The current leading case in the UK is *Royal Bank of Scotland v Etridge (No 2)* [2001] UKHL 44, [2002] AC 773, which followed *Barclays Bank plc v O'Brien* [1994] 1 AC 180. In Scottish law see also *Smith v Bank of Scotland/Mumford v Bank of Scotland* 1996 SLT 392.

remedies in order to discharge vulnerable guarantors totally or partially from unfair surety obligations.

The history of legal protection from unfair suretyships shows lots of spontaneous convergences between the Member States. For example, the new Articles 341–44 of the French Consumer Code state that if the surety is manifestly disproportionate to the guarantor's capital and income at the time the contract was concluded, the lender cannot rely on the guarantee unless the guarantor's assets at the time the guarantee is called in allow them to face their obligations.[11] This straightforward rule is substantively similar to the ultimate result of long and extremely complex case-law developments in Germany.[12] Yet the formal paths followed by the two countries towards this result are totally different. In France, before the enactment of the Consumer Code, in exceptional cases the Courts denied validity to unfair suretyships by applying the rules of the Civil Code about mistake.[13] The German judges

---

[7] See eg Cour d'appel Paris 18 January 1977 *Juris-Classeur périodique, édition générale* II 19318, commented by P Simler. The decision was approved by Cass 4 July 1979 *Recueil Dalloz* 1979, 538.

[8] Although the first German cases in this field go back to earlier decades, the very starting point of the discussion was a judgment of the Federal Constitutional Court of 1993 (BVerfG 19 October 1993 [1994] *Neue Juristische Wochenschrift* 36) which forced the Federal Court of Justice (BGH) to overrule its precedents so as to ensure effective protection to vulnerable family guarantors. Cf M Habersack and R Zimmermann, 'Legal Change in a Codified System: Recent Developments in German Suretyship Law' (1999) 3 *Edinburgh Law Review* 272; Mr Justice Kiefel, 'Guarantees by Family Members and Spouses: Garcia and a German Perspective' (2000) 74 *Australian Law Journal* 692.

[9] In 1995, the Austrian Supreme Court (OGH 27 March 1005, 1 Ob 544/95) aligned itself with the new German case law. Cf G Graf, 'Verbesserter Schutz vor riskanten Bürgschaften' (1995) *Österreichisches Bankarchiv* 776.

[10] See the Supreme Court judgments HR 1 June 1990, *Signaal Rechtspraak van de Week* 1990, 119, *Nederlandse Jurisprudentie* 1991, 759; HR 3 June 1994, *Signaal Rechtspraak van de Week* 1994, 126. Cf RPLJ Tjittes, 'Verplichtingen van de schuldeiser jegens de borg' (2000) *Tijdschrift voor Privaatrecht* 28; O Cherednychenko, 'The Constitutionalization of Contract Law: Something New under the Sun?' (2004) 8 *Electronic Journal of Comparative Law* 4, 10ff, available at http://www.ejcl.org/81/art81-3.html; CE du Perron and M Haentjens, Boek 7 Titel 14 ('Borgtocht'), aant. Inl. 3, in *Artikelsgewijs commentaar op het Burgerlijk Wetboek* (Deventer, Kluwer, forthcoming), with further references.

[11] 'Un créancier professionnel ne peut se prévaloir d'un contrat de cautionnement conclu par une personne physique dont l'engagement était, lors de sa conclusion, manifestement disproportionné à ses biens et revenus, à moins que le patrimoine de cette caution, au moment où celle-ci est appelée, ne lui permette de faire face à son obligation.'

[12] For a recent overview of the German case law see S Braun, 'Von den Nahbereichpersonen bis zu den Arbeitnehmern als Bürgen: Ein Überblick über die Rechtsprechung des BGH zur Sittenwidrigkeit von Bürgschaften' [2004] *Juristische Ausbildung* 474; A Krafka, 'Die Rechtsprechung des BGH im Bürgschaftsrecht' [2004] *Juristische Arbeitsblätter* 668; U Drobnig, 'Die richterliche Neuregelung des Bürgschaftsrechts in Deutschland' in U Drobnig, HI Sagel-Grande and HJ Snijders (eds), *Neuere Entwicklungen im Recht der persönlichen Kreditsicherheiten in Deutschland und den Niederlanden* (Sellier, Munich, 2003), 1; HI Sagel-Grande, 'Bürgschaft in Deutschland: facts and figures', *ibid*, 63.

[13] See the judgments quoted in n 7.

have instead had recourse to the general clauses of good morals and good faith in the German Civil Code.[14]

The British law of family guarantees differs from the French and German ones with regard to both the formal paths and the substantive results. In English law, the House of Lords has tackled the problem of unfair suretyships by relying on the equitable doctrine of undue influence, which empowers the courts to set aside a transaction which is the result of abuse of a relationship of trust and confidence.[15] Undue influence, however, is out of the question when the lender has taken reasonable steps to satisfy itself that the guarantor had understood and freely entered into the transaction.[16]

In Scottish law, the House of Lords has come to similar conclusions moving from the principle of fair dealing in good faith.[17] Also the Dutch Supreme Court (Hoge Raad) deduced from the principle of good faith a duty of professional lenders to provide clear information to non-professional guarantors about the legal consequences of the suretyship.[18] The Dutch case-law of family suretyships also presents spontaneous convergences with the French jurisprudence:[19] according to the Hoge Raad, the creditor's breach of his information duty gives rise to a surety's mistake, which makes the suretyship invalid.[20]

The British and Dutch solutions, however, do not go quite as far as the French, German and Austrian ones, which deny validity to suretyships of family members when grossly disproportionate, irrespective of whether or not the creditor failed to advise the guarantor. Yet an amazing spontaneous convergence can be found also between the English and German case-law on family guarantee.

In 1993, the German Federal Constitutional Court stated that if a contractual party is so powerful that it can define unilaterally the content of the contract, this means heteronomy for the other party, and in this case the fundamental right of private autonomy of the weaker party is affected. If a contract is unusually burdensome for one party and there is a 'structural

---

[14] Cf M Habersack and R Zimmermann, above n 8.

[15] Cf HG Beale, 'Duress and Undue Influence' in HG Beale (ed), *Chitty on Contracts* (29th edn, Sweet & Maxwell, London, 2004), 7-047ff.

[16] In *Royal Bank of Scotland v Etridge (No 2)* [2001] UKHL 44, [2002] AC 773, the House of Lords has specified in great detail the steps reasonably to be expected of a lender. In relation to past transactions, it has to 'bring home to the wife the risk she was running by standing surety, either a private meeting with her or by requiring her to take independent advice from a solicitor on whose confirmation the lender might rely that she had understood the nature and the effect of the transaction. In respect of future transactions the lender should contact the wife directly, checking the name of the solicitor she wished to act for her and explaining that for its protection it would require his confirmation as to her understanding of the documentation to prevent her from subsequently disputing the transaction.'

[17] See *Smith; Mumford*, above n 6.

[18] HR 1 June 1990, above n 10.

[19] See n 7.

[20] HR 1 June 1990, above n 10; HR 19 May 1995, *NJ* 1997, 648. Cf also for further references in Dutch jurisprudence and academic literature du Perron and Haentjens, above n 10.

inequality of bargaining power,' civil courts have a duty to intervene and correct the content of the contract by making use of the general clauses of private law.[21]

Thirty years ago, a strikingly similar doctrine had been also recognised in English law. In a 1975 case concerning a father's guarantee for his son's debts, Lord Denning tried to unite the doctrines of duress, unconscionable transaction and undue influence in a new principle of inequality of bargaining power.[22] However, in 1985 the House of Lords rejected this doctrine. It held that there was no need to erect such a general principle, since Parliament would place such restrictions upon freedom of contract as are necessary (such as in the Unfair Contract Terms Act 1977 and the Consumer Credit Act).[23]

III. 'CRYPTOTYPES' IN UNFAIR SURETYSHIP LAW

All these convergences shed light on what Rodolfo Sacco's comparative law theory calls 'cryptotypes.'[24] Cryptotypes are implicit rules and patterns which substantively shape the solution given by a certain legal system to a particular problem, although they are not explicitly formulated as legal rules. They remain cryptic, hidden behind the veil of other norms and doctrines explicitly applied. Sometimes certain principles are formal legal rules in some legal systems and cryptotypes in others. Moreover, within one and the same legal system certain principles may be born as cryptotypes and then, years later, become formal legal rules.[25]

Both phenomena can be observed in the field of unfair suretyships. For example, in a French decision of 1977,[26] the legal rule explicitly applied by the Paris Court of Appeal in order to annul the suretyship of a poor widow was Article 1110 Code Civil (nullity on the ground of essential mistake). In fact, however, the Court deducted the essentiality of the widow's mistake from the manifest disproportion between her financial means and the amount of the obligation, after having taken into account her age and low level of education.[27] Therefore it could be argued that in this case the decisive

---

[21] BVerfG 19 October 1993 [1994] *Neue Juristische Wochenschrift* 36. For a description in English of the facts of this case, see Cherednychenko, above n 10, 2ff.

[22] *Bundy*, above n 6.

[23] *Morgan*, above n 6.

[24] R Sacco, 'Legal Formants: A Dynamic Approach To Comparative Law' (1991) 39 *American Journal of Comparative Law* 1 and 343, 384.

[25] *Ibid*, at 386.

[26] Cour d'appel Paris 18 January 1977, above n 7.

[27] *Ibid*: '... (l)orsqu'il existe une disproportion frappante entre la pauvreté des ressources de la caution, personne agée et ignorante, et l'enormité du cautionnement souscrit par celle-ci, l'erreur commise par celle-ci au moment de la conclusion du contrat, a porté non seulement sur l'étendue et les conséquences du contrat mais encore sur l'objet même et sur la cause de l'opération envisagée, c'est-a-dire sur la substance même de l'engagement. Cette erreur entraîne la nullité du cautionnement.'

rule was a cryptotype: 'invalidity of manifestly disproportionate suretyships of weak persons.' On the enactment of the French Consumer Code in 1993, this rule left its cryptotype status and became explicit.

In German law, the norm explicitly applied to unfair suretyship cases is the nullity of immoral contracts (section 138 BGB). However, according to a consolidated German jurisprudence, if there is a 'gross imbalance' between the amount of the debt and the surety's financial means, and the surety is a close family member of the debtor who does not have an economic interest in the suretyship, it may be presumed that the bank has taken unfair advantage from the surety's lack of experience or affection for the debtor. In other words: grossly disproportionate family suretyships are presumed to be immoral.[28] Thus it may be argued that in Germany the rule 'invalidity of manifestly disproportionate suretyships of weak persons' is a quasi-cryptotype.

Even more important than the specific cryptotype 'invalidity of manifestly disproportionate suretyships of weak persons' is the general cryptotype 'invalidity of severely imbalanced contracts concluded under structural inequality of bargaining power.' The German Constitutional Court made it explicit. Lord Denning tried to do the same, but failed because such a general doctrine does not fit into the picture of traditional English private law.[29]

IV. DISPARITY OF SURETY PROTECTION STANDARDS IN EUROPE

This brief comparison shows how an equally effective protection of the same interests in the same situations could be achieved either by legislation or case-law, by applying widely different norms and doctrines.[30] However, this comparison also shows that the intensity of protection may vary notably from country to country. The highest standard of protection of vulnerable sureties (invalidity of grossly disproportionate obligations) is found in France and Germany. An intermediate standard (creditor's duty to advise) is found in Britain and the Netherlands. The lowest standard (absence of any special rule protecting non-professional sureties) corresponds, for example, to the situation in Italy.[31]

---

[28] See eg BGH 26 April 2001 [2001] *Zeitschrift für Wirtschaftsrecht* 1190.

[29] However, equitable relief is possible in certain cases of harsh and unconscionable bargains. As HG Beale puts it, 'the real question is the scope of the principles involved, particularly that of relief against unconscionable bargains with persons suffering from some form of bargaining disadvantage' (above n 15, 7-111). On the advantages of a general doctrine of unconscionability, see E McKendrick, *Contract Law* (6th edn, Palgrave Macmillan, Basingstoke, 2005), 378ff.

[30] See also Cherednychenko, above n 10, 13.

[31] In the 1980s, Italian courts did not remain insensitive to the problem of disproportionate family guarantees. Sometimes the lower courts declared the nullity of such contracts because of the indeterminacy of their object (Arts 1346 and 1325 Italian Civil Code). However, the Corte

Spontaneous convergence is therefore not sufficient to ensure an equally effective protection of the same interests in the same cases throughout Europe. To render both the European citizens and the European banks more equal, top-down harmonisation—although of a non-legislative nature—would be necessary.

V. HARMONISATION OF STANDARDS OF PROTECTION THROUGH HORIZONTAL EFFECT OF FUNDAMENTAL RIGHTS AND CONSTITUTIONAL PRINCIPLES?

The mechanisms for ensuring top-down harmonisation of case-law in the EU are available already. The judgments of the European Court of Justice (ECJ) and the European Court of Human Rights form legally binding guidelines to be complied with by the Member States. However, the competence to review private law cases decided by national courts is given to the Strasbourg Court only insofar as a violation of the European Convention on Human Rights (ECHR) is alleged, and to the Luxembourg Court only in so far as a breach of the Treaties or secondary EC law is at stake. Therefore the question arises whether unfair surety agreements concluded between a professional lender and a non-professional guarantor have a human rights and/or an EU law dimension. The answer in both regards seems to be 'yes'.

According to a consolidated jurisprudence of the European Court of Human Rights, Article 8 ECHR does not merely protect private life in a strict sense, it also protects personal autonomy in general.[32] Private autonomy and freedom of contract can be considered as a specific aspect of the fundamental right to self-determination and personal autonomy.[33]

The whole discussion on unfair suretyships gravitates to the fundamental question of personal autonomy and freedom of contract. When someone is asked by both a beloved family member and a bank employee to sign a standard form of guarantee, her or his substantive self-determination is heavily limited.[34] This limitation concerns both core aspects of freedom of contract: the freedom to enter or not to enter into the agreement, and the content of the latter. One may argue that the personal autonomy of vulnerable sureties is even more severely restricted than that of consumers willing to buy a certain

---

di Cassazione rejected this argumentation (see eg Cass 15 March 1991 *Foro italiano* 1991, I 2060). The 1992 Act on transparency in the banking sector (Legge 154/1992) modified Art 1938 of the Italian Civil Code. This provision now requires the maximum amount guaranteed to be indicated in a surety agreement concerning future debts.

[32] See *Goodwin v United Kingdom* (1996) 22 EHHR 123, para 59; *Pretty v United Kingdom* (2002) 35 EHRR 1, para 62; *Mikulić v Croatia* (2002) 1 FCR 720, para 53.

[33] The embedding of freedom of contract in Art 8 ECHR has been convincingly demonstrated by H Snijders, 'Privacy of Contract' in K Ziegler (ed), *Human Rights and Private Law: Privacy* (Hart Publishing, Oxford, forthcoming).

[34] Cf Fehlberg, 'The Sequel', above n 5; Geary, above n 5.

product. Indeed, to renounce a certain product might be less difficult than refusing to help one's own father, son, husband or employer whose small enterprise urgently needs a loan. If it is true that in the context of consumer contracts 'the idea of free negotiation is a myth' and '(t)he bargain has lost its sanctity as an expression of individual will,'[35] the same must also be true with regard to suretyships concluded between a bank and a non-professional guarantor for one of his or her close family members, employer, etc.

The lack of protection from unfair suretyships may clash not only with Article 8 ECHR, but also with Article 6 EU. The latter provision makes clear that there are common European fundamental rights and constitutional principles which are already in force as applicable law. Although Article 6 EU does not create a general competence for the EC in human rights matters, there may be an overlap of competence between the ECJ and the European Court of Human Rights wherever the interpretation of a European constitutional right or principle is at stake. Indeed, the fundamental rights and constitutional principles mentioned in the Treaties are European constitutional norms like the fundamental freedoms. Being part of EC law, they have to be interpreted uniformly in all Member States, and national law must comply with them. The institution competent to interpret EC law—and the European Constitution—in the last instance is the ECJ.

Of course, the lender's freedom of contract and property rights are also constitutionally protected. The European Courts need therefore to strike a balance between competing constitutional rights, in order to assess the appropriate level of protection for both the surety and the lender. Both the assessment of the required standards of protection and the corresponding adaptation of national law by the courts of the Member States can be achieved via a horizontal effect of the European constitutional norms, such as Article 8 ECHR and Article 6 EU Treaty.

Horizontal effect is not a new phenomenon. In EU law, the four fundamental economic freedoms and some principles of the Treaties (such as equal pay for men and women) have been applied horizontally by the ECJ since the early 1970s,[36] as have EU fundamental rights since 1991.[37] Also at the level of national law, at least a weak and indirect horizontal effect of fundamental rights and constitutional principles is now generally acknowledged throughout Europe.[38]

---

[35] S Weatherill, *EC Consumer Law and Policy* (Longman, London, 1997), 77.
[36] Case 4/73 *Nold v Commission* [1974] ECR 491.
[37] Case 219/91 *Ter Voort* [1992] ECR I–5485.
[38] On the horizontal effect of fundamental and constitutional rights in France, see JP Marguénaud, *CEDH et droit privé* (La documentation française, Paris, 2001); in Germany, CW Canaris, *Grundrechte und Privatrecht—Eine Zwischenbilanz* (de Gruyter, Berlin, 1999); in Italy, A Di Majo, *La tutela civile dei diritti* (4th edn, Giuffré, Milan, 2003); in the Netherlands, JH Nieuwenhuis, 'De constitutie van het burgerlijk recht' (2001) *Rechtsgeleerd Magazijn Themis* 203; SD Lindenbergh, 'Constitutionalisering van contractenrecht. Voer de werking van fundamentele rechten in contractuele verhoudingen' (2004) *Weekblad voor Privaatrecht,*

This method of harmonisation can be applied to every private law matter touching upon European fundamental rights, not only suretyship law. Since every citizen of the EU should enjoy the common European fundamental rights without any discrimination on the ground of nationality,[39] one may argue that the standards of private law protection of these rights in their horizontal dimension should become equal. This could be easily achieved through case-law convergence.

Notariaat en Registratie 977; in Portugal, JC Vieira de Andrade, 'Os Direitos Fundamentais nas Relações entre Particulares' (1981) 5 *Documentação e Direito Comparado* 181ff; in Spain, MP García Rubio, 'La eficacia inter privatos (Drittwirkung) de los derechos fundamentales' in *Libro Homenaje a Ildefonso Sánchez Mera* (Fundación General del Notariado, Madrid, 2002) 297ff; and in Sweden, J Nergelius, *Konstitutionellt rättighetsskydd: svensk rätt i ett komparativ perspektiv* (Fritze, Stockholm, 1996) 261. In England it is still controversial whether or not human rights can have a horizontal effect. For an overview of the debate, cf P Craig, *Administrative Law* (5th edn, Sweet & Maxwell, London, 2003) 599, and see further M Hunt, 'The Horizontal Effect of the Human Rights Act' (1998) *PL* 429; N Bamforth, 'The True "horizontal effect" of the Human Rights Act 1998' (2001) 117 *LQR* 34; R Buxton, 'The Human Rights Act and Private Law' (2000) 116 *LQR* 48; HRW Wade, 'Horizon of Horizontality' (2000) 116 *LQR* 217. For discussion of the impact of the Human Rights Act on contracts, see S Whittaker, 'The Human Rights Act 1998 and Contracts' in HG Beale (ed), *Chitty on Contracts* (29th edn, Sweet & Maxwell, London, 2004) 1-029ff.

[39] This follows from the non-discrimination principle enshrined in both Art 12 EC Treaty and Art 14 ECHR.

12

Harmonisation of European Insurance Contract Law

I. INTRODUCTION

In order to enhance the internal market which is defined in paragraph II of Article 14 of the Treaty establishing the European Community as an 'area without internal frontiers in which the free movement of goods, persons, services and capital is ensured in accordance with this Treaty,' the European Commission has launched an initiative which aims at developing a more coherent European contract law. In its two Communications of 2001[1] and 2004[2] and its 'Action Plan—A More Coherent European Contract Law',[3] published in 2003, the Commission has set out different measures to achieve this aim in the area of contract law. One of these measures is the elaboration of a Common Frame of Reference (CFR), which shall, as soon as it is adopted, serve as a set of model rules, designed to improve the quality and the coherence of the current and future *acquis communautaire*, in order to harmonise general European contract law.[4] Another measure discussed by the Commission is the creation of an optional model that could in the end serve as an optional European civil code.

This chapter discusses a possible harmonisation of European insurance contract law since it is designated to be granted a special position within the CFR. In order to deal with this sensitive and, for the time being, still very

I wish to thank Julia Kolbe, Legal Support Lawyer at Clifford Chance, Frankfurt office, for her valuable assistance in the preparation of this contribution.

[1] Communication from the Commission to the Council and the European Parliament on European Contract Law, COM(2001) 398.

[2] Communication from the Commission to the European Parliament and the Council on European Contract Law and the revision of the *acquis*: the way forward, COM(2004) 651 final.

[3] Communication from the Commission to the European Parliament and the Council on A More Coherent European Contract Law: An Action Plan, COM(2003) 68 final.

[4] *Ibid*, paras 55–64.

abstract topic of European insurance contract law, some key questions shall be considered before further examining this topic.

Why special treatment of the insurance sector? Even though insurance contract law is not independent from general contract law, certain aspects of the laws differ. The fundamental principles of insurance contracts vary in the different legal systems of the EU Member States, although they have common origins and similar structures.[5] In contrast to general contract law, which predominantly contains provisions that may be varied by agreement between the parties, insurance contract law within Member States consists of a multitude of mandatory or semi-mandatory clauses. Mandatory clauses are those that may not be deviated from by the parties, whereas the parties may deviate from semi-mandatory clauses if the terms agreed upon benefit the customer more than the provisions set out in the law.[6] The vast majority of mandatory and semi-mandatory clauses that differ from Member State to Member State may form impediments to cross-border insurance transactions and thus to the establishment of an internal insurance market.[7]

Other particularities of insurance contracts ensure that, within the envisaged CFR, insurance contract law merits special treatment. Insurance contracts often cover remarkably long policy periods compared with most other kinds of contracts (eg purchase contracts, lease contracts). In particulr, life assurances can be regarded as 'life long' contracts. Because of this, insurance contracts require a high protection level for consumers—eg by means of understandability and legibility for all consumers. This high protection level is also appropriate because several insurance contracts are compulsory, eg motor vehicle third party liability insurance for every vehicle owner.

Another particularity of insurance contracts is their nature as a mere legal and intangible product,[8] which renders them particularly suitable for cross-border sale. Increased possibilities for cross-border sales of insurance contracts together with the feasibility of placing mass risks within the EU would increase the viability of a single internal market.

Is the insurance sector such a key component to breaking down the barriers in the creation of the single market to merit special treatment? The contribution of the insurance sector to the European economy in terms of both sales volume and employment is undisputed.[9]

---

[5] European Economic and Social Committee (EESC), Opinion of 15 and 16 December 2004 on 'The European Insurance Contract' [2005] OJ C157/1, para 1.1.

[6] *Ibid*, para 4.2.2.4.

[7] Compare COM(2003) 68, above n 3, para 26.

[8] As regards financial services as a whole, compare Recital 5 of the Directive 2002/65/EC of the European Parliament and of the Council of 23 September 2002 concerning the distance marketing of consumer financial services OJ L271/16; R Gärtner, 'EG-Versicherungs-binnenmarkt und Versicherungsvertragsrecht' [1994] *Europäisches Wirtschafts- und Steuerrecht* 114.

[9] In 2004 European insurance total domestic premiums amounted to €927 billion, ie a real growth rate of 5.5% (inflation-adjusted); with €875 billion, the 25 EU markets accounted

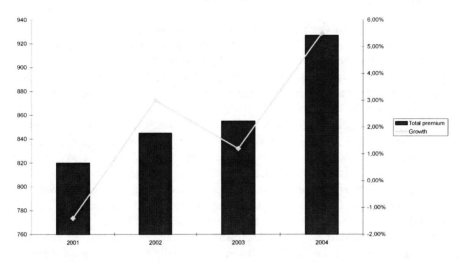

Figure 1: European insurance total domestic premiums.

Due to increasing risks[10] and the growing necessity for each individual to develop a private pension scheme,[11] the importance of the insurance sector for society as a whole is becoming evident. Nevertheless, cross-border insurance transactions are, as Eurostat[12] indicates, still very rare. Eurostat states that

> the absence of harmonisation on consumer protection, [and] the lack of a single European contract law . . . may explain the relatively low level of take-up of cross-border insurance by households.[13]

All these factors—(i) the importance of the insurance business for the economy and the society within the European Union; (ii) the basic suitability of insurance contracts for cross-border trade; and (iii) the completion of the internal insurance market, which should have been reached in the early 1990s—have not, however, led to the desired results. Insurance contract law is still shaped by the different mandatory and semi-mandatory provisions of national insurance contract laws, which are likely to create barriers up to the

---

for 94.4% of total premium income: Comité européen des assurances, 'CEA Executive Update' (1 July 2005), available at http://www.cea.assur.org/cea/v1.1/actu/pdf/uk/ actu222.pdf, 1, from which Figure 1 is taken.

[10] Eg by natural disasters, terrorist attacks.
[11] Mainly due to the 'demographic explosion associated with ageing population,' EESC, Opinion of 24 January 1998 on 'Consumers in the insurance market' [1998] OJ C95/72, para 1.3.
[12] Eurostat, *European Business—Facts and Figures* (Luxembourg, 2002) 351.
[13] *Ibid.*

final completion of the internal market.[14] Not only do differing insurance contract provisions turn out to be an impediment to cross-border trade; different legal systems also hamper the development of an internal market. In particular, the differences between the English case law system and the civil law that is predominant in Continental Europe frustrated former attempts of harmonisation.[15]

Furthermore, insurance contract law is highly affected by other branches of the law, such as general contract law,[16] tax law, surety law, inheritance law and liability law. A harmonised European insurance contract law would have to take into consideration all these other branches. Insurance contract law does not generally regulate any matters that are sufficiently dealt with by general contract law.[17] Thus, insurance contract law always depends on the underlying general contract rules. Basedow gives examples for potential problems that would arise were insurance contract law alone to be partially or wholly harmonised in the absence of any harmonisation of general contract law.[18] In this context, he mentions the different legal systems, and in particular the differing provisions regarding the formation of contracts, as well as the rules concerning the conceptual framework of a transaction, eg agency.

Is European general or insurance contract law a front-line priority for the insurance sector? In the consultation process for the European Commission's Action Plan on a more coherent European contract law,[19] many stakeholders spoke in favour of a special solution for the insurance sector that is most likely to be separated from the general elaboration of a more coherent European contract law.[20] The different expert groups that have been working on an elaboration of a European Civil Code for several years already followed this approach of a separation for European insurance contracts. Based on the Principles of European Contract Law (PECL)[21] that were developed by the 'Lando Commission',[22] the project group on a 'Restatement of European

---

[14] EESC, above n 5, para 1.2.

[15] A proposal for a Council Directive on the coordination of laws, regulations and administrative provisions relating to insurance contracts was presented by the Commission in 1979, OJ C190/2 (28 July 1979); EESC, above n 5, para 5.

[16] J Basedow, 'Insurance Contract Law as Part of an Optional European Contract Act' [2003] *LMCLQ* 498, 500.

[17] *Ibid*, 500.

[18] *Ibid*, 500.

[19] COM(2001) 398 final, above n 1; answers and statements are available at http://europa.eu.int/comm/consumers/cons_int/safe_shop/fair_bus_pract/cont_law/comments/index_en.htm.

[20] COM(2004) 651, above n 2, para 3.1.3.

[21] O Lando and H Beale (eds), *The Principles of European Contract Law, Parts I and II* (The Hague, Kluwer, 2000); O Lando, E Clive, A Prüm and R Zimmermann (eds), *Principles of European Contract Law, Part III* (The Hague, Kluwer, 2003).

[22] Commission on European Contract Law ('Lando Commission') (1982–2001); the Study Group on a European Civil Code emanated from the Lando Commission (2000).

Insurance Contract Law'[23] has drafted specific insurance related provisions, based on the PECL, in order to avoid duplications.[24]

Certain stakeholders, especially the Comité européen des assurances (CEA—European Insurance Association), highlight that there are other, more relevant topics to be reviewed before a general revision and harmonisation of the insurance contract law should proceed.[25] The consolidation process, as seen in the consolidated Directive on Life Assurances,[26] is not yet complete and the inefficiencies that result from different provisions in the various insurance Directives need to be abolished according to the CEA before the harmonisation process is pushed further.[27] Additionally, the CEA demands—after a tidal wave of regulations in recent years—a pause in regulations for the insurance industry.[28]

Insurance contract law in the European Union today is still very incoherent with regard to consumer insurance contracts despite the fact that the first attempts at harmonisation took place as long ago as the 1960s.[29] The

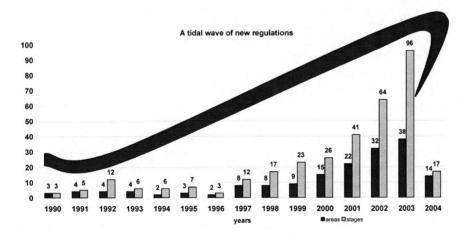

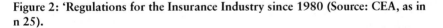

Figure 2: 'Regulations for the Insurance Industry since 1980 (Source: CEA, as in n 25).

---

[23] See www.restatement.info.

[24] J Basedow, above n 16, 501.

[25] Comité européen des assurances, 'Views on the Common Frame of Reference (CFR)' (2005), available at http://www.ania.it/rel_internazionali/attivita/MU5074eann1CEAviews-regardingtheCFRMarch2005.pdf, 3; Comité européen des assurances, 'Annual Report 2004–2005', available at http://www.cea.assur.org, 10, stating that there are other priorities for the legislator to focus on, eg insurers' and reinsurers' supervision, their accounting framework and pension portability.

[26] Directive 2002/83/EC of the European Parliament and of the Council of 5 November 2002 concerning life assurance (recast version) OJ L345/1.

[27] Compare part III of this chapter.

[28] Comité européen des assurances, 'Annual Report 2004–2005', above n 25, 3.

[29] Compare B Bühnemann, 'Zur Harmonisierung des Versicherungsvertragsrechts in der Europäischen Wirtschaftsgemeinschaft' [1968] *Versicherungsrecht* 418.

present chapter covers the history and the current status of European insurance law, as well as the recent developments and discussions regarding an optional instrument of European insurance contract law and its possible impact on insurance practice. It focuses on the question of whether a general harmonisation of insurance contract law could improve the internal insurance market and does not deal especially with the relevant legal aspects. Finally, a summary taking into consideration the pros and cons of a possible harmonisation of European insurance contract law and an outlook on the possible future development is provided.[30]

II. HISTORY OF EUROPEAN INSURANCE CONTRACT LAW

The first attempts to achieve harmonisation of European law in general and also of the insurance sector were made with the founding of the European Community. In the Treaty of Rome of 1960 the main objectives regarding the establishment of a common market[31] were characterised by the abolition of obstacles to free movement of goods, persons, services and capital,[32] as well as the approximation of the laws of Member States to the extent required for the functioning of the internal market.[33] The basic principles of the internal insurance market are set out in Article 43[34] (freedom of establishment) and Article 49[35] (freedom to provide services) of the Treaty of Rome.[36]

Several Directives on insurance[37] and reinsurance[38] law followed the Treaty of Rome in an attempt to harmonise both the general supervisory and solvency margin requirements of insurers, along with specific Directives regulating certain insurance branches. The so-called 'three generations' of

---

[30] This paper shall particularly deal with consumer insurance law. The insurance of large risks is due to its more international character mainly based on the principle of contractual freedom and does not require further harmonisation to the same extent as consumer insurance law.

[31] Article 2 EC.

[32] Article 3c EC.

[33] Article 3h EC; U Mönnich, 'Europäisierung des Privatversicherungsrechts' in RM Beckmann and A Matusche-Beckmann (eds), *Versicherungsrechts-Handbuch* (Munich, CH Beck, 2004), para 2.

[34] Formerly Art 52.

[35] Formerly Art 59.

[36] In its Interpretative Communication 'Freedom to Provide Services and the General Good in the Insurance Sector' of 2000 (OJ C43/3) the EU Commission stated that the differentiation of both freedoms is not sufficiently clear; they set out that the scope of the freedom to provide services covers 'all cases where a person providing services offers those services in a Member State other than that in which he is established, wherever the recipients of those services may be established.'

[37] Three generations of insurance Directives (see below).

[38] Council Directive 64/225/EEC of 25 February 1964 on the abolition of restrictions on freedom of establishment and freedom to provide services in respect of reinsurance and retrocession OJ 56/878.

Directives govern both general insurances and life assurances by means of developing the freedom of establishment, the freedom to provide services and eventually the completion of the internal insurance market in 1994. Several additional Directives regulate, for example, motor vehicle insurance,[39] tourist assistance,[40] legal expenses,[41] and credit insurance and suretyship insurance.[42] This chapter concentrates on the three generations of insurance Directives as they have mainly prepared the ground for the current status of the single insurance market.

1. First Generation of Insurance Directives—Freedom of Establishment

From 1973 to 1992 several EC Directives on the coordination of laws, regulations and administrative provisions relating to direct life assurance[43] and

---

[39] Motor insurance Directives: Council Directive 72/166/EEC of 24 April 1972 on the approximation of the laws of Member States relating to insurance against civil liability in respect of the use of motor vehicles, and to the enforcement of the obligation to insure against such liability OJ L103/1; Council Directive 72/430/EEC of 19 December 1972 amending Council Directive 72/166/EEC of 24 April 1972 on the approximation of the laws of the Member States relating to insurance against civil liability in respect of the use of motor vehicles and to the enforcement of the obligation to insure against such liability OJ L75/29; Second Council Directive 84/5/EEC of 30 December 1983 on the approximation of the laws of the Member States relating to insurance against civil liability in respect of the use of motor vehicles OJ L8/17; Third Council Directive 90/232/EEC of 14 May 1990 on the approximation of the laws of the Member States relating to insurance against civil liability in respect of the use of motor vehicles OJ L129/33; Directive 2000/26/EC of the European Parliament and of the Council of 16 May 2000 on the approximation of the laws of the Member States relating to insurance against civil liability in respect of the use of motor vehicles and amending Council Directives 73/239/EEC and 88/357/EEC OJ L181/65 (Fourth Motor Insurance Directive).

[40] Council Directive 84/641/EEC of 10 December 1984 amending, particularly as regards tourist assistance, the First Directive (73/239/EEC) on the coordination of laws, regulations and administrative provisions relating to the taking-up and pursuit of the business of direct insurance other than life assurance OJ L339/21.

[41] Council Directive 87/344/EEC of 22 June 1987 on the coordination of laws, regulations and administrative provisions relating to legal expenses insurance OJ L185/77.

[42] Council Directive 87/343/EEC of 22 June 1987 amending, as regards credit insurance and suretyship insurance, First Directive 73/239/EEC on the coordination of laws, regulations and administrative provisions relating to the taking-up and pursuit of the business of direct insurance other than life assurance OJ L185/72. For a complete compilation of insurance Directives and Directives that indirectly influence the insurance sector, refer to http://europa.eu.int/comm/internal_market/insurance/legis-inforce_en.htm.

[43] Three Directives on Life Assurance: First Council Directive 79/267/EEC of 5 March 1979 on the coordination of laws, regulations and administrative provisions relating to the taking up and pursuit of the business of direct life assurance OJ L63/1; Second Council Directive 90/619/EEC of 8 November 1990 on the coordination of laws, regulations and administrative provisions relating to direct life assurance, laying down provisions to facilitate the effective exercise of freedom to provide services and amending Directive 79/267/EEC OJ L330/50; Third Council Directive 92/96/EEC of 10 November 1992 on the coordination of laws, regulations and administrative provisions relating to direct life assurance and amending Directives 79/267/EEC and 90/619/EEC OJ L311/43.

general insurance[44] were adopted by the Council. These so-called 'three generations' of Directives had the joint objective of establishing a common insurance market and abolishing obstacles to cross-border transactions.

The first generation of insurance Directives, which were adopted in 1973 (non-life) and 1979 (life), tried to obtain the freedom of establishment by partially harmonising the insurance supervisory law within the European Union. This objective was achieved by means of abolishing any discrimination on the basis of nationality whereas the duplicate control by the supervisory authorities of both the home Member State and the host Member State was retained.[45] The relevant provisions between the general Directive and the life insurance Directive differed only slightly.

The supervisory authority of the home Member State was to be competent for the supervision of the solvency of an insurer whereas the supervisory authority of the country of activity was to be responsible for the residual supervision.[46] Permission by the competent authorities had to be obtained by both a national insurer and a branch of an EU-foreign insurance company.

The policyholders should have enjoyed, by means of the Directives, the same standard of consumer protection irrespective if they were insured by an insurance company of their home country or by an undertaking of a foreign insurer. Insurance companies should have been in the position to conduct their business in a foreign Member State without being hampered either by different supervision requirements or by being discriminated against by means of, for example, an economic needs test (*Bedürfnisprüfung*).[47] Exempted from the Directives were both small mutual insurance companies and certain public insurers.

2. The Directive Proposal of 1979/80

In 1965[48] an EC initiative to harmonise national contract law in relation to insurance contracts was launched. This initiative culminated eventually in a

---

[44] Three Directives on general insurance: Council Directive 73/239 of 24 July 1973 on the coordination of laws, regulations and administrative provisions relating to the taking-up and pursuit of the business of direct insurance other than life assurance OJ L5/27; Second Council Directive 88/357 EEC of 22 June 1988 on the coordination of laws, regulations and administrative provisions relating to direct insurance other than life assurance and laying down provisions to facilitate the effective exercise of freedom to provide services and amending Directive 73/239/EEC OJ L172/1; Third Council Directive 92/49/EEC of 18 June 1992 on the coordination of laws, regulations and administrative provisions relating to direct insurance other than life assurance and amending Directives 73/239/EEC and 88/357/EEC OJ L228/1.

[45] EESC, above n 11, para 2.3.

[46] H Müller, *Versicherungsbinnenmarkt* (Munich, CH Beck, 1995) 13.

[47] *Ibid*, 13; the economic needs test was at that time customary especially in German supervisory practice.

[48] B Bühnemann, above n 29, 418.

Directive proposal in 1979, aimed at the harmonisation of European insurance contract law.[49] The proposal was put before the European Parliament in October 1980. The main purposes of the proposed Directive were to facilitate the provision of insurance services as well as to introduce a free choice of applicable law for all parties involved, and finally to harmonise certain fundamental principles, especially protecting the interests of the insured.[50] Marine, aviation and transport insurance were excluded from the scope of the Directive due to their character as being widely international and their traditional balance of powers between the contractual parties. Because of their special features, health insurance and credit and suretyship insurance classes were also to be exempted from the coordination of the Directive.

The provisions of the Directive proposal basically covered the following areas:

— minimum pre-contractual information of the parties involved;
— general terms of the conclusion, modification and termination of insurance contracts;
— contractual obligations of the parties involved;
— certain questions relating to the existence of cover pending the payment of the premium and the position of insured persons, who are not policyholders.[51]

Whereas the Member States were generally not free to adopt different solutions than set out in the Directive, the parties involved should be able to deviate from the provisions pursuant to the adoption of the Directive provided that such deviations favour the policyholder, the insured person or the injured third party.[52]

The proposal was envisaged to enter into force on 1 July 1983, but, even though the European Commission and the European Parliament recognised the necessity for a harmonised European insurance contract law, the Directive in the end did not come into force. There were several reasons for this: the European Economic and Social Committee (EESC) identified a lack of political will in some of the Member States;[53] an agreement on the content and the extent of the coordination could not be reached;[54] and eventually some of the Member States doubted that the Treaty provided a legal basis for a harmonisation because harmonisation is not a prerequisite for the

---

[49] Proposal for a Council Directive on the coordination of laws, regulations and administrative provisions relating to insurance contracts OJ C190/2 (28 July 1979).
[50] EESC, above n 5, paras 5.1–5.5.2.
[51] *Ibid*, footnote to para 5.2.2.
[52] Article 12 of the Directive proposal, above n 49.
[53] EESC, above n 5, para 5.6.1.
[54] Pursuant to the law applicable then, decisions on the adoption of directives demanded for unanimity; compare Treaty on the Establishment of the European Community.

completion of the internal market.[55] The ultimate withdrawal of the proposal to harmonise national insurance contract law took place in 1993.[56]

3. Four Major Judgments of the European Court of Justice

In four major judgments of 4 December 1986,[57] the European Court of Justice decided that the applicability of the Articles 59 and 60 (freedom to provide services) of the Treaty is not dependent on the harmonisation of the laws of the Member States. Therefore, any discrimination against a provider of services due to its nationality and any restrictions on its freedom to provide services by reason of the fact that it is established in another Member State other than the one in which the service is provided is a violation of the Treaty and has to be abolished.[58]

The freedom to provide services for insurers as a fundamental principle of the Treaty might only be restricted under certain circumstances. Within a three-step examination the European Court of Justice held that any restrictions have to be (i) justified by the 'general good'[59] and (ii) may not be applied in a discriminatory manner and only in so far as the public interest is not safeguarded by the home Member State; furthermore, (iii) the objective to safeguard the public interest must not be obtainable by less restrictive rules.[60] However, in cases where those conditions are met, Member States can impose certain restrictions, especially in cases where policyholders and insured persons need particular protection.[61]

These four major judgments led to an important shift in European insurance legislation due to the statement that harmonisation and coordination of the laws is not a condition for the establishment of the freedom to provide services. The attempts to achieve a far-reaching harmonisation of substantive insurance law were relinquished, and the European legislator limited itself to conflict law issues for insurance contracts[62] and the extensive harmonisation of insurance supervisory law.[63]

---

[55] H Müller, above n 46, 39.

[56] Compare   Prelex   at   http://www.europa.eu.int/prelex/detail_dossier_real.cfm?CL=de&DosId=124614.

[57] Judgments of the Court of 4 December 1986—Case 205/84 *Commission of the European Communities v Germany*; Case 220/83 *Commission of the European Communities v French Republic*; Case 252/83 *Commission of the European Communities v Kingdom of Denmark*; Case 206/84 *Commission of the European Communities v Ireland*; all: [1986] ECR 3663.

[58] Summary, point 3 of the Judgment of the Court of 4 December 1986, Case 205/84, *ibid*.

[59] The 'general good' was later defined and specified by the Commission's Interpretative Communication, above n 36.

[60] Clifford Chance, *International Insurance Regulation: Current and Proposed Regulation Explained* (London, Reactions Publishing Group Ltd, 2002) 26.

[61] *Ibid*.

[62] Second generation of insurance Directives.

[63] Third generation of insurance Directives. Compare H-L Weyers and M Wandt, *Versicherungsvertragsrecht* (Frankfurt, Luchterhand Fachverlag, 2003) 42.

4. Second Generation of Insurance Directives—Freedom to Provide Services

In light of the aforementioned four major judgments, the second generation of insurance Directives was enacted with the intention to substantiate freedom to provide services in the insurance sector. Particularly for large risks, the second Directive on General Insurance provided a far-reaching completion of the freedom to provide services. By the implementation of the Directive,

> policyholders who, by virtue of their status, their size or the nature of the risk to be insured, do not require special protection in the state in which the risk is situated should be granted complete freedom to avail themselves of the widest possible insurance market.[64]

Since then a single authorisation system has been established, offering insurers of large risks the opportunity for cross-border insurance services, the insurer itself being regulated solely by its home Member State supervisory authority.

Whereas the second generation of insurance Directives that was adopted by the Council in 1988 (non-life) represented a step forward in obtaining the freedom to provide services for large risks,[65] mass risks have generally been exempted from the liberalisation of the freedom to provide services.[66] Insurers of mass risks still had to comply with the provisions of the first Directive,[67] namely the retention of the supervision by the competent authority of the Member State where the risk is situated.[68]

Regarding life assurances, the second life assurance Directive had found a way to slightly modify the differentiation of the freedom to provide services as compared with the non-life insurance Directive. Due to the lack of feasibility to divide between the qualities and quantities of the insured risk,[69] this Directive distinguished between the active freedom to provide services and the passive freedom to provide services by determining that the active freedom to provide services derives from the insurer's initiative and the passive freedom to provide services from the initiative of the insured

---

[64] In case large risks are concerned, as defined in Art 5 of the second Directive on general insurance law (88/357/EC), above n 44, as far as the policyholder exceeds the limits of at least two of the following three criteria: balance sheet total: €6.2 million; net turnover: €12.8 million; and/or an average number of employees during the financial year: 250.

[65] Although each Member State was given the choice to apply the principle of the freedom to provide services to mass risks as well, only the Netherlands and the United Kingdom did so: Clifford Chance, above n 60, 29.

[66] *Ibid*, 27.

[67] Article 5 of the first Directive on general insurance law (73/239/EEC), above n 44.

[68] W-H Roth, 'Die Vollendung des europäischen Binnenmarktes für Versicherungen' [1993] *Neue Juristische Wochenschrift* 3029.

[69] H Müller, above n 46, 32.

party.[70] Only in the latter case did the complete principle of the freedom to provide services apply; for example, when the policyholder sought insurance coverage from an EU-foreign insurer,[71] no further obligation to obtain a permit would arise for the insurer and the supervision would fall in the area of responsibility of the supervisory authority of the Member State of establishment.[72]

The provisions of the second generation of insurance Directives were largely superseded by the third generation, especially regarding the passive and active freedom to provide services in life assurance.

5. Third Generation of Insurance Directives—Completion of the Single Market

The third generation of insurance Directives, which were adopted by the Council in 1992, should have led to the completion of the internal insurance market by the implementation of the principle of the country of origin and a single licence system ('European passport').[73] Therefore, establishment of an insurance business was thereafter subject solely to prior official authorisation from the competent authorities of the home Member State.[74]

Due to the principle of the country of origin, the home Member State's supervisory authority is the competent authority for the complete supervision of the insurer in question. It is in their responsibility to furnish the authorities of the Member State where the risk is situated with the relevant information.[75] This mutual recognition of the authorisation and control of insurance companies and undertakings led to a certain degree to a simplification of the authority system within the European Community and the European Economic Area (EEA).

The single licence enables the insurer to apply for an authorisation by its home Member State's supervisory authority that is valid for the entire European Community and the EEA, even if the insurer intends to open an undertaking in another Member State or to provide cross-border insurance services. The authorisation is be granted for a particular class of insurance and covers all the risks pertaining to that class unless the insurer wishes to cover only some of them.[76]

---

[70] EESC, above n 11, 4.

[71] H Müller, above n 46, 32.

[72] In analogy to the regulation model for large risks in the second Directive on direct insurance other than life assurance, W-H Roth, above n 68, 3029.

[73] U Mönnich, above n 33; R Gärtner, above n 8, 115.

[74] Article 4 of the third Directive on general insurance law (92/49/EEC), above n 44, and Art 6 of the third Directive on life assurance (92/96/EEC), above n 43.

[75] Articles 32–35 of the third Directive on general insurance law (92/49/EEC), above n 44, and Art 14 of the third Directive on life assurance (92/96/EEC), above n 43.

[76] Article 7 of the third Directive on general insurance law (92/49/EEC), above n 44, and Art 32 of the third Directive on life assurance (92/96/EEC), above n 43.

In addition to the two principles—country of origin and single licence—introduced by the third generation of insurance Directives, the prior approval of the Standard Terms and Conditions by the supervisory authorities for both life and general insurance was abolished and replaced by solvency checks and accounting rules for insurance companies.[77]

In 2002 a consolidated life assurance Directive[78] was adopted to recast in a single text the existing legislation in this field to facilitate the comprehension and application of the Directives in force.[79] The consolidation of the life assurance Directives is based on the third phase of the SLIM (Simpler Legislation for the Internal Market) initiative by the European Commission.[80] Apart from mere codification of the existing Directives, the new Directive includes minor changes, which do not substantially affect the meaning of the provisions.[81]

The general insurance Directives should have already been consolidated as proposed in the third phase of the SLIM initiative, but this has not yet happened. However, in its new Communication on the simplification of the regulatory environment[82] the EU Commission envisages to recast all existing insurance Directives (except the motor insurance Directives) into one single instrument in 2006. The legal nature of this single instrument is not further specified. Currently, as outlined in the Communication, the Commission is undertaking an evaluation process which shall exploit the possibilities to replace existing Directives (needing implementation in the Member States) by Regulations (with immediate application) in order to ensure a more consistent implementation of EU rules. According to the EU Commission, this would lead to a further simplification and prevent divergent national implementations.[83] Regarding the insurance Directives, this consolidation would most likely lead to a clarification and improvement of the legibility of current insurance legislation, to a reduction of administrative costs for insurance companies and to an enforcement of the consistency of the *acquis communautaire*.[84]

Given that even more time has run from the original general insurance Directives to date than between the original life assurance Directives and the

---

[77] EESC, above n 11, 5.

[78] Directive 2002/83/EC of the European Parliament and of the Council of 5 November 2002 concerning life assurance (recast version), above n 26.

[79] Consolidated Directives: Directive 79/267/EEC (first generation life assurance); Directive 90/619/EEC (second generation life assurance); Directive 92/96/EEC (third generation life assurance); Directive 95/26/EC (prudential supervision); Directive 2002/12/EC (solvency margins requirements for life assurance undertakings).

[80] Compare http://europa.eu.int/comm/internal_market/simplification/index_en.htm.

[81] See www.europa.eu.int/comm/internal_market/insurance/life-nonlife_en.htm.

[82] Communication of the Commission to the European Parliament, the Council, the EESC and the Committee of the Regions, 'Implementing the Community Lisbon Programme: A strategy for the simplification of the regulatory environment', COM(2005) 535.

[83] *Ibid*, para 3d.

[84] As demanded by the stakeholders in the consultation process for the Communication, COM(2005) 535, annex 1.

consolidated life assurance Directive, there is even more of a risk that, contrary to the current attempts for better regulation,[85] such as applying the 'less is more' principle,[86] changes or additions will be made to the general insurance Directives. Europe has moved on, and consolidation or recasting is a difficult exercise. In any event, the problems resulting from the current status of European insurance contract law would remain just as outlined in the next part of this chapter.

III. CURRENT STATUS OF EUROPEAN INSURANCE CONTRACT LAW

1. General

European insurance contract law is mainly shaped by European Directives. National insurance contract laws contain several regulations that are based on the aforementioned Directives on general insurance and life assurance. Whereas insurance supervisory law is substantially harmonised in the European Union and the EEA,[87] there are nonetheless still many differences in the various insurance contract laws of the Member States. These differences mainly derive from either different legal systems, different standards of consumer protection or even from mere gold-plating, ie the 'over-implementation' of European Directives. When striving to achieve a common minimum standard in the EU, the issue of over-performance in the form of gold-plating is seen as a major obstacle. The issue was raised once more by the European Commission in its 'Green Paper on Financial Services Policy (2005–2010)',[88] where it states that

> Member States should avoid adding layer upon layer of regulatory additions that go beyond the Directives themselves . . . thus stifling the benefits of a single set of EU rules and adding unnecessary burden and cost to European industry.[89]

---

[85] Compare the Better Regulation Initiatives available at http://europa.eu.int/comm/enterprise/regulation/better_regulation/index_en.htm.

[86] Compare Speech 05/178 by Günther Verheugen of 16 March 2005 on Better Regulation.

[87] EESC, above n 5, para 4.1.2.1.

[88] COM(2005) 177.

[89] *Ibid*, 6. In its White Paper on Financial Services Policy 2005–2010 of 5 December 2005 the European Commission additionally highlighted that the barriers to the integration of retail financial markets mainly derive from their origin in the fragmented European financial services market and that integration of these markets is therefore very complex and demanding: MEMO/05/465, available at http://europa.eu.int/rapid/pressReleasesAction.do?reference=MEMO/05/465&format=HTML&aged=0&language=EN&guiLanguage=fr, 3.

In any case, harmonisation of substantive insurance contract law has so far only taken place in specific sectors and on specific issues, eg motor vehicle liability insurance.[90]

2. Law Applicable to Insurance Contracts

The interaction of the various national insurance laws is governed by the relevant insurance Directives. The Rome Convention of 1980,[91] which governs the law applicable to contractual obligations, only includes insurance contracts inasmuch as risks are covered that are situated outside the European Economic Community. Critics of current European insurance legislation have often described the current status of the conflict law of consumer insurance contracts as an impediment to cross-border transactions and thus the completion of the single market.[92]

Regarding large, industrial risks,[93] the insured are generally free to choose the law applicable to insurance contracts, unlike the parties to consumer contracts, since the law applicable to mass risks and life assurance is regulated solely in the relevant insurance Directives.[94] The law applicable to life insurance contracts is generally the law of the Member State of commitment, ie the Member State where the policyholder has his/her habitual residence.[95] When the policyholder's habitual residence is in a Member State other than that of which he/she is a national, the parties may choose which law applies.[96]

In general insurance, the choice of law is regulated in Articles 7 and 8 of the second non-life Directive. Generally, the law applicable to insurance contracts is the law of the policyholder's habitual residence or central administration. In cases where the law of a Member State allows, the parties may choose the law of another Member State. When the risk is not situated in the Member State of the policyholder's habitual residence or central administration, the parties to the contract may choose which law is applicable between the Member States in question.[97] As regards compulsory insurance, the parties may generally conclude insurance contracts in accordance with the above-mentioned rules unless a Member State imposes an obligation to take out insurance. In this case, the insurance contract shall only satisfy a specific

---

[90] EESC, above n 5, para 4.1.2.3.

[91] Convention on the law applicable to contractual obligations opened for signature in Rome on 19 June 1980 (80/934/EEC, OJ L266/1).

[92] COM(2003) 68 final, above n 3, para 48; J Basedow, above n 16, 499.

[93] See n 64.

[94] In general insurance the law applicable is governed by Arts 7 and 8 of the second Directive on general insurance law (88/357/EEC), above n 44; as regards life assurance, the law applicable is governed by Art 32 of the consolidated Directive 2002/83/EC, above n 26.

[95] Article 32(1) of the consolidated Directive 2002/83/EC, above n 26.

[96] Article 32(2) of the consolidated Directive 2002/83/EC, above n 26.

[97] Article 7(1) of the second Directive on general insurance law (88/357/EEC), above n 44.

obligation insofar as it is in accordance with the relevant provisions imposed by the Member State in question.[98]

The Rome Convention on the law applicable to contractual obligations will be converted into a Community instrument (ie a Regulation[99]) in the next few years.[100] Whether the conflict of law rules for insurance contracts will experience changes by the transfer of the Rome Convention to a Regulation is not yet decided, but it could well have a significant impact on the current status of European insurance contract law as regards the choice of the law that is applicable.[101]

3. Possible Solutions

The current status of European insurance conflict law poses severe problems to insurance undertakings wanting to market their insurance policies across different Member States. Every Member State applies its own insurance regulation. As a consequence, cross-border insurance transactions are relatively uncommon[102] within the European Union and its 25 Member States.[103] The lack of choice of the law applicable to consumer insurance contracts leads to a 'surprising deficit of market integration.'[104] Would it thus be advisable for the European legislator to simply permit a general freedom of choice on the law applicable in order to maintain the internal insurance market? This approach would be relatively easy to enforce and would at first sight indeed help to promote cross-border insurance transactions. But it would result in further problems.

First, due to the complexity of insurance contracts, it would be too difficult for the consumers to differentiate and choose between the providers of contracts under various jurisdictions without an adequate consumer protection level to be ensured. This would confuse the consumers and does not conform to the high consumer protection level that is pursued by the European legislator. The European Commission has always emphasised that an adequate level of consumer protection needs to be achieved.[105]

---

[98] Article 8(1) and (2) of the second Directive on general insurance law (88/357/EEC), above n 44.

[99] Compare M Fricke, 'Kollisionsrecht im Umbruch—Perspektiven für die Versicherungswirtschaft' [2005] *Versicherungsrecht* 726, 730.

[100] Green Paper on the conversion of the Rome Convention of 1980 on the law applicable to contractual obligations into a Community instrument and its modernisation, COM(2002) 654.

[101] For further details, see Fricke, above n 99, 726–41.

[102] Compare the recent survey conducted by the European Commission on 'Cross-border consolidation on the EU financial sector' (SEC (2005) 1398), Part III, para 1.3, in which the main obstacles to cross-border consolidation were identified, eg the lack of integration of the internal market for retail financial products.

[103] Compare Eurostat, above n 12, 351.

[104] Basedow, above n 16, 499.

[105] Compare, eg COM(2004) 651, above n 2, para 2.1.1.

Secondly, another point that presents an obstacle to this approach is the fact that the courts of the policyholder's Member State deciding on insurance issues would have to apply foreign law in cross-border contracts that are concluded under a foreign jurisdiction, pursuant to Articles 9–13 of the Council Regulation 44/2001.[106] This would cause severe problems for the courts within the European Union and would also not contribute to consumer protection.[107]

Due to the above reasons, this solution should not currently be pursued. Another possible approach to achieve an internal insurance market would be a general harmonisation of European insurance contract law potentially by an optional instrument as envisaged by the European Commission. How such a harmonisation could be shaped and whether it would be feasible will be discussed in the following parts of this chapter.

IV. MODEL OF AN OPTIONAL EUROPEAN CONTRACT ACT

It needs to be thoroughly verified whether unification, harmonisation or convergence by means of an optional instrument is advisable. Taking into account the potential problems that could arise in the case of a unification of law, eg by means of substantial changes to the well-established systems of (insurance) contract law, this option seems less attractive. In the Communication on European Contract Law of 2001, the Commission proposed four different possible solutions to achieve a more coherent European contract law. These were (i) to leave the solution of any identified problems to the market; (ii) to promote the development of non-binding common contract law principles; (iii) to review and improve existing EC legislation in the area of contract law to make it more coherent or to adapt it to cover situations not foreseen at the time of adoption; and (iv) to adopt a new instrument at the EC level.[108]

A great majority of the stakeholders in the consultation process argued for the third option, whereas the fourth option, ie a unification of European contract law, met a broad rejection.[109] The Action Plan that was published in 2003 mainly collected suggestions within the third option, ie the elaboration of the CFR and the introduction of an optional model. Following this, the European Commission proposed, in its Action Plan of 2003, three actions that would be taken in concert with the current sector specific approach[110] in

---

[106] Council Regulation (EC) No 44/2001 of 22 December 2000 on jurisdiction and the recognition and enforcement of judgments in civil and commercial matters OJ L12/1.

[107] J Basedow, above n 16, 500.

[108] COM(2001) 398, above n 1, 2.

[109] Reactions to the communication on European contract law, para 4.4.

[110] Some count the introduction of appropriate sector-specific interventions as a separate measure; compare Basedow, above n 16, 500.

order to achieve a more coherent contract law: (i) the elaboration of a CFR,[111] 'to increase quality and the coherence of the EC *acquis* in the area of contract law,'[112] including general principles, definitions of abstract legal terms, and model rules, including specific regulations for contracts of sale and for insurance contracts;[113] (ii) the compilation of standard terms and conditions applicable to cross-border transactions; and (iii) the development of an optional instrument in the area of European contract law.

Even though the latter is the least concrete and most long-term measure, it is also the focal point of the discussion. The reason for this high, seemingly premature interest in a European contract law is the vague description of such an instrument by the European Commission and the extensive amount of research work that has already been invested so far.[114] Fears are spreading among stakeholders that a European civil code could be introduced through the back door, without allowing enough opportunities to express their views.[115]

In order to include the stakeholders into the elaboration process of the CFR and to give them a possibility to express their views, the so-called 'CFR-net', consisting of about 180 members[116] from all Member States, was created.[117] At the moment, the CFR-net holds regular meetings on different contract law issues, in close coordination with the researcher network,[118] aiming at developing the model rules for the CFR. Unfortunately, members of the CFR-net describe the current working procedure as complex and the whole process as very complex and difficult to understand.[119] The outcome of the evaluation process of the CFR will depend on whether the procedure can be improved.

Peter M. Wiesner, of the Federation of German Industries and a member of the CFR-net, has recently raised the issue whether a European civil code can still be stopped.[120] In his view, an optional model containing general principles, guidelines and model rules would be able to reach the envisaged goals of an internal insurance market as long as it is practice-oriented. However, he doubts whether the door to an open discussion among stakeholders remains open due to the highly focused expert drafts that were presented as a basis for

---

[111] An overview on the structure of the CFR was given in annex 1 to the Communication on European Contract Law and the Revision of the *acquis: The Way Forward*, above n 2.

[112] COM(2003) 68, above n 3, 2. Compare Communication from the European Commission on updating and simplifying the community acquis, COM(2003) 71, annex 2.

[113] COM(2003) 68, above n 3, annex 1.

[114] Cf nn 21–23.

[115] P Wiesner, 'Ist das Europäische Zivilgesetzbuch noch zu stoppen?' [2004] *Der Betrieb* 871.

[116] A list of the members of the CFR-net is available at http://europa.eu.int/comm/consumers/cons_int/safe_shop/fair_bus_pract/cont_law/common_frame_ref_de.htm.

[117] For an overview on the functioning of the CFR-net, see M Fricke, 'Entgrenztes Zivilrecht?—Zu den Perspektiven des Common Frame of Reference und der europäischen Schuldrechtsharmonisierung für die Versicherungswirtschaft' [2005] *Versicherungsrecht* 1474.

[118] Ie the Study Group on a European Civil Code under the direction of Christian von Bar.

[119] Fricke, above n 117, 1478.

[120] Wiesner, above n 115, 871.

a discussion by the European Commission, leaving little room for equally detailed research with perhaps a different emphasis.[121]

Currently there are very few reliable surveys on European contract law and those which do exist represent a very strong emphasis towards this issue. Because of this, Clifford Chance has developed and conducted jointly with the Institute for European and Comparative Law of the University of Oxford, and with the assistance of Gracechurch Consulting, a business survey on European contract law. In this survey most of the enterprises that took part expressed their general support for and their potential willingness to use a European contract law.[122] Wiesner also expresses the wish of the business community that European contract law be implemented thoroughly and most preferably on an opt-in basis. The advantages of an instrument on an opt-in basis instead of full harmonisation or unification of contract law would be that such an instrument could be developed in practice without replacing the traditional concepts of contract law in each Member State, and would thus be more acceptable to the parties concerned. Having established an optional instrument that would be of practical use for the insurance business, a convergence through market pressure would be likely to appear, forcing the insurers to adopt the optional instrument. Additionally, the parties to a contract would have the opportunity to choose between either the applicable contract law or the so-called '26th regime'[123] of contract law.[124] Critics of an optional instrument often mention the Vienna Sales Convention[125] as an example for a very slow approval of optional artificial rules, but, as Basedow[126] indicates, it is dangerous to generalise and draw conclusions from different experiences.

The EC Commission also invited the stakeholders to express their views on the possible structure and legal nature of the CFR and an optional instrument. The question on the precise design in form of Recommendations, Regulations or Directives, possibly with opt-in/opt-out provisions, [127] should be left to be debated by academics, lawyers and the CFR-net.

A concept that would solve many problems relating to the legal nature of the CFR is currently being proposed. Pursuant to the transfer of the Convention of Rome into a Regulation and the connected revision of the international law of conflicts, whether the choice of law applicable to

---

[121] *Ibid*, 874.

[122] Of the respondents, 83% were in favour of a European contract law and 82% were likely or very likely to use it (see above pp 130–35).

[123] Ie the 25 existing national contract laws of the Member States plus the optional instrument.

[124] Compare M Clarke and H Heiss, 'Towards a European Insurance Contract Law?—Recent Developments in Brussels' [2006] *Journal of Business Law* (forthcoming).

[125] United Nations Convention on Contracts for the International Sale of Goods (adopted 11 April 1980, entered into force 1 January 1988) 1489 UNTS 3 (CISG).

[126] Basedow, above n 16, 502.

[127] J Basedow, 'Ein optionales Europäisches Vertragsgesetz—opt-in, opt-out, wozu überhaupt?' [2004] *Zeitschrift für Europäisches Privatrecht* 1.

contracts could be expanded to private supranational Regulations, eg the CFR, is being considered.[128] This would provide the opportunity to market consumer insurance contracts within the European Union based on the CFR without the restrictions of current European insurance contract law.[129] Because this concept has yet to be elaborated on, and many challenges could arise from it, eg as regards consumer protection laws, it is still unclear whether and how this approach should be pursued.

V. REACTIONS TO A HARMONISED EUROPEAN INSURANCE CONTRACT LAW

As with general contract law, so it is with the insurance contract law: there are various different views on how to further deepen and integrate the internal market and whether or not a harmonisation of insurance contract law is needed.

1. Views on the Current Status of European Insurance Contract Law and a Possible Optional Instrument

Whereas the EESC, in its own-initiative opinions 'The European Insurance Contract' of 15 December 2004 and 'Consumers in the Insurance Market' of 29 January 1998, states that the 'total lack of harmonisation at the level of substantive law, in other words, a minimum level of regulation on insurance contract law in the European Union'[130] poses a major obstacle to the 'effective implementation of the single insurance market,'[131] the CEA does not see a harmonisation of European insurance contract law as a front-line priority but identifies a need for improving the quality of the existent *acquis communautaire*. This opinion reflects the current initiatives in the European Union that are trying to simplify European legislation and to cut unnecessary red-tape and over-regulation,[132] which is already much in line with the Better Regulation Initiatives[133] of the year 2005. In the CEA's view, the current status of European insurance contract law does not represent the main obstacle to cross-border insurance transactions; there are various other factors, eg language, culture, social environment and tax regulations, that hamper the integration of the insurance market.[134]

---

[128] Compare, inter alia, Fricke, above n 99, 732.
[129] Compare part III of this chapter.
[130] EESC, above n 11, para 2.3.1.1.1.
[131] EESC, above n 5, para 2.1.1.
[132] Compare, inter alia, COM(2005) 535, available at http://europa.eu.int/comm/enterprise/regulation/better_regulation/index_en.htm.
[133] Compare part IV of this chapter.
[134] Comité européen des assurances, above n 25, para 4.5.

(a) Comité européen des assurances

The CEA has established a working group that in 2004 published its report 'The European Retail Insurance Market(s)', which is targeted at individuals acting outside of business. In this report, the CEA points out that competition and Europeanisation of the retail insurance markets has developed satisfactorily in the meantime under the freedom of establishment, whereas cross-border retail insurance commerce under the freedom of services remains little developed.[135] This is not only due to legal obstacles but also derives from the nature of insurance contracts. CEA states that policyholders are not interested economically in foreign insurance products as long as they have no real difficulties with their own national insurance companies.[136] Additionally, the intangibility of insurance contracts is said to lead to a high degree of proximity between the contracting parties which cannot be filled by foreign insurers without a sufficient aftersales service.[137]

Taking into account these prerequisites, the CEA underlines that it is desirable not to adopt a major legislative measure but to take a series of legal and practical measures towards the establishment of a single retail insurance market, ie give permission for retail insurance companies to expand their business in other EU markets and the facilitation of cross-border insurance transactions.[138] This facilitation should include the improvement of the legal regime of the freedom to provide services,[139] ensuring better information for the consumers and insurance companies as to the possibilities of the European insurance markets[140] and initiatives towards a common legal framework.[141] This common legal framework could provide maximum harmonisation in some issues, ie regulations on unfair commercial practices, and provisions regarding the law applicable to insurance contracts and pre-contractual information, as well as the taxation of insurance products.[142] For certain insurance products that are already very similar in most of the Member States, a principle of mutual recognition could be introduced.[143] Finally, the CEA is also contemplating the idea of a 26th regime, applied optionally to cross-border insurance contracts.[144]

---

[135] Comité européen des assurances, CEA Policy Report on 'The European Retail Insurance Market(s)' (2004), available at http://www.cea.assur.org/cea/download/publ/article192.pdf, first part, s III. According to CEA, cross-border commercial transactions vary between 0.001% to 1 or 2% of the total turnover in the various national markets.

[136] *Ibid*, first part, s III, A 1.

[137] *Ibid*, first part, s III, A 2.

[138] *Ibid*, first part, s II.

[139] *Ibid*, second part, s II A.

[140] For the insurers especially as regards the legal rules of foreign Member States, see *ibid*, second part, s II B.

[141] *Ibid*, second part, s II C 1.

[142] *Ibid*, second part, s II C 1.

[143] *Ibid*, second part, s II C 2.

[144] *Ibid*, second part, s II C 3.

Furthermore, the CEA believes that the insurance industry is suffering from a regulatory fatigue after a 'tidal wave of regulations' in recent years.[145] The CEA does not expressly object to the CFR and the EC initiative to harmonise European insurance contract law, but interprets the CFR merely as a tool to simplify the regulatory environment, particularly with regard to insurance contract law, and to improve the quality and the coherence of the current *acquis communautaire* in order to attain the internal insurance market. Additionally, it is a key concern of the CEA that a thorough cost–benefit analysis should take place before any action is taken and that no additional costs and administrative burden should be imposed on the insurers. The CEA demands that any instrument must meet the practicability test, including feasibility, efficiency and utility. In summary, the CEA asks for a legislative moratorium, stating that rationalisation and simplification of the existent regulation, together with its effective and homogeneous implementation, should be priorities,[146] and that the specific features and realities of the insurance sector need to be taken into account.[147] Thus, the industry representatives insist on a true impact assessment, not only in theory but also in practice, as an absolute prerequisite for the next steps.

(b) European Economic and Social Committee

In contrast, the EESC identifies the fact that insurance contract law is to a large degree shaped by mandatory rules as a major barrier to the internal market. They explain the impact of a possible harmonisation, irrespective of the discussion on the extent and shape, of insurance contract law from the perspective of three main groups of stakeholders—the insurer, the policyholder and the insurance intermediaries—and show how a harmonisation could affect and to a large degree improve their position as a party to an insurance contract.

(i) Assumed Impact of Harmonisation on Insurers

On the one hand, insurers[148] with EU-wide business strategies,[149] as producers of insurance coverage, could, in the case of a harmonised insurance contract law, apply the same designs and calculations to their policies and would be able to pool mass risks on an EU-wide basis. The impediments resulting from the differing mandatory regulations applicable to insurance contracts would diminish. Regarding foreign branch offices of insurers, the possibility of marketing standardised insurance products would have a great

---

[145] Compare Figure 2, above.

[146] Comité européen des assurances, CEA Policy Report on 'Prospects for simplifying European insurance legislation' (2004), available at http://www.cea.assur.org/cea/download/publ/article191.pdf, para 4.

[147] *Ibid*, para 2a.

[148] Compare EESC, above n 5, para 4.2.3.

[149] Basedow, above n 16, 506.

impact on the development of the internal market, as the EESC states, thereby contradicting those critics[150] who state that insurance by its very nature requires geographical closeness.

(ii) Assumed Impact of Harmonisation on Policyholders

On the other hand, policyholders[151] would be able to acquire foreign insurance products. This would be an advantage for the so-called 'Euromobile policyholders' who change their habitual residence and move within the European Union.[152] They would not have to adjust their insurance policies every time they move to another Member State. The tedious and often expensive obligation to adjust their insurance coverage would no longer apply. For the other policyholders who stay within their Member State and whose insurance policies do not require adjustment every time they move, the question of whether a harmonisation would ameliorate their position is not so easy to answer.

The CEA has identified, in its publication on the retail insurance markets, further potential customers for cross-border insurance transactions: first, residents of frontier zones, because they live in proximity to borders between Member States; and secondly, high net worth individuals who try to maximise their life insurance investments by spreading them throughout several European countries.[153] On the one hand, more competition among insurers would probably lead to more policyholder-friendly contracts, but on the other hand, as the CEA has also indicated, insurance contracts are very complex and there are many other factors that affect them just like cultural aspects, language, economic environment and tax regulations. Additionally, insurance contracts require intensive post-acquisition consumer support.[154] With the third generation of insurance Directives, deregulation and greater competition among insurers was envisaged, especially with the abolition of the preliminary regulatory approval for standard terms and conditions and the opening of the national insurance markets.[155] Yet these initiatives did not lead to the envisaged results.

As regards the German insurance market, this deregulation did not result in significantly greater competition through cross-border transactions. There are various reasons for this, most of which legislation cannot change. One reason is that, on the one hand, the differing standard terms and conditions made it harder for policyholders to compare the products and services of insurers, while on the other hand the above-mentioned cultural and linguistic

---

[150] Like, eg the CEA.
[151] Compare EESC, above n 5, 4.2.4.
[152] Compare Basedow, above n 16, 506.
[153] Comité européen des assurances, above n 135, s C-1.
[154] *Ibid*, s C-1.
[155] Eg by the abolition of the (economic) needs test (*Bedürfnisprüfung*) pursuant to Art 9(3) of the third Directive on general insurance law (92/49/EEC) and Art 9(1) of the third Directive on life assurance (92/96/EEC).

factors are often underestimated. Additionally, German policyholders are regarded as being very conservative, and are purported to avoid concluding insurance contracts with foreign insurers. Thus, the access of foreign insurers to the German insurance market still occurs mainly via acquisition of existing national insurers.[156]

(iii) Assumed Impact of Harmonisation on Insurance Intermediaries
Insurance intermediaries[157] play an important role in the distribution of insurance contracts and are thus a key element in the establishment of the internal market, which has recently been strengthened by the Directive on Insurance Mediation.[158] In this Directive, which is still not implemented in many Member States,[159] the advice and documentation duties with respect to the insurance product have extended significantly and thus the liability of the insurance intermediaries has risen.[160] Additionally, insurance intermediaries are currently not in a position to avail themselves easily of foreign insurance markets for placing mass risks. Accordingly, it represents a major issue for them to distribute insurance contracts within the European Union without any knowledge of the specific provisions of the relevant national insurance contract laws. A harmonised insurance market could help them to reduce their liability risks, to lower their transaction costs and eventually to enhance the functioning of the internal market.

Regarding whether a full harmonisation is required in order to achieve the envisaged goals or an optional instrument is sufficient, the EESC has compared both approaches and come to the conclusion that for the first step an optional model would be acceptable but that all terms and components of such a model must be mandatory for the parties in their entirety as soon as the model is adopted.[161] This 'optional mandatory law'[162] would only allow deviation to the detriment of the insurer.[163]

2. Possible Contents of an Optional Instrument

Even though the question on the framework of an optional instrument is not sufficiently answered yet, the EESC has already outlined, in its own-initiative

---

[156] Weyers and Wandt, above n 63, para 112.
[157] Compare EESC, above n 5, para 4.2.5.
[158] Directive 2002/92/EC of the European Parliament and of the Council of 9 September 2002 on insurance mediation OJ L9/3.
[159] According to the EU Commission, only 12 Member States have yet sufficiently implemented this Directive; see http://europa.eu.int/comm/internal_market/finances/docs/actionplan/index/transposition_en.pdf.
[160] U Mönnich et al, 'New Regulation of Insurance Intermediaries in Germany', *Clifford Chance Client Newsletter April 2005*, 2.
[161] EESC, above n 5, para 3.4.6; Basedow, above n 16, 504.
[162] Basedow, above n 16, 504.
[163] *Ibid.*

opinion of December 2004, some general issues that need to be covered in a possible instrument.

(a) European Economic and Social Committee

The EESC explains how a harmonisation could take place. The committee favours a step-by-step approach whereby especially the mandatory rules of general insurance law would be harmonised in a first step. Following the argument of the EESC, the harmonisation would 'immediately allow the creation of an internal insurance market in all branches not covered by specific mandatory legal rules.'[164] According to the Committee, the kind of rules which could be harmonised at this first stage are as follows:[165]

— pre-contractual duties, mainly information;
— formation and duration of the contract;
— insurance policy, nature, effects and formal requirements;
— duration of the contract, renewal and termination;
— insurance intermediaries;
— aggravation of risk;
— insurance premium;
— insured event;
— insurance on account of third party.

In a second step, the EESC proposes that the sector-specific mandatory rules of, for example, health and life insurance should be covered.

(b) Comité européen des assurances

The CEA, on the other hand, proposes that the CFR-net should start by providing general principles of general contract law[166] and with consistent definitions of the legal terminology.[167] On this basis, specific provisions of insurance contract law could be developed, especially regarding the pre-contractual information for the consumer.[168]

---

[164] EESC, above n 5, para 7.4.
[165] *Ibid*, para 7.5.
[166] Comité européen des assurances, above n 25, para 5.1: eg legal responsibility and the capacity to act, the requirements and effectiveness of declarations of intent, conditions, time stipulations, consent and approval, representation, time-limits, deadlines and the prescription period.
[167] *Ibid*, para 5.2: eg the concept of the consumer.
[168] Comité européen des assurances, above n 146, annex.

3. Conclusion

Any solution will require a thorough impact assessment. At the moment it is not possible to foresee where the current initiatives will lead, but constantly striving for a solution is clearly in the interests of the industry. The foundation for this solution has got to be laid down now in order to attain the maximum benefits of the internal market. In the preparation of the future framework of European (insurance) contract law, no solution should be excluded from the beginning in order to permit as broad a debate on this topic as possible. An optional instrument or even a European Contract Act should not be the automatic consequence of the CFR even though much work may have been spent on it over the last years by academics and the EU Commission. The elaboration of the future framework of European contract law is a key point in the internal market, having an extensive impact on the functioning of everyday life and business in the EU. Thus, a broad consultation, involving all stakeholders, is needed to guarantee a balanced solution in the end.

The major decisions should not be left to the EU Commission alone; stakeholders' consultation is of the essence and they should be included in the final decision-making process. Therefore, the transparency of the current process needs to be improved to allow all stakeholders to make their voice heard. In order to prevent a solo attempt by the EU Commission, a superior instance could be considered, consisting of the different groups of stakeholders, being provided with the capacity to actively influence the Commission's decisions. It is questionable whether the CFR-net is in a position to afford this.[169] The EU Commission has recently installed a number of advisory groups[170] consisting of stakeholders (and experts). These highly welcome initiatives seem by and large to be more accepted and better organised than the CFR-net. Perhaps the reason for this is not only a less transparent selection process in the case of the CFR-net and general working procedures, but in particular the special challenge arising when the CFR-net is obliged to work on the very elaborate PECL drafts.

Following the Better Regulation Initiatives, which represent the current concept of governance of the EU Commission, the principles adopted in these initiatives, like 'less is more' and 'make it simpler—make it better', need to be pursued in order to assure consistent, simple and economically reasonable legislation in the future.

---

[169] Compare as an example the description of the functioning of the CFR-net: Fricke, above n 117, 1474–84; part IV of this chapter.

[170] Eg the 'Advisory Group on Corporate Governance and Company Law' by the Internal Market Commission.

VI. PROS AND CONS OF A POSSIBLE HARMONISATION

1. Pros

As indicated above and mentioned several times by the different institutions giving their opinion on this topic, a European contract law would mean a step forward on the way to a single internal market. The differing national insurance contract laws are substantial barriers to cross-border transactions.

One important advantage for the insurers would be the possibility of offering to cross-border policies EU-wide risk-pooling, which is still a problem within the EU. Many statements on the European insurance contract law claim that increased competition among insurance companies could be reached by way of easier access to foreign insurance markets for insurers. Insurance intermediaries as well as insurers would profit in the long run from lower transaction costs. The freedom of movement that is granted by the European Community would possibly be improved, and in particular the so-called 'Euromobile policyholders' would benefit.

2. Cons

Taking into consideration that harmonisation does not necessarily lead to the completion of the single market, the issues and arguments against a harmonisation, howsoever conducted, need to be reviewed.

Insurance law in Germany, for example, is based mainly on case law that has developed in the past 100 years. The introduction of a new regime of insurance contract law would make litigation in insurance matters less reliable and predictable. This situation would, especially in the first years of implementation, produce legal uncertainty for insurers and policyholders dependent on local and foreign court decisions. Choosing an opt-in model, a 26th regime of insurance contract law within the EU is also likely to cause confusion amongst consumers. Almost all other opt-in models within EU legislation are related to B2B transactions.

It is arguable that the benefits of the increased competition for the policyholder will be obvious, since the harmonisation of the supervisory law and the European passport have not yet led to a convergence of insurance contracts. Had there been a true need, competition would have led to convergence. Last but not least, the timescale[171] set by the EC Commission is very tight and this topic is much too sensitive to be rushed. Just like the CEA

---

[171] Eg the adoption of the CFR by the Commission in 2009, compare COM(2004) 651, above n 2, 13.

demanded, a close look at the costs and benefits of an implementation is essential.

VII. OUTLOOK

I want to conclude by saying that action by the EU should be taken, but, before discussing the content of that action, the following must be considered.

Taking into consideration the still existing deficits of the internal market, the CFR would possibly create a more coherent current and future *acquis*, which seems sufficient for the time being regarding general contract law. However, the insurance sector still suffers from underdeveloped cross-border transactions. Additionally, the issue of whether insurance contract law can be harmonised without a coherent general contract law is still subject to debate. On the one hand, the strong dependence of insurance contract law on general contract law makes it difficult to elaborate an optional instrument of European insurance contract law. On the other hand, the existing deficits of the internal insurance market make a swift solution for this sector necessary, which is not possible if handled in conjunction with general contract law.

Although the EU Commission continues to repeat that the benefits of an optional instrument remain to be proven and sees difficulties in reaching an agreement on EU-wide standards, it proposes in the *Green Book on Financial Services Policy (2005—2010)* to launch a feasibility study on an optional 26th regime, eg in the areas of term-life insurance.[172] The European Financial Services Round Table (EFR) highly welcomed this debate on the 26th regime, as it could be a 'last legislative resort' to surmount the difficulties that cannot be solved by harmonisation or mutual recognition.[173]

For the time being, the outcomes of the discussions of the researcher network, the CFR-net, and of the Commission's feasibility study are still awaited, with the hope that the continual influence of the stakeholders will lead to a solution which is not detrimental to the internal market, the insurance industry or the policyholders.

Meanwhile, competition in the insurance market and globalisation of the activities of large insurance companies will lead to increased convergence. This, in turn, may facilitate the CFR and—if appropriate—a 26th optional regime.

---

[172] COM(2005) 177, above n 88, 11. The European Commission confirmed its doubts regarding the benefits of a 26th regime in the White Paper on Financial Services Policy (2005–2010), above n 89, 6, stating that the 'so-called 26th regime might sound attractive in its simplicity, but in practice it will require harmonisation across the board (legal, tax, language etc.).' Additionally, the Commission highlighted that 'widespread scepticism exists among stakeholders about the feasibility and usefulness of 26th regimes in the area of financial services.'

[173] European Financial Services Roundtable, 'Response to the Green Paper COM(2005) 177' (2005) 5.

13

European Contract Law – What Does It Mean and What Does It Not Mean?

DIRK STAUDENMAYER[*]

I. INTRODUCTION

On 11 October 2004 the European Commission adopted the Communication 'European Contract Law and the Revision of the *Acquis*: the Way Forward'.[1] On 23 September 2005 it submitted its first Annual Progress Report,[2] concerning in particular the establishment and working method of the process preparing and elaborating the so-called Common Frame of Reference (CFR). These documents are further steps in the process on European contract law which was launched with the Commission Communication of July 2001[3] and continued with the Action Plan of 2003.[4]

At the conference which was organised by the Institute of European and Comparative Law of the University of Oxford and the law firm Clifford Chance, the contributions to which are collected in this volume, some very interesting results of a survey on European contract law were presented.[5] Among other matters, European businesses were asked about their view on future legislative measures remedying existing obstacles to the internal

---

[*] The author chaired the Commission inter-services working group which prepared the 2001 and 2004 Communications, the 2003 Action Plan and the first Annual Progress Report. However, this article expresses exclusively his personal opinion and does not, in any case, bind the European Commission.

[1] COM(2004) 651 final, [2004] OJ C14/6; available at http://europa.eu.int/comm/consumers/cons_int/safe_shop/fair_bus_pract/cont_law/index_de.htm.

[2] COM(2005) 456 final. See the website referred to in n 1.

[3] Communication from the Commission to the Council and the European Parliament on European Contract Law, COM(2001) 398 final, [2001] OJ C255/1. See the website referred to in n 1. See also D Staudenmayer, 'The Commission Communication on European Contract Law: What Future for European Contract Law?' (2002) 10 *European Review of Private Law* 249.

[4] Communication from the Commission to the European Parliament and the Council on A More Coherent European Contract Law: An Action Plan, COM(2003) 68 final, [2003] OJ C63/1. See the website referred to in n 1. See also D Staudenmayer, 'The Commission Action Plan on European Contract Law' (2003) 11 *European Review of Private Law* 113.

[5] See the contribution of Vogenauer and Weatherill in this volume, p 105.

market. A positive answer was given by 83% of businesses and even 88% of small to medium-sized enterprises. Three options had been given in the questionnaire for the way in which to achieve such results: a more uniform implementation and application of existing EU law (38% of positive answers); an optional European contract law which would run parallel to existing national contract laws (28%); and replacing national contract laws with a European contract law (30%).

In this context, it seems useful to clarify whether the 'European contract law', which the respondents apparently had in mind when participating in the survey, corresponds to what is presently being prepared or discussed at European level. It seems that the survey and the answers refer more to what is known as the 'optional instrument(s)' and also include the option of a European contract law replacing national laws, which is not even discussed at EU level. Furthermore, the survey does not focus on the imminent product of the ongoing process, the CFR.

I therefore attempt here to clarify the debate on the optional instrument in order to remedy misunderstandings on this issue. Secondly, I explain how one can – according to the considerations of the 2004 Commission Communication – understand the 'optional instrument(s)'. Finally, I describe the CFR as the present subject of the European contract law process, focusing on the intentions for its use, its possible contents and the process of its preparation.

II. WHAT IS AN OPTIONAL INSTRUMENT IN THE AREA OF EUROPEAN CONTRACT LAW AND WHAT IS IT NOT?

1. The Debate around Optional Instruments

The Commission Communication treated measure III of the Action Plan, the debate on the opportuneness of an optional instrument, rather briefly. It is true that some contributors to the consultation did show interest in this measure; however, it became clear that the majority of contributors were not prepared to support a political decision on this subject before examining the final version of the CFR, which, according to the Action Plan, should be the basis for possible optional instruments. For this reason, the Commission intends to focus the debate on the development of the CFR. The Commission considers that any discussions relating to a possible optional instrument should be a response to practical needs.

For example, there is some interest among experts on the possible use of such an optional instrument in the area of financial services.[6] It remains to be

---

[6] See http://europa.eu.int/comm/internal_market/finances/policy/index_en.htm; Financial Services Action Plan: Progress and Prospects – Expert Group on Insurance and Pensions, 'Final Report', 19 and Expert Group on Banking, 'Final Report', 20.

seen how firmly that view is held. The Commission Green Paper on this matter[7] mentioned the debate on a 26th regime, which is another term for an optional instrument. In the consultation that followed, a large number of stakeholders dealt with the optional instrument, though the majority remained rather cautious. They focused more on raising questions about the parameters of possible optional instruments than on expressing any need or will of the market to use them, if adopted. However, a possible optional instrument, be it in the specific area of financial services or in general, would only be successful if it were used by market operators. This is only likely if it corresponds to a real need of the relevant market. Consequently, the Commission, in its White Paper on Financial Services Policy 2005–2010,[8] did not consider it possible to take a definitive position. At present, in the area of financial services, it leaves it to the interested business circles to demonstrate the business case and envisages the creation of a Forum Group only in these circumstances.

Given that some suspicions were raised, it is important to emphasise that the Commission has no hidden agenda concerning the development of possible optional instruments or indeed in the process on European contract law.

The process on European contract law has always moved on in a very transparent and open manner. After the two consultative documents, the 2001 Communication and the 2003 Action Plan, the Commission made all contributions to the consultations and their results publicly available in the form of a summary.[9]

If one compares the results of these two consultations and the next step in the process, the consultation after the July 2001 Communication, with the measures proposed in the Action Plan, or the consultation following the Action Plan with the October 2004 Communication, one will note that the Commission follows the broad trends identified in these consultations faithfully. Similarly, as regards financial services, the conclusion again reflects the outcome of the consultation process launched by the Green Paper on Financial Services.

Annex II of the 2004 Communication contains the parameters for any future discussions on an optional instrument, including a number of interesting considerations. These constitute the real contents of the Communication concerning a possible optional instrument. While reading these parameters, one should keep in mind that the optional instrument would probably not be a single, broad instrument, but could consist of many specific instruments. For example, one could possibly imagine an optional insurance contract containing general and specific insurance contract law.

---

[7] Green Paper on Financial Services Policy (2005-2010), COM(2005) 177 final, [2005] OJ C/236/9. See http://europa.eu.int/comm/internal_market/finances/policy/index_en.htm.

[8] COM(2005) 629 final (5 December 2005) 13. See the website referred to in n 7.

[9] See the website referred to in n 1.

2. Relationship with Private International Law and the Legal Nature of the Optional Instrument

First, it should be noted that the consultation after the Action Plan resulted in a relatively large consensus in favour of the opt-in variant of the optional instrument. Under such a variant the parties could apply the instrument through a choice of law clause in their contract. It would not be automatically applicable, in contrast with the opt-out variant.

The relationship with private international law, and in particular the coherence of the process on European contract law with the intended adoption into Community law of the Rome Convention, was one of the central points resulting from the consultation after the Action Plan. The Commission emphasises that the review and adoption of Rome I into Community law must take into account coherence with a possible optional instrument.

With regard to the relationship between an optional instrument and private international law, there are basically three options.[10] These three options have also been submitted in the consultation and are mentioned in the 2004 Communication.

The first scenario would be the adoption of a possible optional instrument as an instrument of international uniform substantive law. In such a case, one would not even arrive at the normal conflict of laws rules, ie the provisions of the Rome Convention.[11] Whilst it is true that international uniform law is at present created by international treaties,[12] this does not necessarily exclude the possibility of creating the former at Community level.[13] The Communication mentions that such an instrument of international uniform law would contain a provision determining the scope of its applicability. It would provide that the parties would first need to choose the optional instrument as the law applicable to their contracts. For cases which fall outside the scope of application of the international uniform law instrument, the applicable law would be determined by the rules of the Rome Convention. The scope of application could include contracts concluded between a party established in a Member State and a party established in another State (not necessarily a Member State). It is interesting to note that such a construction is not without precedent. Article V of the 1964 Hague Convention relating to a Uniform Law on the International Sale of Goods included a reserve, used by the UK, under which the Uniform Law applied only if it had been chosen by the parties pursuant to Article 4 of the Uniform Law.

---

[10] See in more detail D Staudenmayer, 'The Place of Consumer Contract Law within the Process on European Contract Law' (2004) 27 *Journal of Consumer Policy* 282.

[11] Cf, eg K Firsching and B von Hoffmann, *Internationales Privatrecht* (5th edn, Munich, CH Beck, 1997) 24; J Kropholler, *Internationales Privatrecht* (4th edn, Tübingen, Mohr Siebeck, 2001) 94.

[12] Cf G Kegel and K Schurig, *Internationales Privatrecht* (8th edn, Tübingen, Mohr Siebeck, 2000) 71ff.

[13] J Kropholler, *Internationales Einheitsrecht. Beiträge zum Ausländischen und Internationalen Privatrecht* (Tübingen, Mohr Siebeck, 1975) 35ff.

In the second scenario, Article 20 of the Rome Convention would be used to give precedence to a possible optional instrument over the existing rules of the Convention. The latter gives precedence to 'choice of law rules relating to contractual obligations' contained in 'acts of the institutions of the European Communities.' The precedence given to an optional instrument would then guarantee the application of the substantive provisions within it. The precedence granted by Article 20 would refer directly to the provision of an optional instrument in terms of its scope and indirectly to the whole optional instrument. Obviously Article 20 of the Rome Convention was not originally conceived with an optional instrument in mind. It has not yet been applied, and the Commission has stated explicitly that an amendment of Article 20 could be envisaged. Indeed, Article 22(b) of the recent Commission proposal on the Rome I Regulation clarifies the priority of a possible optional instrument over the future Rome I Regulation.[14]

Finally, the third scenario would be for a possible optional instrument to contain only substantive rules and no conflict of laws rules. Such an instrument would need to be chosen under Article 3 of the Rome Convention.

This last point raises the question of the legal nature of such an optional instrument. In the case of the 'opt-in' approach, the most appropriate legal act would appear to be a regulation for any of the three scenarios.

In the case of the first scenario, ie using an instrument of international uniform substantive law, the regulation would be the most appropriate instrument due to its direct applicability.[15] The same reasoning would be valid for an optional instrument being applied under Article 20 of the Rome Convention. A regulation would also seem to be the appropriate instrument for an optional instrument applied under Article 3 of the Rome Convention. It is true that Article 3 of the Rome Convention is mostly interpreted as stating that the applicable law has to be the law of a country.[16] The basis for this

---

[14] 'Proposal for a Regulation of the European Parliament and the Council on the Law Applicable to Contractual Obligations (Rome I)', COM(2005) 650 final (15 December 2005); see p 9 of the explanatory memorandum.

[15] See Kropholler, above n 13, 116ff.

[16] P Lagarde, 'Le nouveau droit international privé des contrats après l'entrée en vigueur de la Convention de Rome du juin 1980' [1991] *Revue critique de droit international privé* 287, 300; U Magnus, in *J von Staudingers Kommentar zum Bürgerlichen Gesetzbuch mit Einführungsgesetz und Nebengesetzen* (Berlin, Sellier, 2003), Art 27 EGBGB, notes 48, 51; D Czernich and H Heiss (eds), *Kommentar zum Europäischen Schuldvertragsübereinkommen* (Vienna, Orac, 1999), Art 3, note 44; R Michaels, 'Privatautonomie und Privatkodifikation: Zu Anwendbarkeit und Geltung allgemeiner Vertragsrechtsprinzipien' (1998) 62 *Rabels Zeitschrift für ausländisches und internationales Privatrecht* 580, 596ff; D Busch and E Hondius, 'Ein neues Vertragsrecht für Europa: Die Principles of European Contract Law aus niederländischer Sicht' [2001] *Zeitschrift für Europäisches Privatrecht* 223, 226ff. The other opinion is represented, for example, by O Lando, 'Some Issues Relating to the Law Applicable to Contractual Obligations' (1996) 55 *King's College Law Journal* 55; K Boele-Woelki, 'Principles and Private International Law – The UNIDROIT Principles of International Commercial Contracts and the Principles of European Contract Law: How to Apply Them to International Contracts' [1996] *Uniform Law Review* 652, 664ff.

opinion is a systematic argument drawn from Article 1(1) of the Rome
Convention which specifically refers to situations involving a choice between
'the laws of different countries'. The discussion, however, does not concern
the application of Article 3 of the Rome Convention to a regulation or a
recommendation, but rather the question of whether soft law rules, like the
Lando Principles of European Contract Law or the UNIDROIT Principles,
can be chosen as applicable law. On the one hand, it is certainly true that a
regulation is not the law of a country in terms of its creation. On the other
hand, because of their direct applicability, regulations automatically become
part of national legal systems by virtue of the EC Treaty. Therefore one could
say that, as far as Article 3 of the Rome Convention is concerned, a regulation
should be treated as part of the law of a country.

This is much more doubtful if one wants to choose a recommendation as
the legal mechanism for the optional instrument. A recommendation has no
binding force and therefore cannot be adapted for the first two scenarios, ie
as an instrument of international uniform substantive law or as an optional
instrument being applied under Article 20 of the Rome Convention. It would
not constitute a viable alternative to an optional instrument applied under
Article 3 of the Rome Convention because the argument drawn from the
direct applicability of a regulation would not work for a recommendation.
For this reason, the Commission mentions that, in the process of modernisation and communitarisation of the Rome Convention, Article 3 could be
clarified accordingly. This has indeed been suggested in the recent Commission proposal on the Rome I Regulation.[17]

3. Contents and Scope of an Optional Instrument

The Commission's Communication of 2004 does not contain any definitive
suggestions on the possible contents of an optional instrument, ie whether it
should include, alongside general contract law provisions, rules relating to
specific contracts and, if it should, which ones. Basically it only refers to
suggestions made by contributors following the consultation on the Action
Plan. The Commission considerations in the Communication seem to make
the contents dependent on the question of whether, and in which areas, an
optional instrument would be necessary. Only then could one sensibly decide
which contents the respective optional instrument should have.

With regard to the scope of the optional instrument, the Commission
Communication differentiates between two questions. The first concerns the
question of the application of the instrument to business-to-business
contracts and business-to-consumer contracts. The Commission focuses here
on the purpose of a possible optional instrument, ie the smoother functioning

---

[17] COM(2005) 650 final, above n 14, see Art 3 and p 5 of the explanatory memorandum.

of the internal market. Therefore one could argue that business-to-business contracts should be included. The same argument would apply to business-to-consumer contracts. In this context, the Commission notes the importance of the mandatory character of some national provisions, in particular in the area of consumer protection. This would constitute the strongest argument for the use of an optional instrument by businesses in business-to-consumer contracts. The inclusion of mandatory consumer protection provisions in the optional instrument would mean that they would only have to respect these provisions, not 25 different sets of mandatory national provisions. This would be the case in the situations covered by Articles 5 and 7 of the Rome Convention. Businesses could therefore use one single contract in order to market their goods or services, which would no longer have to be adapted to different mandatory national provisions.[18] This would result in a considerable reduction of transaction costs for retail businesses and industry. However, such a situation would only be possible if the above-mentioned scenarios concerning the relationship of an optional instrument with private international law, ie an instrument of international uniform substantive law or an optional instrument being applied via Article 20 of the Rome Convention, were chosen.

At the same time one would have to ensure that the mandatory provisions included in the optional instrument would correspond roughly with the level of national protection, otherwise the consumer would not have the necessary confidence to conclude such a contract. Provided that the level of protection was comparable, the consumer in such a situation would have the advantage of having a greater choice of products and services at presumably lower prices.

The issues raised above are interesting in academic terms but are less relevant for the immediate purposes of policies such as the CFR. It is therefore opportune to explain this more immediate objective.

III. THE COMMON FRAME OF REFERENCE

The clear emphasis of the October 2004 Communication, as reflected in its title, is placed on the implementation of measure I of the Action Plan, ie the improvement of the existing and future *acquis communautaire* relevant to contract law, via the CFR. The reason for this lies essentially in the overwhelming support which this measure has received in the consultation following the Action Plan.

---

[18] See particularly the example of the insurance contract, D Staudenmayer, 'Ein optionelles Instrument im Europäischen Vertragsrecht' [2003] *Zeitschrift für Europäisches Privatrecht* 828, 834ff, 840ff.

1. Objectives of the Common Frame of Reference

The two objectives of the CFR had already been mentioned in the 2003 Action Plan and were confirmed in the October 2004 Communication. First and foremost, the CFR aims to improve the quality of legislation and the coherence of the existing and future EC law in the area of contract law. Secondly, and secondary to this, it could be the basis for possible optional instruments of European contract law.

The first aim clearly has to be placed within the context of the Commission efforts for better regulation. When revising the existing EC *acquis communautaire* in the area of contract law or submitting new sectoral proposals, the Commission and the European legislator, the Council of Ministers and the European Parliament (EP), should use the CFR.

Concerning this objective, the Commission had already mentioned in its Action Plan that it intended to use the CFR in the process of reviewing existing and preparing future sectoral measures relevant to contract law. This was confirmed again in the October 2004 Communication. While there are other fields of the *acquis* which are relevant for the first objective,[19] European consumer contract law is of particular relevance for several reasons. First of all, European consumer contract law is the largest coherent field of contract law[20] in the *acquis communautaire*. In addition, the Commission explains its plans for a review of European consumer contract law in more detail in the October 2004 Communication and in the first Annual Progress Report of September 2005. The main task, among others, will be to examine where and how far Member States have gone beyond the minimum standards of the existing directives which are almost all based on the principle of minimum harmonisation. If Member States have, in going beyond the minimum standards, created different mandatory laws, they constitute obstacles to the internal market according to the European Court of Justice case law[21]. In addition, the Commission could identify the implementation and application problems of the existing directives and establish how far these directives have gone in reaching their political goals. The economic impact of the identified weaknesses will also need to be assessed. In light of this analysis, a decision

---

[19] The Communication mentions, for instance, the intended use of the CFR in the framework of the review of Directive 2000/35/EC of the European Parliament and of the Council of 29 June 2000 on combating late payment in commercial transactions [2000] OJ L200/35 ('Late Payments Directive').

[20] Concerning the common denominators of consumer protection law, see D Staudenmayer, 'Die Richtlinien des Verbraucherprivatrechts – Bausteine für ein europäisches Privatrecht' in H Schulte-Nölke and R Schulze (eds), *Europäische Rechtsangleichung und nationale Privatrechte* (Baden-Baden, NOMOS, 1999) 63, 66ff.

[21] Case C–377/98 *Netherlands v European Parliament and Council* [2001] ECR I–7079, at [15ff]; Case C–491/01 *The Queen v Secretary of State for Health, ex parte British American Tobacco (Investments) Ltd and Imperial Tobacco Ltd* [2002] ECR I–11453, at [58ff].

can be taken on which directives and precisely which of their provisions are in need of review. The CFR could be a very useful tool for this.

The CFR is, however, also linked to the implementation of the EU Lisbon Agenda striving for more competitiveness. It is interesting to note that others have also identified this link. For example, the German government had included in its paper for the European Council on the mid-term review of the Lisbon agenda seven priorities for an internal market strategy, the CFR being the sixth.[22] More coherent directives where gaps, inconsistencies and other similar problems are remedied are easier to implement and apply and therefore provide a higher degree of legal certainty – which is desired by market operators.

The contents of the CFR would need to correspond to these objectives. The first Annual Progress Report underlines a need to prioritise the parts of the future CFR which are relevant for the review of the consumer contract law *acquis*.

2. The preparation of the Common Frame of Reference

The October 2004 Communication deals in a relatively detailed manner with the consultation process accompanying the research work. The reason for this is that the success of the CFR depends not only on the quality of the academic preparatory work, but also on the credible involvement of stakeholders and the European institutions. This was a clear result of both the consultation after the Action Plan and a conference jointly organised by the Commission and the European Parliament on 28 April 2004 where the contents and the method of preparation of the CFR were discussed.[23] In addition, the use of the CFR by the Council of Ministers and the EP, which is, as mentioned before, desirable, would only appear realistic if both institutions have been involved from the very beginning.

For this reason the Communication explains in detail how this involvement will be organised in two strands. In the first strand, a network of stakeholder experts (the so-called CFR-net) has been created. In order to prepare this, the Commission published a call for expression of interest in July 2004.[24] These experts are discussing the research work in workshops, and ensure that, through their input, the research results take the needs of economic operators and legal practitioners into account. Experts are using a restricted-access website to consult the respective research documents. The

---

[22] See the paper of the German government for the European Council, 'Growth and Employment for the Years throughout 2010 – Position of the German Government on the Mid-term Review of the Lisbon Stategy, October 2004, 7'. See also the article of Federal Chancellor Helmut Schröder in *Handelsblatt* of 26 October 2004.

[23] Concerning this conference, see the website referred to in n 1.

[24] See the website referred to in n 1.

Commission is producing summaries and conclusions from these discussions after the workshops and transmitting them to the research network. The researchers will respond to these conclusions, ie they will either integrate the stakeholder experts' input or justify why they cannot integrate them.

The kick-off conference on the CFR-net took place on 15 December 2004.[25] A number of workshops have already taken place and the first Annual Progress Report shows that the process faced some criticism from stakeholders. Clearly there were a number of initial problems to overcome. However, the measures announced by the Commission in the first Annual Progress Report demonstrate its determination to tackle these problems in order to make the preparation process more efficient.

The second strand of the consultation process concerns the political involvement of Member States and the European Parliament. This takes place first through a working group, composed of Member States' experts. The Commission informs this group regularly of the progress of the work and the Member States' experts have the opportunity to give their input on the substantive issues. Several meetings of this group have already taken place. In addition, the Commission submits an annual progress report to the Council and the European Parliament giving both institutions the opportunity to create political guidelines.

Of course, in the end, the Commission, in its role as proposer of legislation, and the Council of Ministers and EP, as co-legislator, will define the ultimate outcome.

[25] *Ibid.*

14

Harmonisation of European Contract Law—the United Kingdom Government's Thinking

BARONESS ASHTON OF UPHOLLAND

This article sets out the UK government's thinking on the issue of harmonisation of European contract law, with particular reference to the European Commission's European Contract Law initiative and the review of the *acquis*. I first deal with the government's views in relation to the general harmonisation of European contract law. I then turn to the Commission's current work on the creation of a 'common frame of reference' (CFR) for European contract law and the review of the *acquis*.

By 'harmonisation' of contract law in this context, I mean the enactment of horizontal legislation at European level, which would replace the national contract laws of the Member States. This might take the form of a European Contract Law Code. The government's thinking here can be briefly stated: it is strongly opposed to such harmonisation. We do not believe that such legislation, imposed across the whole of the EU, is an appropriate or necessary way to resolve such problems as there may be in the area of European contract law.

We are not aware of any evidence that shows that the current diversity of national contract laws across Europe causes significant problems for business or consumers, or presents any real obstacles to the efficient functioning of the internal market. Put quite simply, we see no need—and cannot detect any appetite—for such mandatory harmonisation in the area of general contract law. Blanket harmonisation is not an effective or efficient way to resolve problems in civil law and justice.

I should, of course, acknowledge that there are sectors where we do support the idea of harmonisation because there is clear evidence that such harmonisation meets a specific need. A prime example of this is in the area of consumer law. Here, harmonisation, supported by effective mutual recognition and enforcement measures and judicial cooperation, is the most effective way to ensure opportunities for business in the single market and adequate protection for consumers in their dealings across Europe. Harmonisation in such cases is the proportionate answer to the problems that have to be solved. The government sees no such need in the area of general contract law. In that area, the best solution is to be found in the application of the principle of subsidiarity—in using existing national legal systems to deliver real benefits to our citizens in cross-border cases.

This is one of the reasons that we consider individual national legal traditions should be respected. In addition, they provide a diversity that enhances the prosperity of the European Union. The common law of England and Wales, for example, is the international law of choice in a wide range of commercial matters, including finance, insurance and shipping. It is chosen because of its attributes of predictability of outcome, legal certainty and fairness, as well as its well-founded principles, such as the ability to require exact performance and the absence of a general duty of good faith. London—one of the world's most important financial and legal centres—is built upon the foundations of a sound and attractive law of contract. If the ability to choose the common law were to be lost, business would migrate to some other centre, such as New York or Geneva, and the European Union would be the poorer. The existence of the common law therefore enhances the prosperity of the Union.

This is the UK view on mandatory harmonisation, a view that I am pleased to see is clearly shared by the European Commission, which has made it clear on several occasions that it has no plans for mandatory harmonisation of contract law. We welcome this reassurance but feel that this should not prevent us from reiterating our opposition, and the reasons for that opposition, to the idea of a European Contract Law Code.

Harmonisation might, of course, also be effected on an optional basis. This could be by means of an optional instrument or, as it is sometimes called, a '26th regime'. In this case, parties to a contract could choose to govern their contract by the terms of the instrument instead of adopting the contract law of a Member State. We know that the Commission is continuing to contemplate the opportuneness of an optional instrument, but we are unaware of any demand for one and consider that the creation of a voluntary Code would be a huge waste of resources.

That brings me on to the subject of the CFR and the many fundamental questions that still surround it: what is it, what will it look like, and what will it be used for. Regrettably, the form and content of the proposed CFR are still something of a mystery. Some have suggested that it will be useful as something akin to a compendium of comparative information, a European contract law thesaurus or lexicon. It has also been mooted as a precedent book for the busy lawmaker seeking words with which to populate the blank page of a putative instrument.

There is clearly some advantage in a product that promotes better mutual understanding of our respective legal systems. The current work of the academics retained by the Commission could well go a long way to provide a translation tool of this kind for use as a work of reference. Similarly, the European Union can only benefit from improvements to the quality and coherence of the existing and future *acquis*. This sits well with the Better Regulation agendas at the national and European levels, and is to be welcomed. However, it is all too easy to agree that the CFR should be created to achieve these general objectives; it is more difficult to create a CFR that will actually be useful and deliver practical benefits.

How can we achieve such a CFR? The present scheme seems to be that the academics retained by the Commission will produce a draft CFR. This document seems likely to bear strong resemblance to the Principles of European Contract Law. It will look like a Code of Contract Law. We think that this approach needs to be reconsidered. We think that the content and structure of the CFR should be determined by its intended primary function, not by a desire to review the whole of the law of contract and associated areas. The CFR must therefore be constructed as a response to real problems with the *acquis*, not an exercise in abstract legal theory. In this way, the CFR could be an instrument that provides workable solutions to real problems arising out of the consumer *acquis*. It could then deliver real benefits to businesses and consumers. These alone will justify the significant expense in terms of time, money and effort that will undoubtedly need to be spent in creating a CFR.

The Commission's review of the consumer *acquis* is an initiative that the government strongly supports. It presents an opportunity to increase protection for consumers and to increase opportunities for business in cross-border transactions. It is also a good example of the kind of better regulation work that the government is keen to promote. It will create a clearer, more consistent *acquis* in the consumer law area. The CFR, if it is to be a useful, practical tool, will assist in this work. In this respect, we are encouraged that the Commission is taking steps to involve stakeholders from across Europe in the drafting of the CFR. We hope that their participation will help to produce a CFR that provides generally accepted practical answers to real problems with the consumer *acquis*. There are, however, still many unanswered questions about the detailed nature and function of the CFR, and a great deal of work must be done to create something that will be worth putting in place.

In conclusion, the government sees no benefit in either mandatory or voluntary harmonisation of European contract law. On the other hand, we support the Commission's review of the consumer *acquis* and consider that its completion should be a priority so that the present problems can be remedied with the least possible delay. It is our belief that if the CFR is to be useful, it must be directed at answering the real problems of the consumer *acquis*. We are watching with interest to see what steps the Commission will take to achieve this objective.

15

Concluding Observations

DAVID EDWARD

In seeking to summarise the results of the conference, the contributions to which are collected in this volume, there are five points that need to be emphasised.

First, although the European Commission is taking the lead in promoting the harmonisation of contract law, the Commission is not itself the legislator. No legislation binding on the Member States can come into existence without the active concurrence of the Council of the European Union, representing the governments of the Member States. Even if it wished to do so, the Commission cannot force a change in the law.

Secondly, we should accept that there is no hidden agenda. There is no master plan for extensive harmonisation—far less complete harmonisation—of the laws of the Member States.

Thirdly, in a field such as this, careful choice of terminology is crucial. In every legal system, the words and phrases that lawyers use encapsulate concepts and definitions that have developed over years—in some cases, over centuries. While words in one language (eg 'good faith') may appear to be synonymous with equivalent words in another language (eg 'bonne foi'), the underlying concepts or their application may differ to such an extent that it would be misleading, in a legislative context, to treat them as adequate translations of each other.

That is why, for example, in the context of the Brussels Convention on Jurisdiction and Judgments, the European Court of Justice has insisted that the words used by the Community legislator are to be treated as 'autonomous concepts' that have their own Community law meaning and do not necessarily incorporate all the underlying meanings they have acquired in the national legal systems. For the same reason, in its judgments relating to state liability for damages, the Court avoided using the word 'fault', although, at first sight, it might seem to be the obvious word to describe the circumstances in which liability should arise.

In the present context, therefore, it is important either to adopt new terminology that is clearly different from the customary terminology of the national legal systems or, alternatively, if customary terminology is adopted, to spell out what it is to be presumed to mean (or, in some cases, what it is to be presumed not to mean). Detailed analysis and classification of terms and concepts will be an essential preliminary.

Fourthly, this cannot be purely a technical lawyer's exercise. At various stages, it will be necessary to make political choices. For example, it will be necessary to decide how far the legislator should go in protecting the weaker party to a contract against the consequences of his or her own stupidity or folly. The role of the legal expert is not to make the choice, but rather to help the legislator to make a well-informed choice, and thereafter to choose appropriate terminology with which to define the choice that has been made and its consequences.

Fifthly, it should be remembered that it will be the judges who interpret and apply the legislation once adopted. The British constitutional lawyer, AV Dicey, writing about what he called 'judicial legislation' (development of the law through case law), observed that

> Judicial legislation aims to a far greater extent than do enactments passed by Parliament, at the maintenance of the logic or the symmetry of the law.[1]

The interplay between judges and academic lawyers is an essential part of this process. The wise legislator will not seek to answer every question in advance.

The present context is one in which the technique of the directive, prescribed by the Treaty, will be particularly appropriate, concentrating on 'the result to be achieved' rather than 'the choice of form and methods'.

More generally, the conference has touched upon some fundamental issues.

All legal systems develop, in some cases through the search for a better formulation of a legal rule or principle, in others through the search for a rule or principle that is better adapted to changing political, economic or social realities, preconceptions or values. Systems react, more or less speedily, to what the actors want. In some cases there will be direct borrowing from another system, in others two systems will come to a common or similar solution through a sort of osmosis, often as a result of discussions at conferences such as this. On the whole, smaller jurisdictions are more likely to be influenced by larger ones than the other way about.

It is not surprising that, in the context of a developing internal market in Europe and a wider global market, the commercial actors should look for a common set of rules to govern their commercial relations, as indeed happened in the Middle Ages. The search for common rules in the field of contract law should therefore be seen as a normal and natural part of the

---

[1] AV Dicey, *Law and Public Opinion in England* (2nd edn, London, Macmillan, 1926) 364.

development of the national legal systems, and not as an impertinent assault on their autonomy or the purity of their principles.

It is important, too, to recognise that the territory of traditional 'contract law' has been invaded by new forms of law—notably competition law and other forms of modern regulatory law. In many respects, the parties' freedom is restrained, restricted or even excluded to such an extent that it is open to question whether the traditional conception of a 'contract' as an agreement freely entered into remains adequate as a starting point.

In addition, some areas of the law have effectively been excluded from the territory of the law of contract. The legal relationship of employer and employee now owes little or nothing to conventional concepts of contractual relationships. To some extent the same is true of the status of commercial agents and consumers and, for different reasons, of the law governing securities, guarantees and insurance.

So the question arises, what is left for the conventional law of contract? To what legal relationships would a European 'code' of contract law relate? That is perhaps a rather unsettling question, but one that is none the less worth asking as work continues.

Index